A Guide to Tucson Architecture

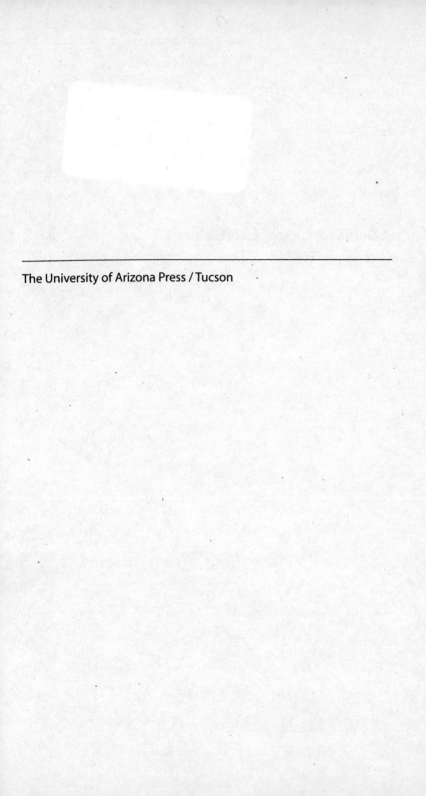

The University of Arizona Press / Tucson

A Guide to Tucson Architecture

Anne M. Nequette and R. Brooks Jeffery

The University of Arizona Press
© 2002 The Arizona Board of Regents
First Printing
All rights reserved

♾ This book is printed on acid-free, archival-quality paper.
Manufactured in the United States of America

Library of Congress Cataloging-in-Publication Data
Nequette, Anne M., 1954–
A guide to Tucson architecture / Anne M. Nequette and R. Brooks Jeffery.
p. cm.
Includes bibliographical references and index.
ISBN 0-8165-2083-6 (pbk. : alk. paper)
1. Architecture—Arizona—Tucson—Guidebooks.
2. Tucson (Arizona)—Guidebooks. 3. Tucson (Arizona)—
Buildings, structures, etc.—Guidebooks. I. Jeffery, R. Brooks, 1959–

II. Title.
NA735.T8 N46 2002
720'.979'776—dc21
2001006511

British Library Cataloguing-in-Publication Data
A catalogue record for this book is available from the British Library.

Contents

Preface

Tucson is a city rich in architectural heritage that spans three cultures, whose history of human settlement defines it as one of the oldest continually inhabited cities in the United States. The remains of pre-historic pit structures and agricultural technologies, the Hispanic presidio and barrios, and the various American architectural forms give Tucson a unique and eclectic identity unlike any other American city. Tucson's architectural character is not yet homogeneous, like that imposed on Santa Fe. But, like many other American cities, Tucson's rich historic and contemporary architectural heritage is threatened by the trend to invent one identifiable "Southwestern" style more easily promoted in today's consumer market. The danger of promoting a purely visual style, as in the case of Santa Fe, is that it does not respond to a complex set of factors including climate, geography, and cultural diversity.

Valiant though efforts have been to document Tucson's rich past during the impetus of the historic preservation movement in the 1960s and 1970s, only a few small publications and unpublished reports were produced that identified the characteristics of Tucson's historic urban neighborhoods. Since that time, little has been done to redistribute or consolidate these publications into one source, and nothing has been done to identify significant contemporary architecture in Tucson, which boomed after World War II.

The purpose of this book is to provide a comprehensive guide to Tucson's significant historic and contemporary architectural resources including buildings, ruins, open spaces, landscapes, and other elements which define Tucson's built environment. The scale of architecture addressed here encompasses urban and geographic patterns, individual structures and spaces, and their particular expressions in form, material, and detail.

Moreover, this book seeks to promote discussion of the critical issues that will determine the quality of our future built environment. By educating readers to be more discriminating observers, producers, and users of architecture, we hope to advocate a unique architectural expression appropriate for this place and this time.

Acknowledgments

This book would not have been possible without scores of people who exhibited a dedication to the purpose of this book equal to ours.

We are truly indebted to Mark Barmann for contributing his financial support as well as countless hours drafting, critiquing, and perfecting the area maps used in this book. He was also instrumental in consolidating biographical information on Tucson's significant architects. It is not an exaggeration to say that without his support and assistance, this book would not have happened. Financial support for securing the historical photos in this book was received from the University of Arizona Provost Author's Fund.

We relied on the expertise of a number of people who guided us through the selection of buildings and sites included in this book. We were blessed with a well-balanced and congenial advisory committee in Kirby Lockard, Jim Ayres, Linda Mayro, Jerry Kyle, Bob Vint, and Luis Ibarra, who gave up many evenings to share their knowledge, challenge our ideas, and provoke discussion on Tucson architecture. In addition, we received valuable comments from a variety of reviewers, including Jim Gresham, Jonathan Mabry, Henry Wallace, Joe Wilder, Laura Hollengreen, Abby Van Slyck, and Dan Brosnan, whose contributions made this a better publication. This book also stands on the shoulders of those whose previous scholarship, contributions, and advocacy on behalf of Tucson architecture are inspirational, including Eliazar Diaz (E. D.) Herreras, Robert Giebner, Gordon Heck, Harris Sobin, Jan Stewart, and Bunny Fontana.

The majority of the photography for this publication was done by

Bill Timmerman, who provided stunning work on a shoestring budget. In addition, the Arizona Historical Society/Southern Arizona Division in Tucson, the *Arizona Daily Star,* El Paso Public Library, Stephen Farley, Jack S. Williams, and Abby Van Slyck all contributed graphic materials from their collections.

We were fortunate to have several teams of University students and friends and family to check and double-check addresses, building descriptions, and maps. Thanks go to Mary Schmidt and Madelyn Cook, who contributed so much support and skill in providing the index.

And finally, this project could not have happened without the patience and support of our families. This book is dedicated to them.

The Guide to the Guide

The purpose of the "Guide to the Guide" is to inform the reader of the conventions used in this book as well as recommendations for how to best take advantage of the body of information presented. The book is divided into five sections: a history of Tucson architecture, architectural examples of buildings as well as sites by area, short biographies of selected Tucson architects, a glossary, and a bibliography. Each section is designed to stand as an independent, yet integrated, element of the entire publication.

The section of examples is the largest and most complex for the reader to use. It provides a listing of Tucson's most significant architecture and includes extant buildings as well as sites of archaeological resources or demolished buildings of architectural significance in order to understand the past and present context. Nominations for inclusion in this guide were solicited from local architectural professionals, which were then reviewed and selected by an advisory committee based on established criteria of significance. These criteria include *design quality; associative value,* representing larger cultural, economic, or stylistic themes, building typologies, or architects; and *national/regional recognition.*

An additional criterion for selection required that the important features of the building be physically or visually accessible or published in available journals. Many of the buildings are open to the public or their significant features can be seen from the street. Those that are not are noted as "inaccessible/published" with citations in the bibliography. When visiting any building, please respect the privacy of all residents and occupants. Some of them will be flattered and others will be intensely irritated by your interest. Always ask before taking photographs. When visiting schools, permission to view the buildings must be obtained from the principal's office. A building's inclusion in this publication does not guarantee you access or the right to trespass on private property.

Buildings and districts listed on the National Register of Historic Places are indicated by the use of the symbol [NRHP]. The actual National Register Historic District boundaries are not delineated on the area maps to avoid potential confusion between the "perceptual" boundary of a neighborhood and the boundary of the historic district, which in most cases don't correspond. A good reference map and listing of Tucson's historic districts can be found in *Celebrating Tucson's Heritage,* and comprehensive documentation about these districts can be found at the State Historic Preservation Office in Phoenix. Buildings listed on the National Register of Historic Places for their association with a historical event or theme, and not their architectural value, are not included in the examples section.

The examples are divided into geographic areas with corresponding maps drawn at three levels of scale: walking maps for dense historic neighborhoods, driving maps for suburban areas, and inset maps for denser areas within the larger driving maps. The maps are intended to help you find the buildings referred to in the section, but a current version of a Tucson street map is needed before setting out beyond the walking map areas.

Each geographic area is introduced with a descriptive overview, an area map, and a listing of significant buildings with numbers matching locations on the maps. Entries with no reference numbers and prefaced by "Site of" denote buildings that no longer exist but were located on the site described in the entry. Many of the areas include a final paragraph with additional buildings "also of note." Some of these represent buildings submitted too late to be included on the maps but whose significance merited inclusion in the book. In an attempt to recognize the collaborative nature of the building process, the section identifies many of the individuals who significantly contributed to the realization of the building, including architects of record, designers, structural engineers, landscape architects, developers, building contractors, and others. Photographs in the inventory section were intentionally limited to those buildings of exceptional quality that should not be missed in any critical study of Tucson architecture. Photographs are also used to illustrate buildings that are no longer extant or are otherwise inaccessible.

For buildings and sites with multiple names, the original or historic name is always listed first, followed by the current name. The most commonly used name, which often varies between the historic and the current, is in boldface. There are some buildings for which there are no street addresses or reference numbers at the request of the owners. In each of these cases, there is a publication reference allowing the reader to "visit" the building through published photographs, drawings, and text. Information not included in the building description indicates no corroborative source for the building's architect or date.

And finally, a caveat from the authors. This publication is still a work in progress. We welcome comments, criticisms, more accurate information, and recommendations for flagrant omissions. As much as we strive for perfection, we know how human we are. Please contact us through the College of Architecture, Planning and Landscape Architecture (CAPLA) Web site: http://architecture.arizona.edu/architecture.

A Guide to Tucson Architecture

Tucson Architecture: A Historical Introduction

One can view architecture, and the built environment generally, as an agent of cultural expression representing the particular place and time in which it was created. Many people look at architecture simply as an aesthetic expression without understanding the importance of what architecture can tell us about the time, people, and values that created it. Understanding any architecture built on the landscape must first be interpreted as representing the variety of forces that created it, including geographic, functional, social, cultural, technological, economic, and political. The significance of architecture, like manuscripts or photographs, must be interpreted through the reconstruction of its context, creating a causal relationship between the built environment and its influences. The built environment must also be studied at various levels of scale: *urban,* referring to how groupings of buildings and spaces create a larger expression; *building,* referring to the form and function of an individual structure and its space; and *detail,* referring to the smaller elements that, when combined, compose the larger building.

Geographically, the Tucson Basin is situated in the vast Sonoran Desert and is defined by five mountain ranges. The most significant features that influenced human settlement in this arid landscape, however, were the rivers by which the basin is outlined. The Santa Cruz, Cañada del Oro, Rillito, Tanque Verde, and Pantano provided the regular water supply needed for agricultural development, which permitted domestic culture. Of these, the perennial Santa Cruz River was also the corridor on which the transportation of people, goods, cultures, and technologies was conducted for millennia until the twentieth century, when geographic and human forces changed the river's character forever.

Prehistoric Period (10,500 B.C.–A.D. 1400s)

The advantageous geographic features of the Tucson Basin attracted people long before the establishment of permanent settlements. The earliest known human use of the Tucson Basin was by the Paleo-Indians, or First Americans, of the Clovis culture beginning in 10,500 B.C. These big-game hunters left little evidence of their seminomadic lifestyle and by 8000 B.C., the Paleo-Indians shared the Tucson Basin with the first hunter-gatherers of the Southwestern Archaic tradition. These early Archaic people, who expanded their diet to include small game, fruits, and seeds, also exhibited the first architectural traditions, beginning in 3800 B.C., as evidence of early pit and surface structures appeared at their seasonally occupied base camps. In the Tucson Basin, this indigenous Southwestern Archaic tradition is the first of five prehistoric architectural traditions recognized by archaeologists, followed by the Formative Mesoamerican, Upland, Hohokam, and Puebloan.

Sometime between 2500 and 1200 B.C., varieties of corn, beans, squash, and cotton were introduced into the region from Mexico, and the establishment of more defined agricultural settlements near permanent water sources followed. The watercourses of the Tucson Basin at that time were shallow, meandering streams that ran throughout most of the year. Although prehistoric settlements occurred along all the rivers of the Tucson Basin, evidence of concentrated and continuous occupations can be found next to existing mountain peaks, including Martinez Hill (the Bac settlement) and "A" Mountain (Tucson), where underground basalt "dikes" pushed the underground stream channel above the ground surface.

In addition to floodwater farming, the sustainability of these early settlements relied on water-control technologies also introduced from Mesoamerica to the Tucson Basin during this phase. Check dams and the earliest known canals north of Mexico, dating from 1200 B.C., provided a greater diversity of planting seasons and crops. Although the Southwestern Archaic inhabitants became more sedentary through the cultivation of crops, seasonal hunting and gathering practices were still maintained. The diversity of topography and natural resources of the Tucson Basin made it an ideal place to balance the two means of subsistence.

The first imported architectural tradition, the Formative Mesoamerican, was adopted and further developed in the Tucson Basin during the San Pedro phase (1200–800 B.C.). The basic element of settlement during this phase was a courtyard group where individual round and oval pit structures were oriented toward a common space, implying relationships of family, clan, and larger social organization. The much longer Cienega phase (800 B.C.–A.D. 150) was characterized by a more sedentary life, including much larger settlements along the Santa Cruz River and the use of pit structures for more specialized functions. Larger pit structures were found during this period with more complex roof support systems and open floor spaces, which may have served as communal ceremonial buildings with adjacent open "plaza" areas.

At the beginning of the Agua Caliente phase (A.D. 150–550), a new, Upland architectural tradition appeared alongside the early agricultural tradition. The Upland tradition, more applicable to winter occupation, was introduced from the highlands of northern Mexico and may have represented the origins of the architectural traditions of the later Mogollon culture.

The Hohokam, a distinctly agricultural cultural group developed between A.D. 1 and 500, initially established villages along the Salt and Gila Rivers of central Arizona and between A.D. 450 and 650 spread to the Tucson Basin. In contrast to the Salt and Gila River areas, where the Hohokam used a complex system of canals to direct water to their communities, the Tucson settlement was laid out much closer to the river floodplain.

During the Pre-Classic Hohokam period (A.D. 650–1150), the architectural tradition represented a blending of the lowland agricultural traditions: Patterns of communal settlement became more formal, individual pit structures were often grouped around common courtyards, and courtyard groups were arranged around communal plazas. Ball courts, one of the first examples of Hohokam community architecture, were introduced in 800 and were found at most of the major sites in Tucson. The ball game, a vital component of Mesoamerican cultural life, provided a ceremonial and ritual activity that brought people together from various communities.

The Classic Hohokam period (1150–1450) began as outside cultures infiltrated the Tucson Basin, introducing profound cultural, technological, political, religious, and architectural changes. During this period, the Puebloan architectural tradition appeared alongside the Hohokam tradition, as shown by a dramatic shift from pit structures to the aboveground earthen structures of the northern Puebloan cultures. Communal settlement patterns often included the construction of walls to create compounds. Although the functional components of the courtyard group remained relatively unchanged, the settlement unit became much more unified as competition for resources, such as water and stored food, may have caused stress on the culture which required a more defensive enclosure. Two new building types were also introduced during this period. The introduction of platform mounds from Mesoamerica in 1100 marked a venue shift of community ritual away from ball courts. Resembling unfinished pyramids, these flat-topped mounds served initially as a unifying element for communal ritual activities and later as a walled defensive precinct on which an elite class of priests were protected in an increasingly stratified society. The other significant building type that emerged during this period was the great house, exemplified by the ruins at Casa Grande (A.D. 1300), but no such structures have been uncovered in Tucson.

In the era between 1300 and 1350, there was evidence of a significant cultural change including a population decline and changes in social organization, possibly brought about by environmental conditions and the collapse of major cultures in the Southwest and Mesoamerica. Trade during this time seemed also to have shifted away from the northern Salado/Mogollon cultures to the more enduring southern cultures of Mesoamerica. By 1450, the Hohokam as a distinct culture disappeared without evidence of abandonment or direct incorporation into other cultures. At the time of initial Spanish contact in the sixteenth century, the two distinct descendants of the Hohokam, the Pima and Papago (the latter now known as Tohono O'odham), displayed only vestiges of the Hohokam's previous architectural traditions and settlement patterns.

Spanish Colonial/Mexican Period (1500–1850)

The arrival of the Spanish to what is today southern Arizona marked a dramatic shift away from a culture principally defined by geographic determinants and regional influences to one characterized by centralized, external, political-religious power and the importation of new technologies for the purposes of commercial exploitation.

The Spanish process of settlement in the New World began in the Caribbean in 1493 and ended in California by 1781, during which time the Spanish took possession of a land area that was forty times the size of Spain. Spain in 1492 had just completed the Christian reconquest of the Iberian Peninsula, which had been in the hands of the Moors since the founding of Cordoba in the eighth century. Islamic architecture, art, culture, and technological advances during the Moors' reign con-

trasted sharply with a lack of progress in these areas during the Dark Ages in the rest of Europe during the same period. During the reconquest, many Jews and Moors were expelled from Spain, were converted to Christianity and known as *conversos,* or remained as subjugated citizens, *mudéjares.* The *mudéjares,* in particular, contributed significantly to the building of Christian monuments, maintaining many of the Islamic characteristics that defined their pre-Christian works. Many of these *mudéjares,* as well as Jews and non-Castilians, fled to the Americas and made their mark on the architectural, technological, and cultural expressions being formulated in the new Spanish colonies.

By 1521, the Spanish had conquered the Aztec capital of Tenochtitlán in the central basin of Mexico, a remarkable city of temples, canals, and rich farmlands, and quickly converted it into the central administrative and political center for the emerging North American colony of New Spain. Between 1535 and 1604, the Spanish explorers Cabeza de Vaca, Marcos de Niza, and Coronado all traversed through southern Arizona in search of the riches of the fabled Seven Cities of Cibola. They recorded encountering Pima and Papago (now Tohono O'odham) tribes in scattered agrarian settlements, which they named *rancherias*. By 1600, Apaches had arrived in southern Arizona from the north but had little contact with the Spaniards until they began raiding Pima settlements later in that century.

There were two northern royal roads that originated from the newly named capital of Mexico City and became lifelines for the colonization process to and from the northern frontier. The first road terminated in the 1609 establishment of Santa Fe. This occurred only two years after the establishment of Jamestown, Virginia, the first permanent English settlement of North America, and marked the contemporaneous settlement by European cultures on both sides of what is now the United States. The other route ran up the western coast of Mexico, through the Tucson Basin, and terminated in the development of California settlements.

The Spanish colonization of the Americas was meant to provide resources to maintain and enrich the Spanish crown and to expand Spain's power in the world but required an organized campaign that would rival the Romans in the establishment, settlement, and exploitation of the new lands. This imperialistic process was implemented through three frontier institutions—mission, presidio, and pueblo—which were manifestations of the more operative goals of conversion, protection, and civilization, respectively.

San Xavier del Bac, c. 1900. Considered the finest example of Spanish Colonial architecture in the United States, the size and iconographic messages conveyed by this mission church were meant to impress on the native population the superior power of Spain and its Christian god.

During the latter part of the seventeenth and early eighteenth centuries, Jesuits followed the footsteps of the early explorers in the northern provinces and attempted to pacify the native population to make them subjects of the Spanish crown. These Jesuit missionaries established a system of mission sites that corresponded with existing native Pima-speaking populations scattered along the river floodplains in a region that was to become known as the Pimería Alta, a large geographic area defined by the Pima and Papago settlements which occupied the current state of Sonora and the region of southern Arizona.

One of the most prolific builders among the Jesuit missionaries, Eusebio Francisco Kino, began exploratory travels through the Pimería Alta in 1694. He recorded the two largest settlements of his journey, at Bac (meaning "where the water appears"), naming Francisco Xavier as its patron saint, and Chuk Shon (later transliterated as "Tucson," meaning "black base" or "at the foot of the black mountain"), naming San Cosmé as its patron saint in 1699. San Cosmé de Tucson was merely a satellite mission to Bac, and the site never rose above that of a *visita*, not having a resident priest but rather one who visited only periodically to give mass. Tucson at that time was a part of the province of Sonora with its capital at Arizpe. The settlement was merely an outpost from that regional center but became an integral junction where the explorers and missionaries stopped their northern trek and crossed over the harsh desert westward to the California coast.

The construction of missionary settlements in the Pimería Alta introduced building technologies unseen in this part of the country. The limitation for the Spanish frontier builders,

"Convento," Mission San Agustín del Tucson, c. 1890. Until its senseless demolition in the 1950s, this majestic structure was the last visible vestige of the Spanish Colonial presence in the original Pima village of Tucson and was part of a mission complex that included gardens, orchards, and a sophisticated irrigation system.

however, was to find the expertise to interpret their distinctly foreign cultural expression within the vocabulary of available materials and technology. As with their predecessors, the Spanish exploited the locally available construction materials and applied their imported technological knowledge in the service of a cultural expression.

The second frontier institution in the Spanish colonization process was the presidio, a system of garrisons that protected coastal ports and defined the edge of New Spain's northern expansion. In reality, the logistics of distance from both Spain and New World administrative centers, such as Mexico City, restricted missionary expansion in areas where self-sufficiency could not be sustained, as was the case in Tucson. Southern Arizona, however, continued to attract Spanish settlers seeking status through land ownership and cattle ranching on its rich

grasslands. The Santa Cruz River valley also attracted miners after the discovery of silver near Nogales in 1736 and continued to be a strategic link in the road to the missions and riches of California until sea routes replaced land routes by the end of the eighteenth century.

Pima dissatisfaction with European involvement in their community led to an uprising in 1751, which spawned the establishment of a presidio at Tubac, 50 miles south of Tucson, in 1752. In 1767, the Jesuits were expelled from Spanish territories and were replaced by the Franciscans. The newly arrived Franciscans at Bac felt threatened in the unprotected mission and attempted to establish a newly fortified headquarters in the San Cosmé de Tucson mission community in 1768. After repeated Apache attacks in the San Pedro Valley, its Terrenate presidio, and the Santa Cruz Valley's Tubac presidio, the Irish mercenary Hugo O'Conor consolidated the Spanish military presence in southern Arizona into a newly created presidio in Tucson in 1775.

This presidio, San Agustín del Tucson, was built on the east side of the Santa Cruz River, opposite the existing fortified mission community, creating a much more defensible position with fortifications on both sides of the natural corridor of the Santa Cruz. In addition, the black mountain for which Tucson is named (later called Sentinel Peak and now "A" Mountain) became a crucial lookout to watch for Apache marauders.

The third instrument of the Spanish colonization campaign was the pueblo or city. The pueblo was a civilian settlement used to unite isolated groups of Spaniards and also exploit as rapidly and efficiently as possible the human and natural resources of each territory. The Spanish city model, based on a 1573 set of royal ordinances governing the settlement of the Americas, commonly referred to as the Laws of the Indies, reflected the Roman model of an urban grid and defined the major urban features of the town: the plaza as a centering device, the public buildings that surround it, and the private residences and streets that radiate from it. The guiding principle of Spanish Colonial urban and architectural expression was the creation of open space as the central organizing element defined by the surrounding building. These open spaces were created of various sizes and scales, from residential courtyards to urban plazas.

In Tucson, owing to its frontier location, the Spanish urban form never developed to the same degree as in cities in central Mexico. The origins of Tucson's urban layout began in the Presidio compound with the establishment of a church and two relatively undefined plazas.

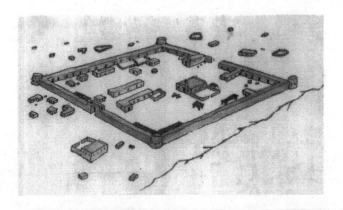

Residential quarters were established against the interior face of the Presidio walls, as well as in the interior of the Presidio's plazas. Tucson's residential architecture, although a frontier, "Sonoran" expression of traditional Spanish Colonial characteristics, bears a remarkable resemblance to the Pueblo-influenced Hohokam structures of earlier centuries. Fear of Apache attacks prevented the expansion of residential neighborhoods beyond the protective walls of the Presidio until the arrival of the Americans in the mid-nineteenth century.

American Territorial Period: Pre-Railroad (1850–1880)

After Mexico gained independence from Spain in 1821, the frontier outpost of Tucson passed from Spanish to Mexican rule and remained a part of the state of Sonora. Although a few American trappers began arriving into southern Arizona as early as 1826, it was the gold rush of 1849 that brought the first wave of Americans through the region. Those who settled here represented the diverse ethnic groups populating the eastern United States: Germans, Italians, Anglos, and French. Although English had become the common language of all of these groups, it is incorrect to generalize these early Americans or their cultural influences as simply "Anglo."

The first generation of new American settlers, as a minority group, adopted local architectural expressions to assimilate into the prevailing culture, and many American men married into local Mexican families. But just as the prehistoric and Spanish inhabitants of the region transported technological skills and used locally available materials to construct the architectural expressions of their cultures, the American settlers slowly transformed Tucson's cultural identity through the use of architectural

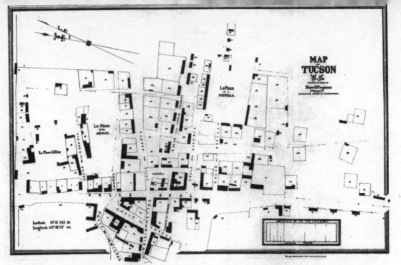

expressions from their many places of origin.

Tucson in the mid-nineteenth century was primarily an agrarian center spanning the Santa Cruz River, a gradual floodplain lined with cottonwood and mesquite trees with year-round water flow for crop irrigation. In 1887, a significant earthquake created a fissure in the ground causing the surface water to sink into an underground river and aquifer. This lack of steady surface water caused increased damming of the river, which, combined with the denuding of the vegetation lining the riverbed, promoted seasonal flooding and deep cutting of the Santa Cruz watercourse, thus deteriorating the agricultural floodplain.

The Mexican-American War (1846–1848) brought little fighting to the Pimería Alta but depleted the troops of the northern presidios. This left the Pimería Alta vulnerable to continued Apache attacks and forced the transfer of Tubac's population to Tucson's presidio. At the end of the Mexican-American War, more than 520,000 square miles, nearly a quarter of Mexico's former territory, was transferred from Mexico to the United States under the terms of the 1848 Treaty of Guadalupe Hidalgo, but this territory did not include Tucson.

The California gold rush brought thousands of people through Arizona, creating supply routes that would quickly connect the American and Mexican areas of what is now Arizona. In 1853, an additional 30,000 square miles, including southern Arizona south of the Gila River, was procured by the American government through the Gadsden Purchase, whose purpose was to secure land for a southern route of the transcontinental railroad. Tucson became part of the United States, and in

Fergusson Map of Tucson, 1862. The Fergusson Map is the first American documentation of Tucson and reveals a town just beginning to break out of its presidial walls. It also delineates Tucson's original plazas, a primary component of Spanish town planning in the Americas, none of which exists today.

1856 the Presidio was officially transferred from Mexican to American hands.

The first generation of Americans in Tucson, arriving in the 1850s, adopted and adapted existing architectural forms and expressions. The population of Tucson, fewer than 500 people, was confined to an area in and around the Presidio, where plazas had begun to form and settlements had started to grow along the original royal road, Calle Real, soon renamed Main Avenue. Tucson was still as isolated from its new American center of government as it had been from its Mexican center, but as more Americans headed west, Tucson became a crucial link in the fast-growing transcontinental travel. Tucson's settlement pattern gradually broke away from its presidial boundaries, and the first structures began to appear in what is now downtown and the Barrio Historico. By 1858, American merchants began

to settle permanently in Tucson and established commercial enterprises, while mail and stage lines, established in 1857, advertised Tucson as a developing commercial and transportation center on the way to California.

The 1860s and 1870s brought tremendous change to Tucson. The American Civil War (1861–1865) again forced the transfer of presidial troops to fight in the East, leaving Tucson vulnerable to more Apache raids, and the town's population declined. When Union forces returned in 1862, Major David Fergusson was charged with protecting the fatigued town and documenting land ownership in Tucson to settle disputes among Mexicans and Americans. This first map of Tucson reveals the timid attempts to settle outside of the Presidio in spite of the Apache threat. In 1863, Arizona became a territory of the United States with its capital in Prescott. As the largest city in the Arizona Territory,

Tucson was designated its capital from 1867 to 1877, the official buildings of which consisted of a series of Sonoran adobe structures on Ochoa Street near Stone Avenue. This architectural testament was one reason that the capital was subsequently returned to the more "American" town of Prescott.

In 1866, the most significant obstacle to a growing and prosperous American settlement was still the Apaches. Efforts to pacify the Apaches became concentrated with the establishment of a permanent military camp, Tucson Post, soon renamed Camp Lowell, within the city limits. In 1873, at the request of the civilian population, the army troops were moved away from the town to the distant confluence of the Rillito and Pantano watercourses, and established Fort Lowell.

Two pieces of federal legislation had tremendous impact as engines of development in western settlements such as Tucson. In 1862, the Homestead Act was passed to provide a system of land ownership that would guarantee titles, both for new claims and for those remaining from the Spanish and Mexican periods. The Homestead Act allowed anyone to acquire 160 acres located in the public domain, as long as there were no residual claims on the land at the time of the Gadsden Treaty. This procedure required a nominal filing fee, continuous occupancy, and a promise to "improve" the land, usually implying the construction of a house or some other structure to give the land a purpose. As in previous centuries, this type of land-settlement policy encouraged the American population to spread into the unsettled West and take claim to land with very little money, thus "Americanizing" the territory. The 1877 Desert Land Act increased homestead allotments from 160 to 640 acres; this was a

Roskruge Map, 1893. This map represents the orthogonal grid plan surveyed by S. W. Foreman in 1872 as part of Tucson's incorporation as a township. In contrast to the plaza-based Spanish urban pattern, this American grid was an efficient means of subdividing land and became the model for Tucson's subsequent growth throughout the twentieth century.

blocks 400 feet square. The original boundaries of the township—Speedway Boulevard to the north, First Avenue to the east, 22nd Street to the south, and Main Avenue to the west—now include the current historic districts of Barrio Libre, El Presidio, Armory Park, Ironhorse, and West University.

In contrast to the Spanish use of a street pattern around a plaza to create a sense of a community center, Tucson's new grid, based on the American traditions of William Penn, was more a device of democratic division of land for economic speculation and expansion. This American grid became the model for all subsequent growth as the city acquired more land and as the unincorporated areas of the Tucson Basin began to expand.

During the 1870s, businesses of all varieties began to appear as Tucson became a commercial and transportation center. These businesses represented the

boon to cattle ranchers but also created an industry of land developers who speculated on the growth of settlements such as Tucson. After the passage of the Desert Land Act, hundreds of people filed claims and pursued livelihoods ranging from ranching and farming to real estate speculation and development, and whose dependence on new residents and growth as an industry is still evident today.

In 1871, Tucson incorporated as a town with 2 square miles of federal land set aside for the township. In 1872, S. W. Foreman surveyed and patented the town plan, laying out an orthogonal grid of north-south avenues and east-west streets that defined

diversity of ethnicity and religious affiliation that was the foundation of Tucson's rich cultural heritage: German, English, Mexican, French, African American, Chinese, Catholic, Protestant, and Jew. In addition to the ubiquitous saloon and two red-light districts for male entertainment, family destinations were provided by three parks. Carrillo Gardens (later called the Elysian Grove) and Levin's Park provided everything from billiards and bowling to restaurants and dancing. Water to supply these parks and much of Tucson's drinking water came from a natural spring, called El Ojito, located in the Santa Cruz floodplain. The Santa Cruz River was dammed at a number of places along its course through Tucson, providing power for a variety of mills and forming Silverlake, another recreational destination. Hotels, including the Cosmopolitan and the Palace, provided increasingly sophisti-

cated accommodations for visitors and single residents.

The establishment of Tucson's municipal and cultural institutions represented the growing confidence of an increasingly American town despite the continued, but subdued, presence of the Apaches. The Catholic Church, a dominant presence throughout Tucson's Spanish Colonial period, was not well represented in the American period until the arrival of Bishop Salpointe in 1866. He was instrumental in establishing Catholic education and, in 1880, an adobe cathedral, San Augustín, built on the Plaza de la Mesilla. In 1878, the first protestant (Presbyterian) church was built on the more northern Plaza de las Armas, in a French Gothic style, in distinct contrast to the Sonoran architecture surrounding it.

Although new stylistic expressions were being introduced through piecemeal

Silverlake, c. 1890. The Santa Cruz River was the focus of all activities for most of Tucson's history until the twentieth century. In addition to providing an agricultural floodplain for settlers, it provided irrigation canals for a variety of purposes and was dammed in a number of places to provide power for mills and to create recreational areas, such as Silverlake.

architectural elements, most of the prominent Americans continued to build their homes in the Sonoran style. Freight wagons brought occasional loads of construction materials, but at a cost well beyond the means of most Tucsonans. Adobe was still the most available, economical, and climatically reasonable form of construction for all types of buildings. Lumber, the other structural component in the Sonoran construction system, was obtained by cutting down trees from the local riverbanks or, if funds permitted, the tall straight pine trees of the Santa Rita and Santa Catalina Mountains. Technological innovation was soon to spawn the primary agent of change in the West for the next century: transportation.

American Territorial Period: Post-Railroad (1880–1914)

By far the most significant impact on Tucson during the American Territorial period was the arrival of the railroad in 1880, also the year that Tucson's population surpassed 7,000. By 1886, when Geronimo surrendered, the worst of the Apache wars were over and Tucson was the major trading and urban center for people arriving in southern Arizona seeking opportunities in mining, agriculture, ranching, and the businesses that supported them. The railroad brought to Tucson both culture (in the form of eastern tastes in everything from food to architecture) and technology (in the form of mass-produced materials), enabling the rapid transformation of Tucson from a Sonoran pueblo to an American town.

The new railroad tracks cut a diagonal line across the northeast quadrant of the new township but acted as a magnet, drawing development away from the presidial center. This shift in Tucson's geocultural center marked the first of many such shifts as new development was

Church plaza. In the Hispanic tradition, the shady park plaza in front of
San Agustín Cathedral was a gathering place for religious, civic, and social functions
and was the geographic, cultural, and perceptual center of the town. The church building
was abandoned for the larger, and current, cathedral in 1897;
the original building was demolished in 1936.

aided by the increased mobility brought about by the technological advances in transportation. Understanding this impact, land speculators and developers began subdividing their homesteads east of the townsite in anticipation of the growing urban population. Unhampered by geographic boundaries, the growth potential of the Tucson Basin seemed endless and was made affordable through homestead legislation. In the years between 1880 and 1912, when Arizona became the forty-eighth state, Tucson experienced a dizzying pace of growth that defined it as the region's economic and cultural center.

Tucson's buildings were also seeing a dramatic transformation. In contrast to Sonoran buildings that defined open space, American buildings were defined as detached objects on a property. The single Sonoran building form that accommodated a variety of functions was replaced by architectural forms as diverse as their functions. Ornamentation, relatively nonexistent in the Sonoran architectural tradition, was celebrated in the American buildings and followed prescribed architectural styles codified in widely distributed pattern books. This multi-scaled transition from a Sonoran to an American architectural expression was not immediate and resulted in the creation of many hybrid buildings composed of a combination of the two expressions. Ubiquitous to most of the newer houses was the emergence of the sleeping porch at the rear, to take advantage of the cooler temperatures outside during summer nights. The sleeping porch was an American adaptation to the previous tradition of sleeping outdoors in courtyards or on the roof.

Adobe continued to be used but took on imported stylistic characteristics. Milled lumber, glass, and bricks were added to

existing Sonoran buildings in the form of projecting porches, door frames, windows, and parapet coping. These changes were representative of a larger cultural transformation that distinguished the American community from the Mexican community, evolving into the ethnic division of neighborhoods after the turn of the twentieth century.

The University of Arizona, considered an undesirable appropriation from the territorial legislature, was awarded to Tucson in 1885, contingent on the procurement of land; 40 acres were subsequently obtained (donated by two gamblers) in 1886. Its location northeast of the township was quite accidental, and it was inconveniently placed a half mile away from railroad facilities, but nevertheless attracted growth for the next few decades. In 1887, the first campus building, the School of Mines (now called Old Main), was built, and its eclectic mixture of

vernacular and historical references made it an unlikely but appropriate model for Tucson's future architectural expression.

The city's infrastructure soon began to catch up with the advancements brought on by the railroad. Telephone lines appeared in 1881, followed by gaslights, electricity, and water in 1882, all of which eventually became operated by municipal companies. By 1898, a mule-car street railway system connected downtown and the train depot with the main gate of the University, and a few years later the system was extended to include Carrillo Gardens and Armory Park, a fashionable residential district growing up along S. 4th Avenue. The expansion of the mule-car street system encouraged real estate development along the corridor between downtown and the University because the periphery of town was now accessible to public transportation. In 1899, the

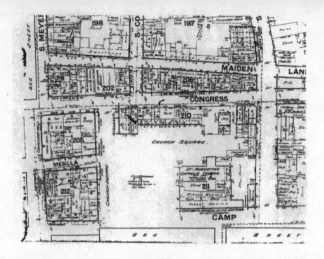

automobile was introduced to Tucson and it would become the dominant form of transportation by 1920, again fueling the direction of growth, this time beyond the corporate limits of the city, and promoting the subdivision of homesteads throughout the Tucson Basin.

A chamber of commerce was established in 1896 to promote not only the entrepreneurial interests of Tucson but also its landmarks of cultural affluence. Tucson boasted an opera house, a variety of first-class accommodations (including the elegant Santa Rita Hotel), and a bustling retail district whose center, at the corner of Stone Avenue and Pennington Street, was marked by Steinfeld's Department Store, the successor of the pioneering mercantile Zeckendorf's. Tucson's commercial architecture also used imported styles as an expression of the growing American cultural trend. In contrast to the accommodation

of a variety of functions within a single Sonoran building topology, American residential, commercial, civic, religious, and educational buildings distinguish their function through unique architectural forms and styles. Specific buildings often used architectural styles to associate their values with their exterior images, such as conservative neoclassical banks and aspiring Gothic churches. As Tucson was searching for an image appropriate for its identity as a prosperous mining, ranching, agricultural, and commercial center, architecture was used as a vehicle to express the town's new, American identity.

The American Territorial period also marked an increased specialization of building skills and the creation of an independent building industry. In contrast to previous periods where the buildings were designed and built by one person, this period distinguishes itself by

Sanborn Insurance Map, 1883. In the twenty-one short years since the Fergusson Map documentation of Tucson, the urban pattern outside the Presidio walls was beginning to take shape, indicating a continued preference for the Spanish model of street-abutting buildings and open space in the center of the block.

the emergence of architects as a profession distinct from builders. Architects designed their buildings for clients, and the structures were subsequently built by specialized craftsmen who shared little of the value systems of the other two. Although architects were employed in Tucson from the 1880s, it wasn't until the turn of the twentieth century that professionals, such as David Holmes, Henry Trost, and Henry Jaastad, began to design a significant number of unique buildings that were distinguished from those of pattern-style builders.

Residential construction, regardless of external stylistic expression, became standardized, typically built of brick exterior walls with wooden floors, roof framing, interior walls, and cabinetry. The emergence of brick as a dominant building material would seal the economic and cultural division between the "old" adobe-built Sonoran

buildings and the "modern" brick-built American buildings. Architect and builder Quintus Monier established Tucson's first brickyard at the end of the nineteenth century, using the rich clay deposits along the Santa Cruz River. He later founded the Tucson Pressed Brick Company, which supplied the material for most of Tucson's prominent early-twentieth-century buildings.

Tucson in the American Territorial period quickly evolved from an agrarian settlement alongside a river floodplain to a commercial trading center whose limits for growth seemed endless. The Santa Cruz River, once the city's original lifeline, was transformed from a rich agricultural floodplain for feeding its community to a source of raw materials for building. The random street layout and irregular plazas of the Presidio had become subordinate to an American ideal: an urban grid

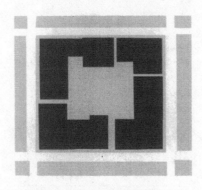

Typical Sonoran and American blocks. The Spanish urban typology included attached row houses with a contiguous street facade protecting the communal inner-block courtyard. In contrast, the American model included large yards surrounding detached houses with no common area. This contrast distinguishes the Spanish and American urban morphologies of defining open space versus defining objects, respectively.

which formalized the open spaces and made land distribution more efficient. The newly arrived railroad not only transported Americans to Tucson, but also transformed the town's cultural identity, expressed in the architectural forms and stylistic vocabulary of the new arrivals. As Arizona's largest city on the eve of its statehood, Tucson was now connected to a nation of numerous architectural expressions that changed as quickly as newly developing technologies were able to transport them.

Interwar Period: 1914–1945

Both before and after World War I (1914–1918), Americans suffering from respiratory diseases (in particular, tuberculosis) came to Arizona and Tucson for treatment in its dry, mild climate, building Tucson's reputation as a destination for "health seekers." The rush of people with respiratory ailments, known as "lungers," was accommodated by sites throughout Tucson known as "tent cities." Because lungers were feared, they were prevented from renting in town, so hospitals, sanatoria, and preventoria were constructed on the outskirts of Tucson, including Pastime Park, Desert Sanatorium, St. Mary's Hospital, and the Veterans Hospital, leading to the development of a health industry in Tucson. This, in turn, led to zoning and building regulations that increased ventilation and restricted the amount of land which a house could occupy, all in attempts to prevent the spread of disease. Political instruments such as these would begin to have an increasing impact on the architecture of Tucson.

Tucson, and the West in general, was also a destination for tourists seeking to explore the exotic landscape and culture that they had only read about. Personal travel, now dominated by the automobile, increased tremendously after World War I.

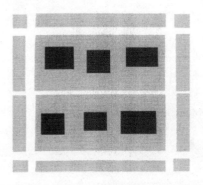

Tourism operators, such as the Harvey Hotel Company, marketed this exotic quality and the unfamiliar architecture to promote a romanticized image of the Southwest. Just as the eastern states had chosen to use English Colonial Revival styles beginning in the nineteenth century, promoters and architects in the West extracted architectural characteristics from previous cultures to produce the romanticized revival styles for this region. This romantic revival movement was crystallized and then disseminated through the buildings of the 1915 Panama-California Exposition in San Diego (today's Balboa Park). Designed by Bertram Goodhue, Richard Requa, and others, these buildings promoted the Spanish Colonial Revival style as an appropriate regional architectural expression. Other architects, including Mary Colter and John Gaw Meem, defined similarly romantic expressions for other regions of the Southwest. The exposition also marks a shift in Tucson's cultural and architectural inspiration from the East and Midwest to California.

By 1920, Phoenix had surpassed Tucson as Arizona's largest city. It had benefited from the Reclamation Act of 1902, which facilitated the development of the Salt River valley and overshadowed the mining interests that had fueled Tucson's growth in the early twentieth century. Up until that time, Tucson was the largest and most important settlement in Arizona owing to its dominance of the five C's of the Arizona economy: copper, cattle, cotton, citrus, and climate. Now a health destination for the ailing, Tucson had to change this negative image to attract new residents, businesses, and the economic prosperity associated with them. In 1922, the Tucson Sunshine Climate Club was formed to promote the attractions of southern Arizona for the

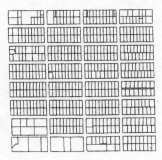

Tucson subdivision patterns, 1928. The orthogonal gridiron subdivision, used in Tucson through World War II, was becoming associated with middle-class living standards. New subdivisions, drawing on California models, emphasized irregular lot sizes, curvilinear streets, dense vegetation, and deed restrictions, all of which were designed to attract affluent residents to Tucson.

benefit of local merchants and hoteliers. Tourism and boosterism became important factors in the growth and prosperity of Tucson and soon were represented by the phenomenon of winter visitors.

Subdivision development in Tucson, outside the city limits, was rampant. The original 1872 grid street pattern expanded to the north and east away from the original townsite, with the University as a primary destination for urban growth. Transportation had an increasing impact on growth: Developments previously outside the perceived limits of the town were becoming not only accessible but desirable as an escape from the growing automobile congestion of the urbanized city. During the boom years of the 1920s, great portions of the desert were developed in anticipation of continuing high demand for residential subdivisions. By the mid-1930s, the 1929 stock market crash had put the

real estate market into a tailspin except for the very wealthy, who were still coming to Tucson.

The orthogonal grid, formerly associated with equitable land distribution, was now becoming associated with the middle-class living standards of small lots and equally small houses, some as small as 900 square feet. Beginning in 1915, subdivisions were developed with deed restrictions intended to ensure property values through exclusivity. As a way of distinguishing affluent neighborhoods from those of the middle class, alternatives to the gridiron subdivision layout were introduced by California developers and architects. In 1928, three innovative subdivisions were planned, and these began to attract the affluent to Tucson: El Encanto Estates, Colonia Solana, and the Catalina Foothills Estates.

Each of these subdivisions was designed to provide a unique environment, and they became models for subsequent subdivi-

sion development. Although unique, each subdivision incorporated common characteristics: curvilinear street patterns, in direct contrast to the existing gridiron standard; protection of the existing landscape and its use as a marketing tool; exploitation of the romantic image of Tucson's relationship to its Spanish heritage; and deed restrictions, which controlled homeownership, set minimum construction costs, and defined the architectural expression of individual residences. In a city where new residents arrived constantly, land and houses increasingly became speculative commodities, bought and sold as the promise of future growth increased their value. Real estate entrepreneurs purchased large tracts of land, developed services, built houses without specific clients, and sold them with a marketing strategy associating the architecture with an ideal image of Tucson.

Supervising architects were hired for these subdivision developments to oversee adherence to architectural control standards of house size, construction costs, building materials, and stylistic expression. In the case of the Catalina Foothills Estates, its developer, John Murphey, maintained control over every aspect of the development process from land purchase, lot placement, and water distribution to the architectural services of Murphey's architect, Josias Joesler, and construction by Murphey's building company. Murphey's development was located 4 miles from the city limits and had a profound impact on shifting the geographic orientation away from the western Tucson Mountains and toward the northern Santa Catalina Mountains.

Winter visitors often bought second homes in Tucson in many of these exclusive subdivisions. Residential architects and builders during this time continued to promote revival architectural styles, especially Spanish Colonial, Mission, and Pueblo. These styles all represent architectural expressions external to Tucson's cultural heritage, but they were nonetheless accepted as representing a generic Southwestern architectural vocabulary dictating the appearance of Tucson's residential buildings.

The attached, screened sleeping porches of the previous generation of houses were built into the new house forms as exterior living rooms and were referred to as Arizona rooms. The mid-1930s also brought the introduction of mechanical cooling systems to Tucson. Houses were retrofitted with evaporative (or swamp) coolers, which added humidity and thus lowered the temperature during the dry summer months, although many residents continued to sleep outdoors or in sleeping porches. Air condition-

ing first appeared downtown in 1929 in the Fox Theatre, which became a popular spot for escape from the heat of the summer. These innovations, especially as they continued to be refined, resulted in fewer residents leaving Tucson during the summer; the new technology also encouraged the larger, rambling house plans of the upscale subdivision developments. The impact of the automobile on Tucson's culture elevated the role of the garage from a detached shed facing the back alley to an attached and integral piece of the overall street facade.

As winter visitors became increasingly more common, hotel facilities were required not only to provide accommodations but also to project the desired image of Tucson as a grand tourist destination. Resort hotels, such as the Arizona Inn and El Conquistador Hotel, and guest ranches, including the Tanque Verde Guest Ranch, promoted luxurious

accommodations amid the serene qualities of the desert. As air-conditioned movie theaters became cool destinations to escape the heat, drive-in theaters, introduced in 1940, gave people alternatives for entertainment during summer evenings. The impact of the car and mobility on American culture was also represented by the growth of motor courts along Tucson's major travel arteries: The Miracle Mile, Florence, Nogales, and Benson Highways were dotted with neon-clad respites that allowed weary travelers to park right next to their rooms. In addition, Arizona's first suburban shopping center, Broadway Village, was built to lure shoppers away from downtown. Just before the depression, Tucson, previously devoid of vertical expression, also gained two high-rise buildings: The Consolidated National Bank (now Bank One) and the Pioneer Hotel were built in an era of prosperity and represented the growing importance of commerce and tourism to Tucson.

The years between the two world wars also brought tremendous growth to the University of Arizona, which, by this time, was a vital contributor to Tucson's economic, cultural, and urban character. The campus had grown from a dispersed collection of individual buildings with an incoherent identity to a formally planned, parklike setting with an increasingly consistent architectural character. This consolidation was achieved by the hiring of Roy Place as the University's architect; Place unified both the University's built environment and its identity as an appropriate place for higher education.

Like the rest of the nation, the depression hit Tucson hard. The 1930s saw the abandonment of many of the speculative development projects on which Tucson had become partly dependent for its economic viability. Tucson

survived the depression primarily because of tourism. And during World War II, Tucson became a hub for troops being transported from coast to coast. Dozens of buildings were used or converted by the military during the war, which brought in much-needed funds to revitalize the local economy. Because construction supplies in Tucson were scarce, very little building activity occurred, which resulted in the relaxation of building and zoning codes and even the use of recycled building materials. To accommodate training facilities, the meager Davis-Monthan airfield, southeast of Tucson, expanded its operations during and after the war and created another urban economic center, which attracted the next generation of subdivision development.

Post–World War II Period: 1945–present
World War II introduced Tucson to thousands of men who, in their desire to start a new life after the war, returned to Tucson as permanent residents. These people flooded into Tucson and Arizona for its mild climate, inexpensive living, and new employment opportunities. Mining was a strong economic generator for southern Arizona, and the aerospace industry burgeoned during and after the war. But by the 1980s, both industries began to leave the area, taking with them the economic prosperity that drove Tucson's growth. The national economic prosperity of the late 1990s brought another population explosion and a new service-oriented workforce, as well as decentralized work environments.

Urban development during the late 1940s rapidly extended beyond the corporate limits of Tucson. Subdivisions prematurely platted in the 1920s north and east of the urban core were consumed by an expanding

Aerial view of eastern Tucson subdivisions, c. 1950. Post–World War II development in Tucson was characterized by low-density suburban sprawl throughout the Tucson Basin. "Leapfrog" land development pushed Tucson's growth outward, left behind undeveloped "infill" tracts of land, and began encroaching on the fragile ecosystems of the valley's edges.

growth unforeseen by local officials and planners. The restrictions on building during the war also left a profound housing shortage, which, combined with an exploding population, made Tucson a haven for land developers, real estate agents, architects, and builders, who built an industry based solely on growth.

As in earlier periods, new centers of development drew the population away from the city core. Low-density semirural housing, no city taxes, and relaxed county building standards encouraged continued development beyond the perceived geographic boundaries of the Tucson Basin. Initial development north of the Rillito River expanded farther into the Santa Catalina foothills. A new corridor of development consolidated northward along the alignment of U.S. Highways 89 and 80 (Oracle Road), overtaking an area known for its citrus groves. Low-

density suburban development spilled over the eastern watercourse, the Pantano Wash, and began to consume most of the available land in the basin. Land development, however, was not contiguous, but rather used a "leapfrog" approach, jumping over more expensive open land in favor of pushing farther outward and encroaching upon the fragile ecosystems of the eastern, northern, and western foothills of the basin.

By 1950, two-thirds of Tucson's metropolitan population lived outside the city limits and were under the jurisdiction of Pima County planning. Aggressive annexation policies between 1952 and 1960 under Mayor Don Hummel added 61.4 square miles to the city of Tucson, resulting in its population surpassing 200,000 and an immediate increase in the tax base. After 1960, however, annexation programs met with considerable resistance from residents outside the city limits as annexation meant tax increases to cover the cost of additional urban services provided under municipal status, such as police and fire departments, public transportation, water services, and electricity.

Pima County had limited authority to control the urbanization process taking place outside the city limits until 1949, when Arizona established zoning authority in the state's two largest counties, Maricopa and Pima, for the purpose of regulating and controlling land use. In 1959, a comprehensive regional transportation study was conducted, which led to a 1965 proposal that included plans for an extensive system of parkways and freeways to accommodate the growth predicted to occur by 1980. During public hearings in 1970, Tucsonans opposed not only the projected system of freeways and limited-access roads but also the notion of continued growth

inherent in the plan's population and land-use projections. This was considered the initial rallying point for the formation of a no-growth or limited-growth philosophy in Tucson as the prospect of exploding community expansion fueled intense public debate. Controlled growth ultimately was viewed as unattainable because the municipal government ruled it illegal to deny building permits for new construction, thus protecting the community from potentially adverse effects on its economic health.

The once inexhaustible supply of low-cost peripheral land was now becoming limited, which, combined with high interest rates in the 1980s, slowed development in Tucson. Area plans, such as the Rincon Area Plan, held the line against unlimited sprawl, but in other regions, such as the original 1928 Catalina Foothills Estates development, the opportunity to renew initial deed restrictions limiting density was rejected. Tucson's surrounding foothills, whose lush desert was once a marketing tool, were despoiled by the demand for denser development of a kind very much like any suburban tract development. Although other regulatory incentives promoted urban infill on vacant land and encouraged the reuse and renovation of older dwellings within the central city core, these infill programs were not popularly supported. People continued to move farther out, destroying more of the natural desert each year.

Tucson's downtown as a business and cultural center was slowly dying as traffic congestion, higher city sales taxes, and an increasing suburban population encouraged businesses to follow residential development to the suburbs, as in 1960 with the construction of El Con Mall, built adjacent to and subsequently replacing El Conquistador Hotel.

The corollary to Tucson's peripheral urban sprawl was its attempt to revitalize the downtown area through federally assisted urban renewal programs. Federal funds, through the Housing Act of 1954 and the Model Cities Act of 1966, were available to "attack decay and blight" in American cities and "revitalize" downtown areas. Boosters of this proposal argued that the solution to the drain on economic viability downtown was through the development of government and community infrastructure that would reinvigorate commercial and retail interests. In Tucson, initial proposals for "redeveloping" 392 acres of Tucson's original neighborhoods began in 1957, but public outcry led to a smaller, 80-acre proposal, which was approved in 1964. The city created the Committee on Municipal Blight, which produced a planning document justifying its definition of blighted areas. The committee criticized the neighborhood's mix of residential and commercial properties, far from the American suburban ideal, and documented a "lack of front or side yards," referring to the Sonoran architectural tradition. In addition, the city appointed a Historic Sites Committee to identify major locations of historic interest that should be preserved. This 1969 report, the first attempt at documenting Tucson's architectural heritage, recommended the preservation of seventy-five buildings in the affected area, but ultimately only seven escaped demolition.

Demolition took place between 1967 and 1970, removing 250 buildings, the original presidial Plaza de las Armas, and the Plaza de la Mesilla and displacing hundreds of people representing generations of Hispanic, African-American, and Chinese families who had occupied those neighborhoods.

These areas also housed crime, poverty, prostitution, and drugs, but changing the built environment did not alleviate these social problems, as was promoted by city planners at that time; these activities simply moved to other neighborhoods. Built in its place over the next ten years was a city and county governmental office complex, the Tucson Community Center, La Placita shopping and office complex, the Tucson Museum of Art, a police and fire facility, and a large downtown hotel. Beyond working hours, however, the redeveloped area failed to draw people back downtown as it lacked the diversity of activities that would sustain it as a cultural center.

Although some archaeological and architectural documentation was done before demolition, this work relied on separate funds and volunteer workers without regulatory mechanisms for preservation advocacy. The Historic Preservation Act, passed by Congress in 1966, had little impact in Tucson until the 1970s. The urban renewal program and the resultant demolition of Tucson's core neighborhoods raised awareness of historic preservation and ultimately led to National Register of Historic Places designation for all of the residential districts surrounding the downtown urban renewal area within the next decade. By 1972, both the city and county adopted historic district ordinances, but they were too late to save many of Tucson's landmark buildings, including the Jacobs House, Santa Rita Hotel, and El Conquistador Hotel.

Architectural expression in Tucson after World War II was affected by two phenomena: the incorporation of modernism as a national architectural movement and federally insured home loans. The arrival of modern architecture in Tucson is attributed to three architects: Art Brown, William Wilde, and Nicholas Sakellar. Their new materials and forms contrasted sharply with the revivalist architectural expression still prevalent in Tucson at that time. By the 1970s, however, modernist buildings were so disliked that many were demolished or revamped to appear more "Southwestern" as Tucson reverted back to the idea of Spanish Colonial romanticism, bringing, in many cases, a superficial interpretation of its Spanish heritage.

Tucson's postwar housing boom was also greatly influenced by the emergence of federally insured housing loans provided by the Federal Housing Administration (FHA). The FHA required builders to follow design standards to ensure building value, and these standards began to dictate not only the construction materials and building processes but also the basic house form. The standards encouraged the use of prefabricated materials and streamlining the production of houses within a subdivision development. Houses were built with production-line efficiency with separate crews moving down a row of plots to pour the concrete floor slab, erect wooden frame or concrete block walls, and install premanufactured roof trusses; other crews were brought in for finish work. These houses also blended the characteristics of the emerging open interior plan with the appliance-filled and outdoor-oriented ranch-house prototype from California, which conformed well to the FHA guidelines by including features such as outdoor patios with sliding glass doors. Cheap energy and the availability of residential air-conditioning systems expanded development in the desert Southwest; however, the architectural designs showed a lack of consideration of the environmental factors that define the region.

The same FHA financing options used by individual home buyers were also available to building companies, enabling them to enter the marketplace as residential developers. Builders and bankers quickly became the driving force in shaping the bland and repetitive architectural appearance of residential subdivisions. Out-of-town builders and developers colonized the Tucson Basin with a generic architectural image of the greater Southwest that was promotable to an emerging transient homeowner who didn't stay long enough to understand the complexity of Tucson's cultural and architectural heritage. These developers didn't care about Tucson's sense of community, but rather its fertile economic market. The few local developers did attempt to create regionally appropriate housing prototypes, such as the Perfect Arizona Type (PAT) house, but they stood out as exceptions to the rule.

After construction of the

interstate freeway, which began as a limited-access highway in 1954 and followed the northwest/southeast line of the railroad, a corridor of development spread in both directions away from Tucson. Distinct geographic places once associated with farming and ranching were now becoming a blur of urban sprawl typified by communities of anonymous tract-home developments. With the expansion of development in almost every direction, neighborhood shopping centers were established that reinforced the long-standing ethic of distinctly separated residential and commercial zones. These centers became self-sufficient, formulaic mixtures of grocery store, drugstore, restaurant, and specialty shops that were repeated at regular intervals along major streets. Pedestrian activities, once a defining feature of pre–World War II downtown Tucson, were restricted to enclosed, air-conditioned, theme-styled malls of national chain department and retail stores with Tucson merchants, one by one, losing their ability to compete and closing down.

In contrast to the homogeneity of suburban housing developments and shopping centers, other building types in the 1970s and 1980s did project local interpretations of contemporary architecture. Banks, museums, and religious and educational buildings designed by local architects became studies in an attempt to define an appropriate architectural expression for Tucson.

The architectural profession in Tucson also changed dramatically after the war. Traditionally, public work, the bread and butter of architectural practice, was doled out to long-established firms, making it difficult for new or young professionals to get a foothold in Tucson. The Arizona chapter of the American Institute of Architects, formed in 1947, was a gentlemanly community of professionals in an era when advertising and promotion of architectural services were considered unethical and firms shared their projects and employees. In 1964, with the establishment of the Department of Architecture at the University of Arizona, graduating architects entered the local market and formed the basis for a less autocratic and more competitive distribution of public work by the early 1970s. In contrast to the more unified expression of the previous handful of Tucson architects, the city began to see a mix of expressions representing the new diversity of architectural firms. The complexity of architectural projects led to the division of architectural services into specialized subfields that used consultants on a project-by-project basis. Beginning in the 1990s, many local architectural firms were bought by national firms to act as regional offices or to establish project-based joint ventures with internationally recognized firms. Several of today's architectural firms, however, can still trace their roots back to the few firms that dominated Tucson architecture after the war.

When the energy crisis of the 1970s hit the building market, Tucson became a center for the exploration of alternative building materials and construction processes. A resurgence of traditional materials, including adobe and rammed earth, was matched by an abundance of passive solar designs. Tucson's water supply, however, was rapidly depleting due to an imbalance between the amount of water required to supply the Tucson Basin's agricultural, mining, and human needs and nature's ability to recharge the underground aquifer. Fissures in the land surface on the fringes of the basin appeared as physical evidence of this phenomenon.

The energy crisis also ushered in a community-wide ethic of water conservation and conversion to drought-tolerant landscaping, which profoundly distinguishes Tucson from Phoenix's water-consumptive oasis environment. When the Central Arizona Project (CAP), the 300-mile open canal channeling water uphill from the Colorado River, reached Tucson in 1992, it ended the city's long-standing dependence on groundwater. The need to secure water in the Tucson Basin has remained an enduring techno-logical, economic, and political challenge, underscoring the impact of geographic influences on the sustainability of both the built environment and the quality of life.

History as Prologue: Tucson's Architectural Future

Tucson's architectural expression over the last 5,000 years has developed from handmade structures of local materials to complex buildings using premanufactured construction systems. Settlement patterns have transformed from clustering around available resources to dispersion and depending on technological mobility. In this evolution of Tucson's built environment, the geographic, cultural, technological, economic, and political forces that shape the architectural expression are present in each of the historic periods. Each period's architec-tural expression, however, can be defined as a response primarily to one or two of these forces. As exposure to other civilizations increased, cultural and techno-logical forces began to supersede the geographical considerations that had defined the earliest settlements in the Tucson Basin. The economics of mass-pro-duced housing to accommodate an exploding population and the regulatory mechanisms to control that growth defined Tucson's twentieth-century development.

Today, Tucson's built environment is affected by an army of disciplines ranging from planners, architects, landscape architects, and builders to developers, bankers, marketing executives, and real estate agents. The primary decisions regarding the built environment are no longer made by those trained to ensure its architectural quality, but rather by those trained to ensure its economic viability. The current culture of transience has also led to the homogenization of cities across the country, each with the requisite amenities needed to satisfy this transient lifestyle. As cathedrals were a known refuge in a foreign place to medieval European travelers, fast-food restaurants, national chain retail stores, and caricature architecture reinforcing regional stereotypes bring comfort to temporary residents whose commitment to a community is short-lived. Tucson, as a result, is beginning to look like every other city in the Southwest, if not the country.

To create quality communities in today's complex world requires a holistic understanding of all of the influences that define our built environment. The essence of Tucson is that its inhabitants dwell in a desert, a harsh and beautiful physical environment, whose meager resources have attracted and sustained numerous emigrant cultures who have left their mark over millennia. Today, as Tucson's demand for water increases, geography will once again be the primary force that will affect its development. We have chosen to dominate the desert, and its geographic features, to the point where we are no longer aware when our streets cross a river, arroyo, hill, or any other natural feature. Controlling growth in this fragile ecosystem is not an option; it is a necessity. If history is our textbook, the economic and political consequences of

Blackwell House, c. 1980. Controversial in both its construction (1979) and demolition (1998), the house was located in the foothills of the Tucson Mountains and was designed by Judith Chafee. It represents many of the issues facing Tucson's future built environment, including preservation of both the natural environment and the architectural landmarks, historic and contemporary, that define Tucson's unique sense of place.

controlled growth are short-lived, but the consequences of unlimited growth with limited resources would repeat the lesson of extinction.

Tucson's cultural identity has always been eclectic, reflecting diverse migrant populations and frontier architectural expressions brought from other places. Tucson's architectural character is not yet homogeneous, like that imposed on Santa Fe. However, like many other American cities, Tucson's rich historic and contemporary architectural heritage is threatened by the trend to invent one identifiable "Southwestern" style that can more easily be promoted in today's consumer market. Architectural alignment with one style of building may be simpler to promote but ignores and often eliminates the rich diversity of multicultural expression. Moreover, we must move beyond our romantic affair with revival architecture and build a city that

integrates the expressions of the past with an architecture appropriate for this time and the unique qualities of this place.

Tucson's history has also been defined by the accumulation of technological advancements to provide water, construct buildings, and temper the environmental extremes of the Sonoran Desert. Technology, however, has also removed us from the natural rhythms of life in the desert and has allowed us to negate the environmental forces acting on our built environment. We live in a time when technology, as expressed in construction, transportation, and communication systems, determines the building and urban form of our cities. Technology, instead, should be appropriately used in balance with the cultural, economic, and political forces in service to conserve Tucson's natural resources and, ultimately, preserve its unique sense of place.

Economics continues to

dominate the architectural expression of the everyday environments in which we dwell, work, and play. Commercial land and buildings have become expendable commodities, devoid of cultural or aesthetic value. Many of these buildings are demolished within a few decades of their construction, only to be replaced by other expendable buildings. Most of us live in houses that were not designed by architects, were constructed of premanufactured materials, and were placed on lots in such a way as to maximize density and thus profit for the developer. For many, however, affordable housing of any kind is a luxury. In the United States, the world's strongest economy, affordable housing must become a local priority that dignifies the concept of dwelling and contributes to the urban fabric of the community.

In an age where the regulatory,

litigious, and economic aspects of an architectural project overwhelm the design process, many of the architects of Tucson's everyday built environment have chosen the path of least resistance. The blandness of this design ethic is matched by a lack of vision and leadership at the municipal level to define and implement a coherent aesthetic, geographic, and cultural sense of community. Great cities are created when political decision-makers understand the importance of architecture in the expression of a city's identity. The local chapter of the American Institute of Architects, once the dominant voice in the design profession, no longer represents the entire field of design professionals, including architects, landscape architects, planners, designers, and builders. The profession, then, lacks a unified voice to contribute to the larger design issues facing Tucson:

affordable housing, urban sprawl, loss of community, and a holistic aesthetic for defining the city.

Tucson's sense of urban place must also be refocused. Planners abandoned the dense placemaking potential of the Spanish urban morphology and instead chose one of dispersed placemarking in a desert whose subtle and immense power overwhelms any attempt to enhance it. For Tucson to preserve the natural beauty that still remains, its inhabitants must abandon their frontier attitude and declare Tucson an urban city. The city must have a stronger sense of center, become denser, develop efficient transportation systems, create vibrant open spaces, and invest in good public architecture. Tucsonans have a responsibility to be stewards of their natural and cultural heritage for future generations to enjoy. To do this, we must educate ourselves—native, newcomer, and nonresident—to appreciate this comprehensive and holistic balance of influences that has created Tucson's unique architectural expression and defines our common identity.

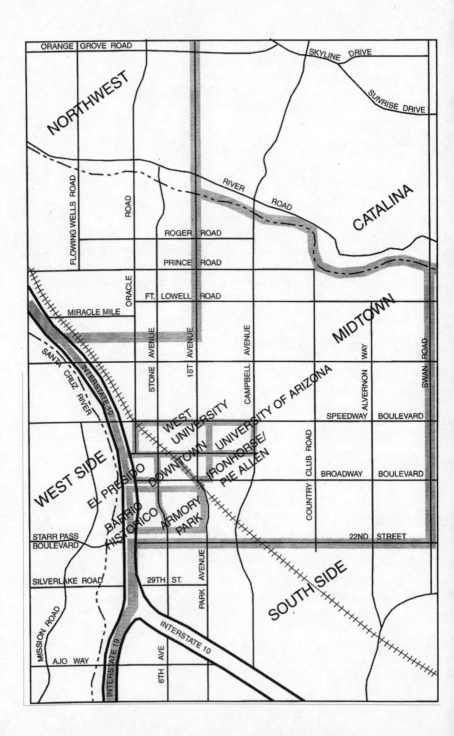

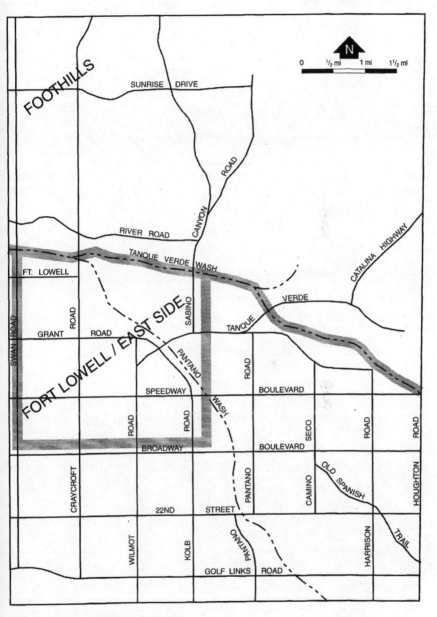

Tucson Basin Reference Map

Architectural Examples by Area

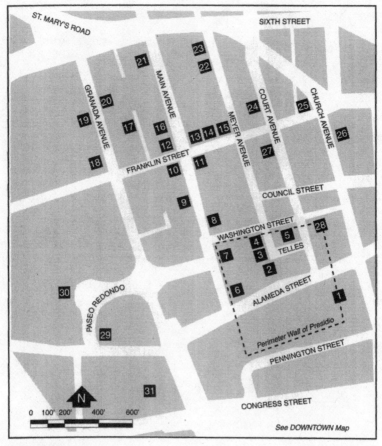

El Presidio

El Presidio [NRHP]

Although the earliest Spanish settlement in Tucson was the *visita* at the base of "A" Mountain, on the west side of the Santa Cruz River, this area to the east soon followed with the construction of the Presidio San Agustín del Tucson. The presence of the Presidio from 1775 until Mexican independence in 1821 helped to secure the area against Apache raiding parties and promote future settlement by both Hispanics and Americans. Civilian settlement grew casually in the small area between the main presidio gate centered on the west wall and the primary *acequia* from the Santa Cruz River. This bend in the canal opened up to the south, promoting expansion in that direction. As settlement in Tucson grew outside the Presidio, it did not follow the more orderly precepts for a pueblo defined in the Laws of the Indies, especially concerning planning around a plaza, but grew instead along established routes of travel—from the Presidio to the river, the *visita*, and the Mission San Xavier. After the Mexican garrison left Tucson in 1856, the Presidio was occupied by soldiers of the United States, but by 1862 they abandoned it to the elements, disrepair, and creative recycling on the part of Tucsonans. The Fergusson Map (p. 14) from that year indicates the boundary of the Presidio by a dashed line and identifies the Plaza de las Armas and the Plaza Militar, but indicates only a dozen or so structures standing along the line of the original wall.

The neighborhood, as it is today, grew north along the Calle Real, today's Main Avenue, with most of the structures dating from about 1860 to 1920. This neighborhood was long referred to as "La Vecindad cerca del Centro," and later "Snob Hollow," but it was designated as "El

Presidio" in its listing as a National Register of Historic Places [NRHP] historic district in 1976. This neighborhood has become the most popular venue for walking tours because of the remarkable variety and quality of buildings in a relatively small area. There are houses that align with the location of the Presidio and whose construction method is consistent with what is known of the Presidio. There are Sonoran row houses, detached Transformed Sonoran and American Territorial houses, bungalows, and two of the finest works by Henry C. Trost, which combine Spanish Colonial and Prairie elements.

Moreover, the range of these examples, from the 1860s to the 1900s, is the key to understanding the larger architectural issue—that the conception of space in the two cultures was antithetical and the transformation which occurred is still evident in this neighborhood. To see the contrast in these urban models, stand in front of the Stevens-Duffield House (p. 54) and the Corbett House (p. 55). The Corbett House is an object sitting in the center of its lot, an excellent example of the American conception of the levels of private versus public space; it layers from sidewalk to front yard, to porch, contrasting sharply with the Stevens-Duffield House, which epitomizes the Hispanic model in its placement of the building as a contiguous wall at the street, relegating private space to the interior of the house and the interior of the block.

Included in this neighborhood are a few structures that exemplify a particular stylistic or construction type; though seen more commonly in other neighborhoods, their presence here is noted as a convenience to the visitor.

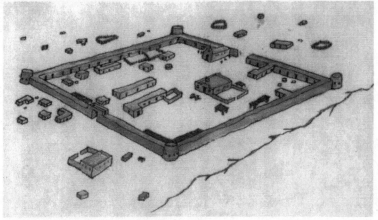

Presidio of San Agustín del Tucson, reconstructed view.

---

1 Site of the Presidio of San Agustín del Tucson; demolished by 1870

The Presidio was built between 1775 and 1783, formed of enclosing walls of whole timbers standing upright with the tops sharpened to points. When the massive adobe walls were finally completed in December 1783, the log palisades were taken down. Above ground, nothing remains of the walled fort described in written accounts or shown in drawings. According to those records, one side measured about 900 feet, and in area the fort was "less than two square miles" with walls averaging 2.5 feet thick and 12 feet high. The main gate was strategically placed on the west side facing the Santa Cruz River, the primary source of water and the transportation corridor. It also faced the direction of the earlier and still surviving *visita* settlement and the irrigated agricultural fields and gardens watered by the Santa Cruz. The rooms built for storage and the barracks lining the interior provided a rooftop defensive position behind the parapet during Apache attacks. In addition to quarters for soldiers working for the Spanish crown and their families, there also were a store, a saloon, a chapel, and two graveyards. To get an idea of the size of the Presidio, walk the walls by following the dashed line on the Fergusson Map of 1862 (p. 14). Be sure to enter the courtyard of the Pima County Courthouse and look for the 2-inch strip of dark brown granite running north to south in the pavement, representing the location of the east wall of the Presidio.

Jacobs House; demolished 1968.

2 Tucson Museum of Art,
140 N. Main Avenue, 1973–1974;
William Wilde & Associates

This building is constructed of exposed concrete and metal sheathing in a bold sculptural expression of space and form typical of the Brutalist architectural aesthetic. The interior plan is defined by a gallery ramp that forms a square, central open space, mimicking Frank Lloyd Wright's Guggenheim Museum, but on a much smaller scale. The original east/west breezeway was enclosed to create a lobby in a 1998 addition.

The museum was built just north of the **site of the Jacobs House** (demolished 1968), located on the northwest corner of N. Meyer Avenue and Alameda Street. The first floor of this two-story Victorian Italianate mansion was built of adobe and the second floor of wood. It was built between 1877 and 1897 by Baron Jacobs, one of two brothers who moved to Tucson from California, bringing with them the fashionable Victorian style. It was probably the first and most elaborate home in that style.

3 **La Casa Cordova** [NRHP],
171–177 N. Meyer Avenue, before
1848; restoration 1973–1975 by E.
D. Herreras, FAIA; stabilization
1996 by Bob Vint, architect/Eric
Means, contractor

This small building is an excellent
example of an early Sonoran row
house typical of the barrios that
originally extended from this site
south to the Barrio Libre.
Although this building has lost its
adjacent structures, it would have
originally shared a continuous
facade abutting the street. A
private outdoor space at the
interior of the block featuring a
well, cooking stove, ramada, and
outhouse was connected to the
street by a *zaguán*. Now under
the stewardship of the Tucson
Museum of Art, La Casa Cordova
is also home to several models
and interpretive exhibits related
to the development of Tucson's
presidio and early settlement.

4 Leonardo **Romero House,**
104–108 W. Washington Street,
c. 1868; remodeled 1999 by Bob
Vint, architect/Philip Rosenberg,
contractor

Based on this building's skewed
alignment with the modern street
and its construction materials
and methods, it may embody a
portion of the original Presidio
wall. Otherwise, a typical
transformed Sonoran row house
with a pitched roof. Currently
being used by the Tucson
Museum of Art.

5 Telles Block **(Old Town Artisans),** c. 1850s–1860s

The entire block between Washington and Telles Streets and Meyer and Court Avenues is defined by Sonoran row houses with only a small gap created by missing structures at the northeast corner. This well-defined block creates an intimate, colorful, and shaded courtyard— a saving grace for anyone living in a hot climate. Benches, a fountain, and shade trees make it one of the most appealing courtyards in Tucson. Also note the remnants of Victorian wallpaper on the interior walls.

6 Edward Nye **Fish House,** 119– 133 N. Main Avenue, 1868, and Hyram **Stevens-Duffield House,** 151–163 N. Main Avenue, 1865; stabilization 1977 by E. D. Herreras, FAIA, and 1999 by Bob Vint, architect/Eric Means, contractor

These attached buildings are typical of the Sonoran row house form transported from northern Mexico during the Spanish and Mexican periods. The interiors are characterized by tall rooms made with materials typical of pre-railroad construction in Tucson, including thick adobe walls and saguaro-ribbed ceilings. These houses are also on the alignment of the original Presidio and may in part date from that structure.

Corbett House.

7 J. Knox **Corbett House,** 179 N. Main Avenue, 1907–1908; Holmes & Holmes

Built by Corbett, one of Tucson's first lumber dealers, not only is this house an excellent example of the Mission Revival style, but it is in good condition and open to the public as part of the Tucson Museum of Art. The colors used both inside and out are typical: The exterior has white walls, deep green trim, and terra cotta tiles; the interior has cream-colored walls with wooden trim at both the wainscot and base molding in a dark stain. The wood trim in the interior is typically plain in shape and used as a contrasting and repetitive element against the light-colored walls, indicative of Craftsman interiors, which were often found in Mission Revival houses.

8 Sam **Hughes House,** 221–223 N. Main Avenue, begun c. 1864

The original adobe house was expanded in 1886 and several times thereafter to accommodate the fifteen children of Sam and Atanacia Santa Cruz Hughes. The exterior doors and windows— especially the main front door— have the very shallow wood pediments typical of the influence of the Greek Revival, which was then the fashionable style in the rest of the country. The main part of the house originally had a *zaguán* with circulation from room to room. Today the house is an L-shaped plan with later roof additions in both gable and lean-to types. Yet the most dramatic alteration occurred when a rock foundation was added to the entire house by Mrs. Hughes in 1934.

Steinfeld Mansion; detail of owl design on spandrel, c. 1900.

9 Olcott House, 234 N. Main Avenue, c. 1890; Arthur Jacobson, builder/contractor

This detached house is a compact block in form, made of fired brick. It was the first house on the west side of Main Avenue to take advantage of the steep slope by creating one story on Main Avenue and two stories to the west. It is similar to many of the American Territorial houses in the Armory Park neighborhood in both style and material. The porch, supported by slender wood posts, wraps the northeast corner and is contained under the pyramidal roof. Brick lintels over doors and windows have a very slight arch. (See photograph, p. 276.)

10 First Owl's Club (Steinfeld Mansion), 300 N. Main Avenue, 1898; Henry C. Trost; renovation 1978 by Gresham Larson Associates

Designed as a residence for the thirteen bachelors who comprised the original Owl's Club, this two-story building reveals Trost's stylistic preference for combining Mission Revival forms, including "tiled" roofs and an arched portico with Sullivanesque ornament. What appear to be Spanish clay roof tiles are actually painted and textured pressed tin, probably from the same Missouri manufacturer who still produces them today. The empty niche in the center of the facade once held a statue of an owl. This public street facade contrasts sharply with the intimate space of the shaded rear courtyard, whose fountain and wall openings serve to cool the building. Oval attic vents and deep roof overhangs

El Presidio Bed & Breakfast.

also help to cool the building. The sensitive renovation in 1978 earned the architectural firm a design award.

11 Kruttschnitt House **(El Presidio Bed & Breakfast),** 297 N. Main Avenue, before 1886; restoration 1980 by Paul Weiner

Beneath the 1899 Victorian dress of this building is a traditional Sonoran row house built of thick adobe walls and a flat roof. This hybrid demonstrates the evolution of stylistic preferences by Tucsonans as a result of the arrival of the railroad and the influence of national trends in building design and aesthetics. This house is also unique for its passive cooling system in which cool air generated by a 4-foot space under the house was drawn through the floorboards by opening a trap door in the roof. The restoration removed many subsequent additions and returned it to something very near its turn-of-the-century Victorian design with gables, porches, brick chimneys, and turned woodwork.

Verdugo House.

12 Francis **Hereford House,**
340 N. Main Avenue, 1902; Henry
C. Trost

From Main Avenue, this two-
story stuccoed brick house
appears to be a large cube with
the projecting flat roofs that are
often associated with the Prairie
style and Frank Lloyd Wright's
Unity Temple. In addition, it is
reminiscent of the work of Irving
Gill, the pioneering California
architect who explored a modern
approach to the Spanish Colonial
Revival styles that resulted in a
simplified version, including very
smooth white walls, round
arcades, and vertical rectangular
window openings. The west side
is a full three stories tall, adapting
to the steep slope. The original
plaster ornament on the fascia is
still apparent, though somewhat
softened by time.

13 Rosalia **Verdugo House,**
317–325 N. Main Avenue, 1877

This especially handsome
Transformed Sonoran house sits
high above the street with steps
leading to each entry. At the base,
built to accommodate the sloped
site, is what appears to be a solid
stone foundation wall. The color
scheme is contemporary—the
deep earthen tone of the stucco
walls is complemented by the
brilliant colors on the Greek
Revival trim at windows and
doors. Although rendered
obsolete, the original canales
were left in place, indicating the
addition of the gabled roof to the
original flat roof.

14 Gertrude **McCleary House,**
241–245 W. Franklin Street,
c. 1872, later additions c. 1888

This Sonoran house with its
symmetrical, central plan was
either painted or stuccoed and
inscribed to resemble stone,
complete with quoins at the
corners, sometime before 1888. It
was then bought by MacTroy
McCleary, a contractor and
carpenter, who transformed it
further with the addition of the
pyramidal roof, with its single
dormer, and the front porch,
which runs along the entire south
facade. The porch makes use of
the new materials only then
becoming available: slender
lathe-turned or chamfered
columns with simple capitals and
brackets.

15 **Corner Market,** 211 W.
Franklin Street, c. 1880

This former market, run by Lin
Silk, has the typical 45-degree
corner cut seen in commercial
properties in Sonoran neighborhoods. Living quarters were
added upstairs, probably at about
the same time as the pyramidal
roof. The steel corner post is a
more recent structural necessity
to support the addition over the
entry.

Second Owl's Club.

16 **Second Owl's Club,** 378 N. Main Avenue, 1902–1903; Trost & Rust; facade restoration 1985 by Rob Boucher

Designed as a larger facility for the fraternal organization, this massive two-story building is an eclectic mix of Mission Revival forms and Sullivanesque orna-ment. Trost incorporated playful references to local architecture, including the immense, oversized canales, typical of Sonoran row houses; a sculpted facade, reminiscent of that of San Xavier; and local flora and fauna. The building was renovated and the facade completely re-created from historic photos by Rob Boucher during an extensive restoration in 1985 after vandal-ism had reduced the building to a ruin.

17 **Carriage House,** in alley behind Second Owl's Club, c. 1902; Holmes & Holmes

Typical of carriage houses for the residences along Main Avenue, this one actually belongs to the Kingan House at 325 W. Franklin Street. The brick structure has a gable roof covered by faux Spanish tiles of pressed tin.

18 Eliza Ward **Rockwell House,** 405 W. Franklin Street, 1907–1908; Holmes & Holmes

This residence represents the English Tudor style with the first story in brick and the second story in contrasting dark wood half-timbering with light-colored stucco. The height and steeply pitched roofs and multiple gables give it a vertical expression, which is echoed by the pine trees in the yard. The plan is laid out along a central hall with the various interior spaces and outdoor verandah. The house was designed from the interior out without regard for the irregular forms on the exterior, though contained under one roof form.

19 Charles W. **Hinchcliffe House,** 330 N. Granada Avenue, 1910; Holmes & Holmes, architect; Orin Anderson, contractor/builder

An excellent, but deteriorating, example of the Western Stick style of bungalow. The front porch is spacious and majestic, providing shade and capturing cooling breezes. The small apartment in the back of the house is a miniature version of the main house. Unfortunately, the design detailing of very small wood members, meant for a Japanese climate, cannot be protected from Tucson's dry heat and monsoon rains.

20 **Hinchcliffe Court,** 405 N. Granada Avenue, 1910–1911; attributed to Holmes & Holmes; extensive interior remodeling 1994

Conceived as Arizona's first resort catering to a public enamored with automobile travel, this auto court of ten small wooden bungalows is arranged in a horseshoe plan, with the open end facing Granada Avenue. The center area, which was originally used for parking, is today beautifully landscaped with a variety of desert and imported plants attractive for their color and scent. The 1994 interior remodeling showcased the work of interior designers but unfortunately did not include a renovation of one of the bungalows to its original style.

21 **Herring House,** 430 N. Main Avenue, 1868; Holmes & Holmes

When it was built, this house was considered to be on the outskirts of town. Despite its traditional Sonoran *zaguán* plan and adobe walls, it was intended to be detached from its neighbors. Its most unusual feature is the Gothic pointed-arch window on the south elevation. The front porch is a later addition.

22 Row Houses, N. Meyer
Avenue, c. 1860–1880

These transformed Sonoran row
houses, primarily on the west side
of the street, run almost continu-
ously from Franklin Street to 6th
Street. The various pitches,
heights, and materials of the
added roofs and the multiple
colors of the exterior walls are an
indication of individual property
ownership. Unfortunately, most
of these are in poor condition,
illustrating the need for financial
support to preserve historically
significant buildings and prevent
occupant displacement due to
gentrification. For examples that
have maintained their traditional
architectural integrity, see 326,
381, 382, 384, and 385 N. Meyer
Avenue.

23 Residence, 405–411 N.
Meyer Avenue

The street facade of this contemporary construction blends well
into the historic context using
compatible forms, materials, and
siting.

24 Residence, 337 N. Court
Avenue

Note the Queen Anne elements:
bay window with overhanging
roof made of pedimental gable;
ashlar block—that is, concrete
block that was produced to look
like ashlar stone.

25 Gustav **Hoff House,** 127 W. Franklin Street, c. 1880

This house typifies the Transformed Sonoran style, with 22-inch-thick adobe walls representing the Sonoran tradition, but placed on the property as a detached structure representing the American tradition. The addition of the pyramidal roof and south-facing stone porch of "A" Mountain stone was done sometime between 1890 and 1900. The original ceiling height was at least 12 feet before remodeling.

26 Wright-Zellweger House **(Wedgewood Court),** 288 N. Church Avenue, 1900; restoration 1976

Tucson's best remaining interpretation of the Neoclassical style, in which its flat roof carries a balustrade with finials. During restoration, the original clapboard siding of painted redwood was discovered under a layer of stucco. Entry porch with Ionic columns has matching pilasters at the door. Interiors feature Victorian ornament including paneled doors in ash and chinoiserie latticework in dark walnut. Art Nouveau gaslight fixtures and stained-glass windows adorn the living room. A recent addition at the back has weakened the stylistic integrity of the original house.

27 Jules le Flein House **(El Charro Restaurant),** 311 N. Court Avenue, 1900; Jules le Flein

Jules le Flein (also known as Julius Flin) was the stonemason brought from France in 1883 to carve the stone rose portal for the San Agustín Cathedral (p. 77). His own house has a central plan with stairway down to a basement lined with stone. Originally, it was set back slightly from the street but adjacent to the houses on either side. The "A" Mountain stone piers of the front porch were added later.

28 **Archaeological Site,** W. Washington Street

In 1954, excavation of this area revealed structures from three distinct cultural groups: a prehistoric oblong pit structure dating from A.D. 700–900, the northeast corner of the Presidio wall, and a Sonoran row house.

29 **Johnson** (Manning-Johnson) **House,** 455 W. Paseo Redondo, 1916; Henry O. Jaastad

Influenced by Spanish Colonial residential types from Mexico, which are urban and attached, this detached house is very American in its independence. It is a symmetrically planned structure suggesting a duplex with pale earthen-colored stucco and brick coping. Two short ornamental columns with bas-relief acanthus leaves topped by urns grace either side of stairs at the entry and can be seen in archival photographs of other homes, which makes one wonder about their origin.

30 Levi Howell **Manning House** [NRHP], 450 W. Paseo Redondo, 1905–1907; attributed to Mrs. Manning

Little integrity remains of this mansion built for Levi Manning, one of the original members of the Owl's Club and the person who commissioned Trost to design the club's first building. The enormous single-story structure gently curves in plan, punctuated by a turreted cylinder in the center and another at the south end. The open arched loggia that joined the two halves has been enclosed, and the interior changes necessary for contemporary use make the original unrecognizable. The last vestige of its former beauty, and the main reason for visiting the building, is the painted interior of the south rotunda. Once the formal entry to the house, the painted ceiling and space between the openings in the dome are a fantasy of exotic birds (including peacocks and phoenix) and floral decoration in the Mexican tradition, but in pale rather than bold colors: shimmering blues, gold, and white. The tile floor, in a combination of geometric and floral patterns in pastel colors, complements the painting.

31 Site of Levin's Park, c. 1870

What began as a brewery at the rear of the property of Alexander Levin grew into a beer garden, saloon, and billiard hall. By the end of the 1870s, the 3-acre Levin's Park included a bullring, shooting gallery, bowling alley, open dance pavilion, restaurant, and even a small theater where opera productions were held. By the mid-1880s, the "pleasure garden" had begun attracting undesirable guests, which, combined with the popularity of the larger Carrillo Gardens, forced its closure for public entertainment.

Also of note is the 1905 **Cheyney House** at 252 N. Main Avenue, designed by Holmes & Holmes; restoration 2001 Bob Vint, architect, and Michael Keith, general contractor. Typical of the affluent "Snob Hollow" residences on Main Avenue at the turn of the twentieth century, this Mission Revival house has a living room bay window projecting from the two-story facade facing the Santa Cruz River and Tucson Mountains. The interior walls were originally painted with landscape scenes and the wooden floors with designs resembling rugs. In 1981, the roof structure was destroyed by fire, and the building was abandoned until recently. To prevent its demolition, two El Presidio residents purchased the house and resold it to the new owners, who restored it to its original elegance—a preservation success story.

Downtown and Warehouse District [NRHP]

Downtown

The urban fabric of downtown Tucson will, for many visitors, be a disappointment, as it lacks the kind of building density and diversity of activities necessary for exuberant interaction. However, there are compelling examples from each of the three major periods of expansion: illustrations of our unique Hispanic urban land-use patterns, a period of rapid commercial growth, and the decentralization of downtown typical of postwar urban renewal.

The decision by the Spanish in 1775 to locate the Presidio on the east bank of the Santa Cruz River opposite the existing Pima village and Spanish *visita* benefited from the large tract of land for growth, whereas there was only a thin strip of land on the west side between the river and the base of the mountains. In the Spanish Colonial and Mexican periods, growth south of the Presidio reached almost to 22nd Street in the typical pattern seen in the Sanborn Insurance Map of 1883—residential Sonoran adobes at the perimeter of blocks with commercial activities at the corners.

With the arrival of the railroad in 1880, copper mining, and American expansion, there were needs for new building types including warehouses, hotels, and rooming houses. By 1893, Congress Street had become the new heart of a linear commercial district linking the Southern Pacific Railroad Depot and the Calle Real (Main Avenue). The unintended result was the abandonment of Church Plaza, Tucson's last urban space, as the commercial structures that once faced the plaza now turned their backs on it to face Congress Street. (See Sanborn Map, p. 22.)

By 1914, there were men's clubs, hotels, shops, and banks designed by architects. Bricks were being produced locally, but ornament was most often ordered by mail from catalogs. A wave of commercial growth north of Broadway Boulevard and east of Stone Avenue replaced residential structures. The natural barrier created by the diagonal cut of the railroad was soon crossed by the now historic underpasses [NRHP] at 4th, 6th, and Stone Avenues. In the late 1920s, downtown Tucson was marked by the vertical expansion that resulted from experimentation with high-rise technologies.

Tucson was not immune to the obsession of American planners and architects with European and International styles of modern architecture and therefore became subject to the dismal results of "urban renewal." Hundreds of buildings were "modernized" by stripping ornament and roofline articulation and covering with a skin of white stucco. But this is nothing in comparison to the wholesale demolition that took place between 1967 and 1970. Buildings such as the Jacobs House (p. 52), blocks and blocks of Sonoran row houses, and open spaces, such as the Plaza de las Armas and Plaza de la Mesilla (p. 77), were lost forever. In their places Tucson now has parking structures, high-rise office and governmental buildings, and Interstate 10 (I-10).

One of the most interesting challenges that Tucsonans face today is the desire to mark or reclaim the area of the earliest settlements (p. 174), yet that very area is now cut off from downtown, on the west side of I-10.

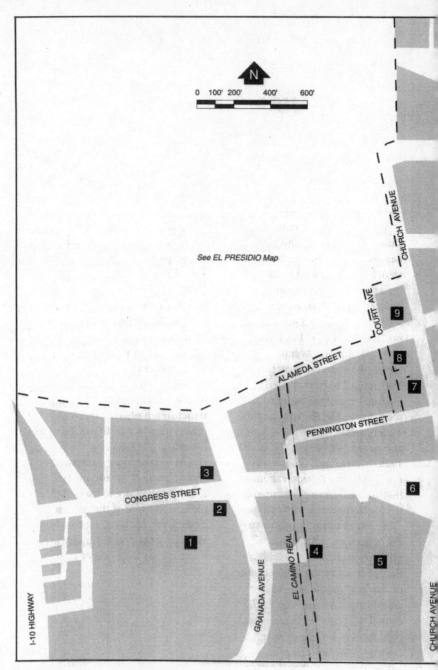

Downtown and Warehouse District

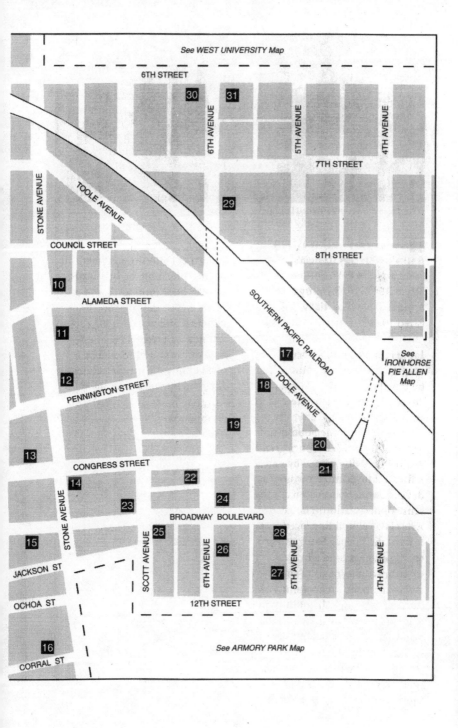

El Paso & Southwestern Railroad Depot.

1 El Paso & Southwestern Railroad Depot (Garcia's Restaurant), 419 W. Congress Street, 1912–1913; Henry C. Trost; remodeled and partially demolished 1982

Little remains of this once magnificent railroad station, built by the Phelps Dodge Company "to serve their copper interests in Bisbee and Douglas" after disagreements with the Southern Pacific Railroad. This once grand station, now dominated by newer, taller buildings and crowding development, no longer has a real sense of destination. The Beaux Arts classical building faced east toward the former Douglas Park (p. 73) and featured a brick exterior with terra cotta entablature, ornament, and columns of Indiana limestone. In addition, Mission Revival elements are present, including the pitched roof covered with clay tile and the arches at the entry. The porticoes on either end were originally open to the air, with a pattern of columns on either side, but not touching the brick corner piers. A huge fountain stood at either end of the 106-foot-long building. Still visible is the central rotunda covered by a stained-glass dome and protected by a skylight. A similar railroad depot designed by Trost in Douglas, Arizona, has been restored for its original use.

Douglas Park; demolished c. 1974.

2 Site of Douglas Park, 1912; demolished c. 1974; Cammillo Fenzí Franchesschi, landscape architect

The park was commissioned by Mr. and Mrs. Walter Douglas and featured tree-lined walkways connecting the El Paso & Southwestern Railroad Depot with the corner of Congress Street and Granada Avenue. The park incorporated two monumental stone fountains, carved stone benches, and many rare and unusual trees and shrubs. Once an elegant prelude to train travel.

Evo A. **DeConcini Federal Courthouse,** 405 W. Congress Street at Granada Avenue, 2000; Leo A. Daly/Hardy Holzman Pfeiffer Associates, design architects, and Sakellar & Associates, architects of record; Swinerton & Walberg, general contractor

This towering structure is a confusion of forms, scale, and materials. The use of smaller volumes to break down the huge mass of the building is a reasonable act; however, the overuse of variety in materials and scale causes the parts to be too distinct from the whole. The building demonstrates an appropriate urban response by defining the street edges with walls, providing a generous entry at the corner, and in the curved form that echoes Granada Avenue. Although overscaled and oddly attached, the prominent entry canopy is reminiscent of commercial structures in early Tucson

Arizona State Office Building, atrium.

Arizona State Office Building, north elevation.

that were always entered at the corner, allowing more space for socializing; in this case, the entry also provides a connection through to the courtyard and parking lot in the back.

3 Arizona State Office Building Addition, 400 W. Congress Street, 1992; NBBJ/ James A. Gresham, FAIA, designer

The expansive atrium space that joins the new north addition to the existing building is shaded by a metal structure high above and on the east and west sides and is cooled by breezes and plants. Entry to the atrium is by way of a bridge above the basement-level patio. Natural light is brought into the basement cafeteria both through the atrium and along the east side, which is separated from the ground level by a sunken garden. In recognizing the disparate climatic conditions of each face of the building, the exterior is ambiguous; each elevation is an individual statement and less a part of the whole. The north elevation on Alameda Street features a curvilinear curtain wall of ribbon windows and patterned brick

Sosa-Carrillo-Frémont House.

reminiscent of Native American baskets or the skin of a snake. The design was actually based on a simple mathematical progression that was easy to construct, and there is only one brick out of place on the entire wall. In addition, while the view looking west on Alameda Street previously ended unceremoniously at the I-10 freeway, closure is now created by the building's curvilinear north wall. 1992 AIA Honor Award/Western Mountain Region.

4 Sosa-Carrillo-Frémont House [NRHP], 151 S. Granada Avenue, c. 1858; remodeled 1879; restoration 1971–1974 by E. D. Herreras, FAIA

Inhabited by a number of influential families in Tucson's history, this Sonoran row house was one of the few buildings saved from the demolition of urban renewal. With the disappearance of its original context—that is, the block of attached row houses and communal rear yard—this building appears as an artificially detached object. It is well preserved and still retains many of the other features characteristic of the Sonoran row house. It is also the best example of the typical *zaguán* plan with a central hall leading from the street facade directly to the rear yard; all of the rooms are located off of the central hall. The building is now a branch museum of the Arizona Historical

Society and includes period
furniture, some from the original
families.

5 **Tucson Community Center,**
260 S. Church Avenue, 1971; Cain
Nelson Wares & Cook and
Friedman & Jobusch, architects

The community center is part of
the 80 acres and ten years of
building spawned by the 1965
capital improvements bond issue,
in which two-thirds of the money
was provided by the federal
government as a Title I renewal
project. The community center is
composed of three buildings: a
Convention Center with arena
and exhibition areas, a 2,400-seat
Music Hall, and the Leo Rich
Theater with 575 seats. These
buildings are placed around a
spacious central plaza with
fountains and other water
features, which unfortunately
have not been well maintained.
On the outside, these buildings
exhibit a Brutalist character and
are monumental in scale,
composed of smooth poured-in-
place concrete and rough
concrete block. The interiors of

San Agustín Cathedral; demolished 1936.

the Music Hall and Leo Rich Theater have a comfortable scale and contain elegant lobby and theater spaces. The design of the 1989 addition to the Convention Center, with pyramidal skylights, is by Anderson DeBartolo Pan, Inc.

6 Site of the First San Agustín Cathedral* and the Plaza de la Mesilla (Church Plaza), c. 1862–1883; church demolished in 1936

The Plaza de la Mesilla appears on the Fergusson Map of 1862 (p. 14) as an open space barely defined by adobe row houses on the north, west, and south. The eastern edge, in the direction of Mesilla, New Mexico, is open but by 1863 would be the site for the first San Agustín Cathedral. The Calle de la Alegría (later Congress Street) and the Calle de la India Triste (no longer extant) run parallel and just north along the row of houses that form the north edge of the plaza. In the construction of the cathedral,

*There are discrepancies in the historical records regarding the spelling of the name of this church, the previous church of the same name (p. 174), and the structure that followed (p. 85). We refer to these buildings by the names most widely used at the time.

adobe blocks were hand-carried to the site by the parishioners and Father Donato Rogieri. The towers were added in 1881 under the direction of Father J. B. Salpointe, and in 1883 the French stonemason Jules le Flein carved the Romanesque facade. It was Salpointe who encouraged church celebrations in the plaza and who later became disillusioned as it devolved into the backyard of the booming commercial activity along Congress Street. In its prime, the plaza hosted public celebrations and processions. In 1871 the city of Tucson took control of the plaza, and by 1897 Salpointe decided that a larger church was needed, purchased land on Stone Avenue, and erected another Romanesque structure (p. 85). When he sold the older building it became a hotel, a boxing ring, and an auto repair shop before its final demolition in 1936. Thanks to the preservation work of

George W. Chambers, le Flein's stone portal now graces the facade of the Arizona Historical Society (p. 143).

Pima County
Courthouse.

7 Pima County Courthouse

[NRHP], 115 N. Church Avenue,
1929; Roy Place, architect; Herbert
Brown, contractor; south wing
addition by Blanton & Cole,
architects, with M. M. Sundt,
contractor

The third Pima County Courthouse exemplifies Place's interpretation of the Spanish Colonial
Revival style defined by the space
of the arcade and courtyard, as
well as through the use of
religious building forms and
ornament, including a central
dome and an elaborate portal
facade. Moorish overtones,
typical of this style, can be seen in
the use of ceramic tiles on the
wainscotting, courtyard fountain,
and dome, whose mosaic form
has become a Tucson icon. The
exterior plaster covers reinforced
concrete walls that are accented
by cast concrete ornament. The
east wall of the original Presidio
lies under the courtyard and is
marked by a thin strip of dark
coppery granite in the pavement.
(See additional photograph, p.
281.)

Second Pima County Courthouse; demolished 1928.

Second Tucson City Hall; demolished 1972.

This is also the **Site of the Second Pima County Courthouse,** 1881; demolished 1928

The second Pima County Courthouse was a symmetrical two-story structure with a base of ashlar stone, brick, and wood in the Victorian style. The most prominent features were the high octagonal drum capped by an elongated dome in the center and the multiple pitched roofs with dormers.

8 **Site of the Second Tucson City Hall,** 1939; demolished 1972

Typical of American governmental buildings of that period, this two-story building was designed in the Classical Revival style with a raised basement, fluted columns, Ionic capitals, a portico with ornamented pediment, and a balustrade at the parapet.

Transamerica Office Building.

First National Bank of Arizona.

9 Transamerica Office Building, 177 N. Church Avenue, 1961–1962; Thomas E. Stanley

Tucson's best example of a modern curtain wall in white, clear (silver color), and gold anodized aluminum. The best view is from the sidewalk below, looking straight up. Stanley was from Dallas, Texas, and the original client was the Phoenix Title Company.

10 First National Bank of Arizona (Office Building), 200 N. Stone Avenue, 1968; Cain Nelson Wares & Cook/William Engelhardt, designer

In an authentic acknowledgment of the importance of the pedestrian experience in the city, this former bank building is both civic in scale and articulated with enough detail to be engaging to the pedestrian. It is a brick-covered steel structure with an arcade of shallow arches providing shade to the inner wall of glass on the south side. The interior space extends to the full two-story height, covered by a shallow brick vaulting. The banking room also contains a fountain and an office mezzanine.

Pioneer Hotel.

11 Bank Building, 150 N. Stone Avenue, 1955; Place and Place

The building facade is in the Italian Renaissance Revival style. It mimics the form of a palazzo, the building that served as headquarters for wealthy merchants and bankers from that period. Those borrowed characteristics include the two-story arcade on slender columns rising from the single-story base. Piers at either end frame the arcade. Elements from the late Renaissance or Mannerist period also appear here in the broken segmental arches with their rectangular windows above, both trademarks of Michelangelo. Lobby murals by Jay Datus were recently restored by the Wells Fargo Bank.

12 Pioneer Hotel (Office Building), 100 N. Stone Avenue, 1928; Roy Place; remodeled in 1970 after fire

Located at the corner of Stone Avenue and Pennington Street, this twelve-story building was at the center of the downtown business district and attracted the social and political elite. The building's vertical composition was defined by a base, middle, and top, articulated by the use of a classical entablature at the second floor, string course at the eleventh floor, and a bold cornice line at the roof. The classical entablature bisected the ornately decorated Spanish Colonial Revival entrance portal of prefabricated concrete elements, similar to that of Place's Pima County Courthouse (p. 79). The rooftop was used as an open-air ballroom whose wall openings framed magnificent views of the Tucson valley. The structural system was unique for Tucson,

Fox-Tucson Theatre.

using poured-in-place concrete, but although the structure survived a terrible fire in 1970, most of the ornately painted walls in the interior were destroyed. After the closing of the hotel in 1974, the exterior of the building was remodeled, retaining only a spiraled column at the corner as the last remnant of the original facade. As part of long-term renovation plans, the entablature is currently being uncovered and restored.

13 Fox-Tucson Theatre, 17 W. Congress Street, 1929; M. Eugene Durfee; closed 1974; under renovation with a planned summer 2003 reopening

This building was one of a national chain of movie theaters showing Fox Studio productions and decorated with ornate Art Deco stylistic motifs expressing the grandeur and opulence of pre-depression moviehouses. It was designed to house vaudeville acts and silent movies, for which it included an orchestra pit and Wurlitzer organ, respectively. Although closed since 1974, renovation is currently under way to revitalize the theater and restore the Art Deco features, including the street facade, neon marquee, interior ceiling mural, gold fluted columns, ornate light fixtures, and even the original organ pipes. (See detail photograph, page 287.)

Consolidated Bank of Tucson.

14 Consolidated Bank of Tucson (Bank One, Arizona), 2 East Congress Street, 1928–1929; renovation 1978 by Cain Nelson Wares & Cook

This eleven-story bank building was a dramatic change from the one- and two-story buildings that then defined Tucson. As Tucson's first high-rise building, its architecture reflected that of other big cities by importing a vertical composition of base, body, and top, marked by differences in the architectural elements and materials of the building. The cosmopolitan interior lobby, defined by decorated columns supporting a mezzanine level, is adorned with rose- and cedar-colored Tennessee marble; the walls are decorated with hand-painted murals depicting the arrival of the missionaries.

15 Charles O. Brown House [NRHP], 40 W. Broadway Boulevard, c. 1840; stabilization 2001 by Bob Vint, architect

This existing adobe structure was actually two houses. Based on tree-ring data of the extant vigas and latillas, the Jackson Street house is the oldest; it was remodeled by Charles O. Brown in 1868, with a new coat of stucco sporting quoins at the corners. The house that faces Broadway Boulevard is connected by a series of adobe rooms to the west and is newer and more American in its expression, with a sloping porch roof that is supported by wooden columns and brackets.

Saint Augustine Cathedral, c. 1896.

Saint Augustine Cathedral today.

16 Saint Augustine Cathedral,
192 S. Stone Avenue, 1896; Quintus Monier, architect; facade remodeling 1929 by Henry O. Jaastad, E. D. Herreras, FAIA, and D. Burr DuBois with John P. Steffes, contractor; remodeling 1968 by Terry Atkinson/M. J. Lang, contractor

Under the auspices of Father Peter Bourgade, Bishop of Tucson, the second Catholic church in Tucson with this name (but now Anglicized) was built in the Romanesque Revival style usually favored by French priests. In the interior, the high vaulted nave and side aisles were supported by Roman arches on brick-clad iron columns. Even though the columns had 900-pound iron pipes inside, two of them collapsed during construction. This "French style" was later considered inappropriate for Spanish and Mexican parishes by Bishop Daniel J. Gercke, D.D., who began to remodel the church by having the pair of truncated towers rebuilt of reinforced concrete and plastering the stone walls inside and out. The facade was then remodeled in the popular Spanish Colonial Revival style based on a design by Jaastad, Herreras, and DuBois, who "made the designs," which were then cast in Los Angeles by J. S. Watkins. In a variation on Catholic church tradition, the facade reveals not only the bronze figure of Saint Augustine but also a saguaro, yucca, horned toad, and various local cacti. In addition, there are symbols of the four evangelists—Matthew, Mark, Luke, and John—and the coat of arms of the Tucson bishops. Ironwork was created by Raúl Vásquez and Ramón Zubiate. The 1968 remodeling reinforced the roof, added a ceiling, and removed the columns separating the nave from the side aisles, which increased the seating capacity from 600 to 982 and completely changed the character

Southern Pacific Railroad Depot.

of the space. To experience an interior space similar to the original 1896 cathedral, see the Benedictine Sanctuary (p. 191).

17 The Second **Southern Pacific Railroad Depot** (Amtrak), 400 E. Toole Avenue, 1907; B. J. Patterson (San Francisco); partially demolished 1942; renovation 2001 by Poster-Frost Associates, Inc.

The shell of the building that is visible was once a magnificent example of a mixture of the Mission and Spanish Colonial Revival styles, attractive to visitors and the pride of Tucsonans. It was subsequently stripped of architectural merit with the removal of its decorative elements in 1942. This is also the site of the first depot, built in 1880, a wooden structure consumed by fire. To make room for the building of the new depot in 1907, the beautiful wooden structure of the San Xavier Hotel was torn down, and thus the need for the Hotel Heidel.

18 Hotel Heidel (**MacArthur Building**), 345 E. Toole Avenue, 1907–1908; Holmes & Holmes; building renovation 1984 by Gresham Larson; interior renovation by Collaborative Design Group/Frank Mascia

Built to serve passengers arriving in Tucson at the new Southern Pacific Railroad Depot, this triangular three-story building has stately proportions. Even though the facade is 173 feet long, the expression is vertical, created by the proportions of the repeated windows. The unique "flatiron" shape of this stuccoed brick structure is not immediately apparent when facing the symmetrical facade composed of a central arcade with paired windows at both ends. Elements from both Mission Revival and Prairie styles are incorporated, but neither style is especially dominant, a feature also seen in Trost's Santa Rita Hotel (p. 91). One of the finest elements of the building is the cornice of painted decorative brackets supporting the deep overhang of the roof. The hotel originally included a restaurant, saloon, and barbershop. The entire building is now used for offices.

Ronstadt Transit Center.

19 **Ronstadt Transit Center,**
215 E. Congress Street and N.
Sixth Avenue, 1991; Fentress
Bradburn Architects

20 **Hotel Congress,** 311 E.
Congress Street, 1919; Roy Place;
renovation 1985 by Eglin Cohen
Architects

This much-needed public
transportation hub is defined by
a trellised arcade at the perimeter,
which includes bricks from the
structures that previously stood
on this site and colorful ceramic
tiles. Two evaporative-cooling
towers provide visual markers
and tiny pools of cool air at their
bases. The second best use of this
space occurs during "Downtown
Saturday Nights," when it
becomes an open-air social
center, just like a traditional
plaza.

The location directly across from
the Southern Pacific Railroad
Depot made it an ideal hotel and
residence for winter visitors.
Exposed-brick bearing wall
construction on the exterior is
complemented by a gracious
lobby with high ceilings opening
onto spaces containing a restaurant, bar, and shops available to
hotel guests and the public. In
1934 a fire destroyed the third
floor and it was never rebuilt.
Second-floor rooms have private
baths, and the sitting areas and
hallways are decorated in the
1919 idea of Southwestern colors
and patterns.

21 **Rialto Theater and Apartments,** 318–322 E. Congress Street, 1919; name changed to Paramount in 1948, closed in 1963, reopened in 1973, fire in 1981, closed after explosion in 1984

The original theater once had an incredibly elaborate interior where all surfaces were ornamented with plasterwork and painted decoration of Islamic character. The theater had 1,300 seats, now all removed, and a stage that was unusually large at 32 feet deep. The second-floor apartments are still in use, and the theater is regularly used for informal parties, performances, and concerts.

22 **Chicago Store,** 130 E. Congress Street, 1903; David H. Holmes

Built for the Los Angeles Furniture Company, this is a good example of twentieth-century main street commercial architecture, with brick bearing walls and a cornice carried on brackets supported by paired pilasters and capitals. With the use of an enormous crane, a new roof structure was added in 1999 above the pressed-tin ceilings and original oak staircase.

23 **U.S. Court House** [NRHP], 55 E. Broadway Boulevard, 1929; James A. Wetmore (Department of the U.S. Treasury); *interior inaccessible*

Originally built as a ground-floor post office with courtrooms on the second floor, the restrained Neoclassical style here is apparent in the corner quoins and decorative pilasters of terra cotta that sport a mottled glaze made to look like stone, but with accents in color. The building is made from various shades of buff-colored brick and uses Roman and Greek ornament with heavy bronze doors and decorative iron lamps at the entry. Even the underside of the projecting eaves has an articulated pattern with accent colors.

24 **Commercial Building,** 41–47 N. 6th Avenue, 1918; Henry Jaastad

Typical of Tucson's commercial structures of this period, this building is built of pressed brick of contrasting colors, which produces a Puebloesque ornamentation above the windows and at the stepped parapet.

25 Site of Santa Rita Hotel,

Trost & Rust/Henry Trost, designer, 1902–1904; addition 1917 by Trost & Trost; demolished 1972

Considered one of the most elegant hotels in Tucson, this five-story building was the tallest building at the time of its construction. It attracted elite travelers, movie stars, big-band orchestras, and cattlemen until the 1950s, when ownership changed and car-oriented motels began to draw guests away from downtown. The hotel contained a beautifully ornamented two-story, balconied lobby, roof garden, and dance hall. As was typical of Trost's work, he combined the Mission Revival features of light-hued stucco and entrance arcade with Sullivanesque attic frieze orna-mentation.

26 Odd Fellows Hall (Barrio Grill, Etherton Art Gallery, Timothy Fuller Photography, Barbara Grygutis Studio), 135 S. 6th Avenue, 1919

A good example of an early-twentieth-century commercial building with large windows at the ground level, which was usually rented to an automobile-related business. Highlighting the spacious second-floor dance hall are three large windows with shallow arches of articulated stonework including keystones. The Fellows have been an active social club since 1881.

27 **Stillwell-Twiggs House,** 134
S. 5th Avenue, 1901–1902

This two-story brick house was
the former Twiggs boarding-
house, used by railroad employees, winter visitors, and business
travelers until the 1930s. The
front porch, which runs the
length of the house, was used by
guests. In addition, each room
had its own wood stove.

28 **Julian Drew Block** [NRHP]
and Lewis Hotel, 178–188 E.
Broadway Boulevard, 1917; facade
renovation 1982–1983 by Eglin
Cohen & Dennehy Architects

The ground floor of this two-
story brick structure has the large
window walls associated with
commercial use. The second
floor, originally a hotel with
screened porches for guests, is
now used as apartments.

Warehouse District [NRHP]

The area of the earliest warehouses built along the railroad
tracks runs between the depot to
the east and Main Avenue to the
west. Sixth Street and the West
University neighborhood became
the northern boundary, and
commercial activity in downtown
encouraged locating warehouses
on the southern edge of the
tracks. However, some of the
better extant examples are north
of the railroad tracks. In many
warehouses, it is the interior
structure that is fascinating but
difficult to see as many of these
buildings are not open to the
public.

29 Corbett Building, 340 N. 6th Avenue

This simple poured-in-place concrete warehouse provides shelter and shade over the public sidewalk in an example of good civic architecture. The arcade of the building sits at the curb of the street and is about 12.5 feet wide and 13 feet high. The rhythm of the piers at the street is reinforced inside by concrete "beams." The smooth exterior walls are accented by cast bas-relief ornament above the arcade made of wreaths, shields, and the profile of a Spanish conquistador. Emphasis is given to the corner by a short tower, and the roof is red tile.

The second warehouse north of the Corbett Building features a tin "Spanish tile" roof supported by exposed wooden brackets. Across the street, at **403 N. 6th Avenue,** sits another warehouse, but this one has had a modern facelift in the form of a perfo-rated metal screen along the street and an ornamental metal piece running horizontally at the top of the screen.

30 Warehouse, 439 N. 6th Avenue

Another good example of adaptive reuse sits on the southwest corner of 6th Street and 6th Avenue. It has a steel sash window that curves around one corner, metal shade structures, and a large canopy at 6th Street.

31 **Warehouse,** 450 N. 6th Avenue

On the southeast corner of 6th Street and 6th Avenue is another great example of the civic-mindedness of the original designer and client in the attractive sidewalk canopy supported by steel cables. Also a good example of adaptive reuse, especially in leaving the canopy and the original steel sash windows.

Also of note is the **Tucson Warehouse & Transfer,** 100 E. 6th Street at the corner of 7th Avenue. The high-rise structure is poured-in-place concrete; for an excellent example of adaptive reuse, visit the office of Sakellar & Associates on the ground floor. The structural system in **Zee's Warehouse** at Stone Avenue and Toole Avenue features steel bowstring trusses of various lengths built to accommodate the irregular shape of the structure itself.

Barrio Historico

The Barrio Historico area includes the historic neighborhoods south of downtown: Barrio Libre [NRHP], El Hoyo, El Membrillo, Carrillo Gardens, and Elysian Grove. Barrio Libre is the largest piece of the historic area, built between the 1860s and the 1920s, which is still standing after the demolition of "urban renewal" in 1967. In the last decade of the nineteenth century, it was called Barrio Libre because it was the "free district" outside of the city's jurisdiction. It is still an area of Hispanic cultural and architectural traditions, with a past in which Spanish was the lingua franca, adopted by Anglo-Saxons, Russians, German Jews, Italians, and later Chinese immigrants. Many of the Spanish residents were families of ranchers living in homes in town to be near church, community, and schools. Among the residents, some were businesspeople and professionals, but the majority were laborers: bakers, blacksmiths, saloonkeepers, and shopkeepers. After the completion of the railroad, Chinese immigration resulted in the opening of restaurants, laundries, and markets.

The major architectural characteristic of the Barrio Libre is the nineteenth-century Hispanic tradition, which makes the street a social space that is clearly defined by a wall of continuous adobe houses at the property line. This initial form, in which residences lined the block perimeter with commercial functions at the corners, was then transformed with the arrival of non-Hispanic Americans. The majority of the earlier buildings are of the Sonoran row style, whether of the earliest types or the later Transitional or Transformed. The later non-Hispanic styles include Victorian, Queen Anne, and American Territorial, located mostly along Stone Avenue, with the edge joining Armory Park, and there are a few even later Mission Revival and Bungalow examples. There are only a handful of commercial and public buildings left, including one open-air shrine, two schools, three churches, and two small markets, of which Jerry's Lee Ho on Meyer Avenue has been open since 1912. The landscape material typical of the period includes chinaberry, tamerisk (salt cedar), rhuslancia, cotton-wood, fruitless mulberry, mesquite, prickly pear, palm and pepper trees, and oleander and elderberry shrubs.

El Hoyo is the neighborhood in the sunken area just to the west of Main Avenue. There was a large spring just north and west of the intersection of Calle de la Mision and South Main Avenue, which supported settlement and growth of this area. Some residents refer to this area as "the Gardens," in memory of Carrillo Gardens, and some call it "the Grove," referring to Elysian Grove.

El Membrillo, located between Sentinal Peak and I-10, was named for the quince trees that grew in the area and is today a tiny remnant of the neighbor-hood that existed before the construction of the freeway.

The entries 1–4 make up much of block 234 on the Sanborn Insurance Map of 1883, bounded by Cushing and Simpson Streets and Convent and Meyer Avenues. Today, the interior of the block is used for parking.

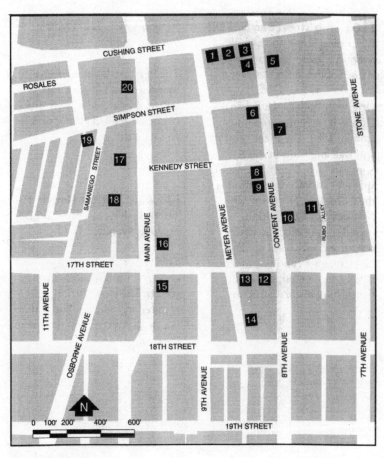

Barrio Historico

1 Cushing Street Bar, 343–353 W. Cushing Street and Meyer Avenue, c. 1869; addition 1973 by Harris Sobin/Blanton & Company

Originally built as the Ferrin House, it was converted into a store in 1880. The corner entry and wall angle are a typical Sonoran form allowing for more space for casual conversation at the front door. South on Meyer Avenue is a 1973 addition, including a small patio and restaurant, which are modern in form, material, and restrained detail and yet compatible with the existing historic structures.

2 Residence, 122–124 W. Cushing Street

The best canales in Tucson are found on this Sonoran row house; they are decorated with birds that look like woodpeckers and with flowers.

3 Manuel Montijo House, 110–116 W. Cushing Street/300–302 S. Convent Avenue, c. 1870

This Sonoran row house grew and grew until it had seventeen rooms. The west portion was restored in 1980, and today there is a small courtyard in the back.

Convent Streetscape.

4 Convent Streetscape, 300–400 block of S. Convent Avenue between Cushing and Simpson Streets

Built throughout the 1880s, this area represents one of Tucson's last remaining intact Sonoran streetscapes, and thereby becomes a snapshot of the urban environment before American influence came to dominate Tucson's architectural vocabulary. With new structures replacing those that have collapsed, and renovation of older buildings, the next block south on Convent Avenue is beginning to have a similar continuous form; however, the breaks occur with the freestanding structures such as the Valencia House (p. 100).

5 Residence, 317 S. Convent Avenue, c. 1890

American Territorial in style, this single-story detached brick house has segmental arches above windows and doors, a hipped metal roof with a projecting gable, and a corner porch with turned wooden posts. The property line is marked by a new wrought-iron fence and gate with a walk that leads directly to the front door. The palm trees in the front yard were as exotic as the style of the house.

6 **Residence,** 360–370 S. Convent Avenue/110–116 W. Simpson Street, before 1883; Simpson Street facade c. 1900

A good example of a Trans-formed Sonoran corner adobe structure. A roof has been added to the rooms on Convent Avenue, but those on Simpson Street have their original flat roofs with parapets.

7 **Residence,** 387 S. Convent Avenue, c. 1880

The curved corner and wood cornice on this building are an unusual and interesting variation on a Sonoran adobe.

8 Diego **Valencia House,** 432–436 S. Convent Avenue, c. 1907; Henry Jaastad

A single layer of brick envelops an earlier adobe building here in this one-story detached American Territorial with its pyramidal roof. Cantera stone was used to protect the base, and the structure accommodated both commercial and residential use—as a carriage shed for hearses, as a market, and, later, as a house.

9 **Brick Row Houses,** 440–446 S. Convent Avenue, before 1909; Henry Jaastad

The most notable feature of this one-story, four-unit structure is that it is an American translation in brick of the Transformed Sonoran row houses in the neighborhood.

Convent Avenue Studios.

10 Convent Avenue Studios,
469 S. Convent Avenue, 1997; Rick Joy; *inaccessible/published*

The most interesting question raised in this design lies in how any architect interprets the secretary of the interior's standard to provide a "clear distinction between old and new." This policy can promote a living architecture *and* one that respects the past, especially on an abandoned property such as this in which only the street facade wall remains. The decision to place the three wedge-shaped studio apartments in the center of the lot and not in the traditional placement on the front property line is questionable. It illuminates an attitude that would ensure the integrity of the historic facade (that is, the streetscape) while ignoring the way in which buildings sit on the land (that is, the urban geography). There must be a middle ground in this polemic. The distinction between old and new here is much more successful at the scale of the building itself and its details: The palette of earth, metal, concrete, bright paint, and native vegetation skillfully complements the existing neighborhood.

11 Studio, 400 S. Rubio Alley, 2000; Rick Joy

Sitting on the lot at the back of the Convent Avenue Studios, this building takes full advantage of the land-use code for this neighborhood, which allows one to build to the property line. The 14-foot-high, rammed-earth walls insulate and enclose a narrow courtyard to the north; the single-room work studio sits to the south. There is a poetic balance in minimalist forms, materials, and details, such as the detached effect of the north wall of the studio.

12 **Pasquale Court** Row Houses, 209–219 W. 17th Street, before 1879

This row of adobes is part of a large family compound begun by Italian immigrant Juan Pasquale in 1879, with the original house on Convent Avenue. With children and grandchildren, the house grew north and west along 17th Street in eight attached houses two rooms deep, forming an inner courtyard as a social center for the family. The front rooms each had a fireplace, and the structure has recently been restored by the owner, Warren Michaels, with the help of Robert and Luis Saenz, adobe masons and plasterers.

13 **Row Houses,** 601–698 S. Meyer Avenue and 17th Street

Adobe row houses in good condition.

14 **Mexican Baptist Church** (Templo de Bethel), 641 S. Meyer Avenue

Now a residence, the stone foundation and steps at the entry lead to a doorway spanned with a very shallow segmental arch with a Palladian or tripartite window above. This simple single-room brick structure also features a gabled roof behind the shaped parapet of the facade.

15 Row Houses, 621–623 Main Avenue and 17th Street, 1912

Very small adobe row apartments.

16 Hardy Residence and Guest House, 585 S. Main Avenue, 1997; Bob Vint & Associates/Bob Vint & Luis Ibarra

Built in the Sonoran tradition, this adobe house is a good example of infill in a historic neighborhood. The L-shaped floor plan creates a patio on the southwest corner that provides passive solar heating in the winter. A central breezeway or *zaguán* connects the patio to the street entrance.

17 Carrillo School, 440 S. Main Avenue, 1930; Merritt H. Starkweather, FAIA, architect, and R. H. Martin, contractor; renovation 1994 by M3 Engineering

Twelve original classrooms were built in the Mission Revival style on the exterior, with Craftsman woodwork inside including the wide doors of dark-stained wood. There were several later additions and renovations, including filling in the pool that the school board had inherited when they purchased the Elysian Grove property from Emmanuel Drachman.

Carrillo Gardens; demolished c. 1925.

18 **Site of Carrillo Gardens/**
Elysian Grove, c. 1870; demolished
c. 1925

The gardens built by Leopoldo
Carrillo covered 8 acres and
included orchards, shade trees,
lakes fed by natural springs, and a
rose garden. City boating races
and concerts were held there
from the 1880s until 1903, when
the land was purchased by
Emmanuel Drachman and
converted for use as a baseball
and amusement park. In 1910 it
was renamed Elysian Grove, and
in 1912 it was visited by Teddy
Roosevelt.

19 **Elysian Grove Market,** 400
W. Simpson Street

Now the Elysian Grove Bed &
Breakfast Inn, this Sonoran
adobe has the corner cut typical
of commercial properties.

20 El Tiradito [NRHP], 221 S. Main Avenue, present location c. 1894–1909

El Tiradito, Spanish for "the little castaway one," refers to the site of a murdered man, which became a traditional place for Mexican Americans to say a prayer for his soul and make a wish; also called "the wishing shrine." The actual location of the incident, and the first shrine, is in the middle of present-day Simpson Street just west of S. Meyer Avenue. The current location is very near the artesian spring called "El Ojito" on the road to the San Agustín Mission. The new site was finally deeded to the city in 1927, the same year that the Tucson City Council chose an official version of the many legends associated with the shrine. The U-shaped adobe wall that serves as backdrop to the shrine was constructed in 1940 by the National Youth Administration.

Armory Park [NRHP]

The Armory Park Neighborhood takes its name from the use of the area between 1862 and 1873 as the Military Plaza and Armory. Public pressure forced the garrison to move to the remote Fort Lowell location as the occasional but undeniably rowdy behavior of the soldiers was considered a threat to families beginning to settle here.

It is the arrival of, and proximity to, the railroad that gives this neighborhood its unique character. When the Southern Pacific arrived in 1880, the neighborhood grew rapidly in a pattern of wide streets and avenues, primarily settled by the families of railroad employees, white-collar workers in the Victorian houses, and laborers in much simpler structures located along the alleys. This pattern created by class segregation is still evident today as the non-Hispanic preference for setbacks creates a rhythm of detached houses along the street, whereas traces of the Hispanic-derived continuous adobe wall define the alley. You can see this most clearly in the block bounded by 12th and 13th Streets and 4th and 5th Avenues. These houses reflect not only segregation in land-use patterns, but also cultural affinity as expressed though building materials. By 1880, materials that were previously unavailable, in very short supply, or very expensive were arriving by rail in abundance. Bricks, milled lumber, pressed tin, paints and wallpapers, furnishings and hardware—all allowed Tucson's newest arrivals to express their tastes in the styles popular in the eastern states: Victorian, Queen Anne, and Greek Revival. Most of the buildings are single- or multiple-family residences, with a few boardinghouses. Groceries and other items could be found in the commercial areas along 6th and S. Stone Avenues. The

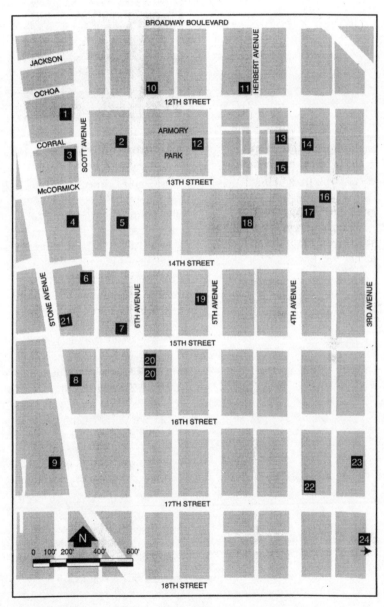

Armory Park

Scottish Rite Cathedral.

establishment of the Plaza School in 1884 was extremely controversial as its location in the sparsely settled area was considered an easy target for Apache raids.

Some houses in this neighborhood are open for the annual Armory Park tour.

1 Scottish Rite Cathedral, 160 S. Scott Avenue, 1915; Trost & Trost/Henry C. Trost, designer; restoration 1994 by Bob Vint, architect/Division II, contractor

A surprising variety of Neoclassical stylistic influences are combined in this Masonic temple. The symmetrical exterior facade of brick and terra cotta meshes the large scale of the Roman Revival with a restrained Greek Revival ornament, seen in the Ionic capitals. Passing through the small entry, the central interior stairway rises to a lobby with Craftsman period elements: dark wooden beams, wall paneling, and decorative light fixtures. Continuing through to the openness of the spacious main hall, the surprise comes in realizing that it is decorated in the High Renaissance style complete with pilasters, Corinthian capitals, and formal raised seating on both sides with a large stage at the far

Carnegie Free Library.

end. Typical of many of the buildings in Trost's short career in Tucson, the resulting combination of seemingly disparate influences is at once odd and pleasing. (See plan, p. 279.)

2 Carnegie Free Library

(Tucson Children's Museum), 200 S. 6th Avenue, 1900–1901; Trost & Trost/Henry Trost, designer; wing addition 1938; dome destroyed 1941; garden wall addition 1961 by Arthur Brown, FAIA

The surest evidence of a good building is one that has survived trials—in this case, of being enclosed by a massive wall, the destruction of its lofty central dome by fire, and the stripping of much of its decorative ornament. This tough little Neoclassical Revival building was the winning competition entry for the Carnegie Library by Trost, who later formed a partnership with one of the other competitors, Robert E. Rust. A sense of solidity is evident in the square proportion of the entry porch framed by piers at either end with a pair of Ionic columns in the center. That central block becomes a module that repeats on both sides. The quality of the remaining materials and the fine craftsmanship, including the reddish-buff stone base, buff-colored brick, terra cotta columns, and staff (or weather-proofed) plaster ornament, contribute to the building's continuing appeal. Placed directly in front of the library is the massive (Merrill P.) **Freeman Memorial Bench,** designed in 1920 by Bernard Maybeck and sculpted by Bejamino Bufano. It is surprisingly cool sitting on this large curved bench in the afternoon, as the western sun is blocked by the high back and the marble itself is cool. Typical of this California architect's work, the proportions of the bench, and especially the planters, seem odd or squat. This is because Maybeck preferred the proportions of Romanesque architecture over those of the ancient Greek; the former is heavy and grounded, the latter in perfect equilibrium. Travertine, onyx, and verde marble create the rich color images. The bench is dedicated to the Arizona pioneers and was recently restored through the efforts of the Tucson-Pima Arts Council.

Temple of Music and Art.

3 Blenman House, 204 S. Scott Avenue, 1878

The Late Transitional style is evident in this one-story adobe house, whose wall thickness can be measured by the depth of the entry. It sits on a stone foundation and features an added porch and pitched roof. The recent renovation as the Royal Elizabeth Bed & Breakfast highlights the wood detailing and leaded-glass skylights in the central hall or *zaguán*, probably dating from the 1890s.

4 Temple of Music and Art

[NRHP], 330 S. Scott Avenue, 1927; Arthur W. Hawes; renovation 1990 by Janus & Associates, architect, and NBBJ/Gresham Larson, architect of record/Division II, contractor

The open side of the U-shaped plan of this Spanish Colonial Revival structure faces the street, creating an inviting courtyard paved in Mexican tile and featuring a fountain. Because Hawes assisted in the design of the Pasadena Community Playhouse in California, it is not surprising that the Temple is so similar. Be sure to see the fully restored and richly decorated interiors, including the spacious 623-seat auditorium with its stage large enough for a symphony orchestra. Other spaces in the complex include a cafe, recital hall, art gallery, and a gift shop. Call for off-season (May–August) tours.

Healy House.

5 **Healy** (Schneider-Healy) **House,** 324 S. 6th Avenue, 1900–1902; Henry Trost

It is possible that the deep porch facing east and the pyramidal roof are additions to this large single-story adobe house. The Greek Revival porch uses fluted columns to support an entablature, above which the hip roof forms the shape of a Greek temple pediment. The dynamic pattern of the Sullivanesque plaster ornament at the entablature is composed of repeated vertical ovals. Note the unusual octagonal or faceted capitals that project beyond the entablature.

6 **Brady Court Bungalows** (Arizona Theatre Company), 40 E. 14th Street, 1915; renovation 1976 by Collaborative Design Group/Frank Mascia

Typical of California Bungalow court apartments, three symmetrical duplex units form a tight courtyard open on the street side and shaded by mature pepper trees. The buildings sit on a raised foundation of dark volcanic stone with concrete slab porches composed of tapered piers and wooden rafters of composite construction and shaped ends. A very rough concrete stucco has been added to the exterior, and the wood is badly deteriorated. In the interior, the original Craftsman woodwork elements in the wainscotting, picture molding, and doors are all intact.

7 St. Joseph's (Immaculate Heart) Academy, 35 E. 15th Street, 1886

One of the largest surviving structures from this date, this two-story building is badly in need of restoration. The original building served as a convent, and the addition housed the first Catholic school in Tucson. The first story is constructed of hand-hewn, rough-cut stone from "A" Mountain, and the second story is stucco over brick. The stonework, including the cantera window surrounds, was crafted by Jules le Flein, the stonemason who created the Romanesque facade of the first San Agustín Cathedral (p. 77). The mature date palms lend a stately and exotic air, which is echoed in the simple Doric columns standing on the front porch. The original second-floor wooden sleeping porches and the belfry have been removed.

8 Velasco House [NRHP], 475 S. Stone Avenue, c. 1850s; addition(s) 1860–1890

This house is an excellent example of a Transformed Sonoran structure in which the earlier simple adobe with its *zaguán* not only lost its adjacent neighbors but was changed in form and detail. In 1878, the walls were covered with lime stucco, and the original flat roof was topped with a gable that included a dormer with fish-scale shingles and an attic vent. Fired-brick chimneys were added at both ends. Although the original lintels of mesquite wood continue to support the walls above openings, simplified Greek pediments above the new panel doors and sash windows were also added. Asphalt roof shingles are a recent application, replacing what was probably corrugated tin as that material typically covered most early wooden roof additions.

9 Temple Emmanu-El **(Stone Avenue Temple),** 564 S. Stone Avenue, 1910; renovation 2000 by Poster Frost Associates, architects

The facade of the first synagogue in the Arizona Territory is an odd combination of a central Greek temple front flanked by towers with Moorish domes. The facade was originally exposed brick, so the effect was less "Moorish" than it is today. The most curious feature is the raised base, with entry through stairs at either side tower, not in the center. Semi-circular arched windows are derived from Roman or Christian churches. No longer used as a synagogue, the recent renovation allows for a variety of community uses.

10 **Willard** (Pueblo) **Hotel,** 145 S. 6th Avenue at 12th Street, 1902-1904; Trost & Rust/Henry Trost; renovation 1990 by Collaborative Design Group/Division II, contractor

The Mission Revival style here is modest in ornament. Viewed from the corner, the towers anchor the arcades of half-circles at the lower floor. The gabled roof is missing the original Spanish tile, and the exposed brick is now stuccoed. A sign from about the 1950s advertising the pool is a classic.

11 House, 219 E. 12th Street, before 1880

The Transformed Sonoran house seen here is more typical of the houses in the Barrio Historico, which were built before 1880 but had gabled roofs and other elements added as the materials became available via the railroad.

12 Armory Park Senior Citizen Center, 220 S. 5th Avenue, 1975; James A. Gresham & Associates/Jim Larson; remodel 1979 by Swaim & Associates

In responding to the opposing character of the existing buildings—the Neoclassical Carnegie Library to the west and the turn-of-the-century residences to the east—the architect had to resolve those differences within the building itself. This extremely difficult proposition is more successful on the exterior, where the building seems to be woven into the fabric of the neighborhood. The entry facade facing the park and the Carnegie Library is grander in scale and expression, with a deep-set, large arched opening and vertical windows. Originally, this facade was a freestanding wall shading the west side of the building, but it was significantly changed in the 1979 remodel, which filled in the area between the two walls. A base course and brick coping are provided for scale on the smooth stucco walls. Matching the scale of the residences on the east side is a continuous covered porch with a sloped roof supported by slender cast-in-place concrete columns.

Site of the Military Plaza,
1862–1873; demolished

Major David Fergusson, in command of the Tucson detachment of the Union Army's California Volunteers, established the Tucson Post (renamed Camp Lowell in 1862) when he carried out his orders to "take possession" of sites necessary to station men and supplies for an American garrison. Several adobe buildings were begun in 1866 for the never-quite-permanent American post, and the troops slept in tents until they were moved to Fort Lowell along the Pantano River. By 1872 it was considered an unfit camp, which may have had something to do with public opinion evident in the 1870 editorial in the *Tucson Weekly Arizonan:* "It is enough that the [towns]people are constantly harassed by Indians without being subjected to the outrages of a depraved and drunken soldiery."

Residence at 228 S. 4th Avenue.

13 Residence, 228 S. 4th Avenue, before 1901

This residence illustrates the qualities of the Queen Anne style, including an irregular, complex plan and building form with a high-pitched roof with multiple gables. This building also maintains many of the intricate decorative features of this style, including fish-scale sheathing at the gable ends and a whimsical widow's walk.

14 Ure Boarding House, 219 S. 4th Avenue, 1888

This two-story building with its pyramidal roof may not look like much, but it may be the only remaining two-story adobe apartment house in Tucson that is still in use.

15 Paddy Woods House, 246 S. 4th Avenue, 1891, 1898

Most of the features characteristic of the Queen Anne style can be seen in this relatively small house.

16 **Roskruge** (Culin-Roskruge) **House,** 318 E. 13th Street, 1895–1896; Creighton & Millard/James M. Creighton

Designed by the architect of Old Main on the University of Arizona campus and the Pinal County Courthouse in Florence, Arizona, the floor plan (p. 278) of this Queen Anne house really needs to be studied or an interior visit is needed to appreciate the informality and dynamic space created by the diagonal walls, octagonal spaces, and bay windows. The exterior features of note include the rosette pattern on the raking fascia and the gracefully carved ornament on the wooden entrance porch gable. The lot to the west with the olive grove also belongs to the house.

17 **Kitt** (Kitt-Peterson) **House,** 319 S. 4th Avenue, 1899; Katharine Kitt

Unusual for the Greek Revival in Tucson, the facade of this house is the only example of a complete classical temple portico. Also surprisingly, the house is built of adobe. The living space is extended through the addition of the deep porch, which occupies the entire west end of the house. The columns are fluted Doric with capitals, and a lunette attic vent sits in the center of the pediment. Diagonal interior walls suggest an interest in the Queen Anne style.

Safford Junior High School.

18 Safford (Junior High) **School** (now Safford Magnet School), 200 E. 13th Street, 1918; Henry Jaastad/Annie Rockfellow, designer; renovation 1992 by Noggle McCarthy, architects

Sitting on the **Site of the old Plaza School,** which was destroyed by fire, this structure is arguably the best surviving example of the work of A. G. (Annie) Rockfellow and her belief that the Spanish Colonial Revival was an appropriate architectural style for the Southwest. This school illustrates the elements she thought to be especially well suited: the elaborately carved portico set against the smooth, white stucco walls and framed by twin towers capped by domes. Deep shadows are created by the overhangs of the red-tiled gabled roofs with the rafters exposed underneath.

19 Lincoln (Lincoln-Brown, Windsor-Davis) **House,** 422 S. 5th Avenue, 1902; Henry Trost

Many of the signature Trost elements are evident in this one-story stuccoed house. His Prairie-style composition is based on a cube from which receding and projecting forms are balanced in the overhanging flat roofs and the columns of the porch. The planes of the smooth stucco walls are unified by setting the oval attic vents within an ornamented rectangle the width of the window below it. The ornamented fascia is also typical of Trost. Altogether, a very appealing small house.

20 **Servin Houses,** 505 and 509
S. 6th Avenue, c. 1902

Almost identical two-story brick
houses in the Queen Anne style.
The paired, low wrought-iron
fences at the sidewalk define the
private space of the front yard.
The house at 505 is fairly well
hidden by mature chinaberry
trees and other vintage vegetation.

21 **Twin Palms Apartments,**
385 S. Stone Avenue, 1903;
renovated 1999 by Oden Con-
struction/Oden Hughes

Quarried stone provides the base
and window trim on this two-
story brick duplex. Simple
columns support the porch roof
and balcony, which features
classical wooden dentils but a
simple balustrade. Deep overhangs on the roof are supported
by exposed rafters with curved
exposed ends. A pair of dark
wooden stairs in the center rise to
the second-floor apartments.

22 **McGinty-Laos** (Muncy-Laos) **House,** 647 S. 4th Avenue, 1897, 1901

Although this house has a bay window with an overhanging gable characteristic of the Queen Anne style, its plan and massing are rather simple and more characteristic of the American Territorial style. Typical of these structures, the house has brick walls on stone foundations, a pyramidal roof, wall openings with flat or segmental arched lintels, wooden eave trim, and porches with gabled roofs and lathe-cut columns. The interior is rich in Victorian details, including wooden lathe-cut or lattice screens.

23 **Lee-Cutler House,** 620 S. 3rd Avenue, 1910

This house is the one of the best examples of the later phase of the Queen Anne Revival. Many of the features can be seen from the street (but through the trees), such as the round turret capped by a conical roof. The turret is the extension of the semicircular bay of the living room, part of an irregular or loosely composed floor plan that includes porches. The variety of color and texture in the exterior surfaces includes a stone foundation, brick walls and chimneys, wooden shingles, and a very rough stucco at the roof gable ends. This house even has a Palladian motif attic vent on the south gable.

24 **Harding House,** 711 S. 3rd
Avenue, 1997; Design & Building
Consultants, Inc./Paul Weiner,
architect

This simple strawbale house
makes reference to the historic
Transitional style in the square
form, with its porch at the corner,
pyramidal roof, simple window
and door openings, and plaster
finish. The thickness of the walls
is not apparent from the exterior,
but it is an excellent example of
an appropriate design in a
historic neighborhood.

Ironhorse and Pie Allen [NRHP], John Spring [NRHP] and Barrio Anita

The Tucson High Magnet School campus and the two historic neighborhoods of Ironhorse, west of Euclid Avenue, and Pie Allen, to the east, make up the area south of the West University neighborhood, between 6th Street and Broadway Boulevard and 4th and Park Avenues.

Even though the John Spring and Barrio Anita neighborhoods are not adjacent to Ironhorse and Pie Allen, they are included here for their characteristic similarities: placement along the railroad, narrow streets, and adobe structures.

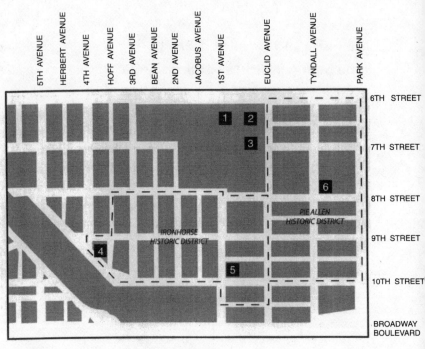

Iron Horse and Pie Allen

Tucson High Magnet School.

1 Tucson High School **(Tucson High Magnet School),** 400 N. 2nd Avenue, 1924; Lyman & Place/ Henry Jaastad, Associate

Monumental and truly civic in scale, the original building for 1,500 students is Neoclassical in style. The west-facing entry porch is almost a continuous wall of massive fluted columns with Corinthian capitals and support- ing a simple white entablature on which the attic story windows continue the rhythm of the columns below. In material there are two shades of buff-colored brick, limestone, glazed terra cotta, and roof tile. The slightly projecting cornice is an elaborate expression of eaves, fascia, and finials formed as stylized badger's heads representing the school mascot. The ends of the facade step back at the corners, reducing the overall length of the facade and creating a more complex articulation at the roofline. One enters the school by ascending a

series of stairs that run the length of the shaded porch, then through the monumental doors into a spacious lobby. The auditorium is the interior space worth visiting.

Three of the buildings on the campus clearly illustrate the progression of architectural styles skillfully employed by the office of Roy Place and are hallmarks of their periods: The original 1924 building is Neoclassical, the 1938–1939 Union or **Gymnasium Building** is in the Art Deco style, and the Vocational Education Building from 1949–1950 is Streamline Moderne.

Tucson High Magnet School Addition.

2 Tucson High Magnet School Addition and Remodel, 1992; James Merry & Associates

This large addition echoes the original building in form, color, and rhythm, using current technology and materials. The brick is very similar in color and texture to the original. Folded receding corners mimic those of the 1924 building, but at the attic level, steel columns and I beams with chamfered ends are an expression of contemporary technology used to take the place of the earlier brick pilasters and wooden eave rafters. The ribbed pattern of the roof decking on the underside of the overhang also provides visual texture on a small scale, similar to the wooden articulation in the original building.

3 Tucson High Magnet School Vocational Education Building, 1948–1949; Place & Place

This is a great example of the Streamline Moderne style, with its horizontal bands of terra cotta–colored brick curtain walls, white concrete trim, and ribbon windows of glass block. (See photograph, p. 288.)

Ironhorse Historic District [NRHP]

In 1879 the Southern Pacific Railroad took the land along the tracks for right-of-way and sold the excess for development of rental properties to house their blue-collar employees. This was one of five neighborhoods that met the Southern Pacific criterion that employees must live within one mile of the tracks in order to hear the "whistle code," the communications system used before the telephone. By the end of World War I, 50 percent of the residents in the district were still railroad employees and their families.

Although the most rapid period of growth occurred here in the early 1900s, in construction of duplexes and rooming houses, there are also adobe houses from the 1880s, several excellent examples of Transformed Sonoran and American Territorial, and a handful of Queen Anne houses. Every conceivable variation of the Bungalow style is represented, and infill along the alleys can be dated by the period revivals then popular, either Mission or Spanish Colonial. A few commercial properties have survived, including a grocery and a laundry, small businesses, and light industry. Today, the neighborhood is characterized by the uneven care given student rental properties versus the owner-occupied homes, the preservation of the arroyo that meanders through the area, and oddities.

4 **Coronado Hotel,** 402 E. 9th Street, 1928; Roy Place; renovation and adaptive reuse 1991 by Collaborative Design Group

This hotel on the edge of the historic 4th Avenue business district is typical for its time: a four-story box of rooms with an elegant public lobby and inviting entry facade. The Mission Revival entry features spiral columns supporting three arches with a curved pediment relief over the recessed entry. The 1991 conversion to single-room-occupancy (SRO) apartments provides a good model for both adaptive reuse and preservation of this common historic Tucson building topology.

5 **Ziegler House,** 126 N. 1st Avenue, c. 1910 (plaque says 1885)

Sitting high above the street, this majestic Queen Anne residence dominates the streetscape with a two-story round tower and a second-story balcony that covers the front porch. Other Queen Anne features, such as the complex house forms and high-pitched roofs, are blended with Victorian details seen in the decorative woodwork and stained-glass windows on both the first and second floors.

Also of note, next door to the north, at 128–130 N. 1st Avenue, is a very simple but attractive duplex that appears to be a Transformed Sonoran, but is probably a more recent remodel. Excellent examples of Transformed Sonorans include the **Riecker Duplex** at 636 and 638 E. 9th Street and **Casas Antiguas** at 3rd Avenue and 8th Street, built in the 1880s. The first brick house built north of the railroad, in

1898, and a classic example of an American Territorial, stands on the northeast corner of 2nd Avenue and 9th Street.

Pie Allen Historic District [NRHP]

The Pie Allen Historic District is the area between Euclid and Park Avenues and 6th and 10th Streets, which was originally developed by, among others, John Brackett (Pie) Allen, a Tucson pioneer and mayor, who used his 1878 land-claim homestead rights to secure and develop the land.

6 Daily Ranch, 8th Street and Tyndall Avenue, c. 1870

Surrounded by a stuccoed wall, this Transformed Sonoran ranch house sits on a large piece of property with mature trees. The original structure was added onto several times, including hipped and gabled shingle roofs, which were then covered with Spanish tile in the 1940s.

For an excellent example of a Transformed Sonoran, see 832 7th Street (c. 1870s), with a recent clay-tile roof. Also of note is the **El Capitan Court** (316–342 Park Avenue); this formal typology in which the individual units are placed around a central courtyard was developed for rental properties and made popular in California.

John Spring [NRHP] and Barrio Anita

John Spring and Barrio Anita are two small neighborhoods within the boundaries of Speedway Boulevard, 6th Street, I-10, and Stone Avenue. Separating the two neighborhoods are the Southern Pacific railroad tracks.

John Spring

This neighborhood, sometimes called Dunbar/Spring after the school, consists of approximately 75 acres between Speedway Boulevard and 6th Street and between Main and Stone Avenues. It was built between 1896 and 1930 and has an intimate feeling because of the narrow streets, small lots, and placement of many of the houses at the front property line. There are three visually distinct areas: the original settlement south of West University Boulevard (now 3rd Street), the bungalow settlement north of West University, and, the heart of the neighborhood, the church and school block bounded by W. 2nd Street and University Boulevard and by N. Main and 11th Avenues. In the latter stand the Mission-style **Holy Family Church** (1913), **School Plaza** (1918), **Dunbar Elementary** (1917 by Jaastad, now closed), and **John Spring Junior High School** (1949 by Jaastad & Knipe, now closed). Paul Dunbar Elementary School was Tucson's only school for Americans of African descent. This block now features a community garden, and there is a master plan by Poster Frost Associates to renovate the elementary school as the Dunbar Museum and Cultural Center. In addition, the neighborhood also includes several grocery stores, other churches, and a splendid variety of houses.

Barrio Anita

This even smaller neighborhood, between the railroad tracks, I-10, Speedway Boulevard, and St. Mary's Road, features very narrow streets and small blocks and includes many Sonoran and Transformed Sonoran houses, Davis School, and Oury Park.

West University [NRHP]

The West University Historic District is fairly close in density and scale
to the original pattern of growth of a middle- to upper-class neighborhood dated from 1890 until about 1930. Before development by
American immigrants, this area was relatively flat with arroyos and
desert vegetation, and the number of wells, windmills, and storage tanks
indicated a water table much higher than it is today. The comfortable
scale of the neighborhood comes in part from its small blocks and
alleys. The majority of the original buildings were single-story detached
houses, often with a carriage house on the alley. The few multi-story
buildings were residential rentals, schools, and churches. The neighborhood originally provided living accommodations for students and
faculty, winter visitors, and tuberculosis patients in lodging houses,
hotels, and apartments. With the growing number of students, many
new multi-story structures were built, and most of the carriage houses,
servants quarters, and rentals for sanatoria were converted for student
use.

An incredibly wide range of sizes, materials, and styles is present,
although about 50 percent of the buildings are some variation of the
Bungalow style. The earliest styles include Transformed Sonoran and
Victorian, with later revival styles such as Spanish, Mission, Gothic, and
Neoclassical. Adding to the diversity are Prairie, Sullivanesque, and Art
Deco. With the advent of architecture as a profession, several of the
houses and all of the schools and churches were designed by architects.
Materials range from local adobe, "A" Mountain stone, brick, and stucco
to imported wood and metal roofing. The large number of brick

buildings is the result of the 1905 city fire ordinance prohibiting the use of wood as a structural material.

Among the architects and contractors represented are Jaastad, with over fifty residences in the district; Holmes & Holmes, also providing a large number of designs; Henry C. Trost; Roy O. Place; Starkweather & Bray; Ely Blount; and the John Murphey Construction Company.

Between 5th Street and University Boulevard is the **6th Avenue Streetscape,** characteristic of the variety of residential styles popular between 1900 and 1920: one- and two-story detached houses, duplexes, bungalows of all sorts, and apartments in Victorian, Queen Anne, Mission, and Spanish Revival.

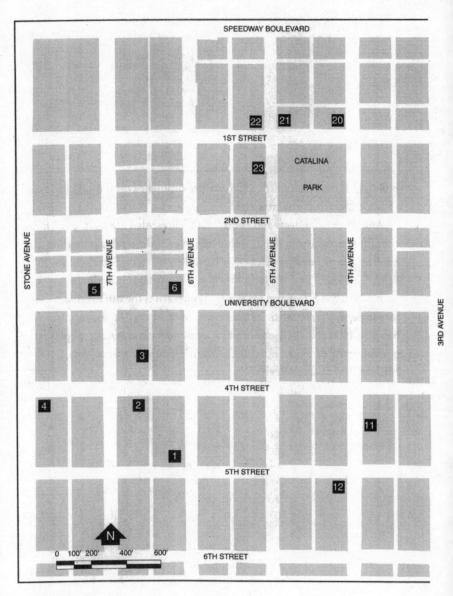

West University

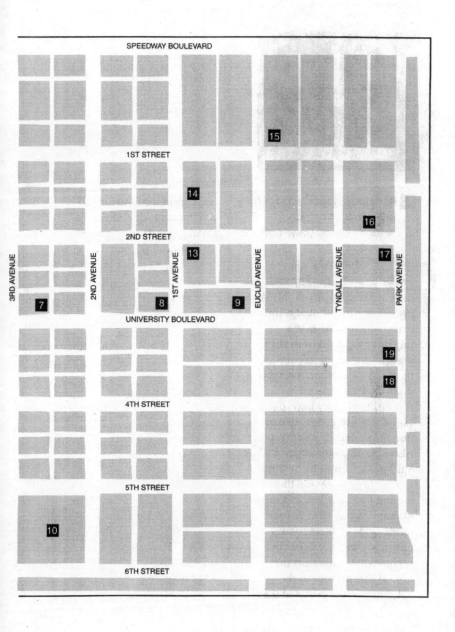

Ronstadt House.

1 **Ronstadt House,** 607 N. 6th Avenue, 1904; Trost & Rust; renovation 1977 by David Goff

Built on a double lot for Frederico and Lupe Ronstadt, the most striking feature of this large two-story stucco house is the entry, which consists of a protruding flat slab roof sheltering a second-story balcony above the porch. The whole assembly is supported and framed by columns with leafy lotus flower capitals, which appear to melt into the underside of the roof. Also of note on the exterior is the Sullivanesque ornament at the face of the balcony. On the ground floor, the house is made of nine-squares (that is, three rooms wide by three rooms deep), whereas the upper floor becomes a cruciform as the central area extends to the balconies. In the center of the house is a spacious two-story hallway and stairs. The Ronstadt family sold the house in 1922, and it was much abused as a rental property until the 1977 renovation.

2 **Office Building,** 140 E. 4th Street, 1994; Bill Mueller

Built for Wheat-Gallaher Associates, landscape architects and planners, this structure is a good example of an infill in a historic neighborhood. It is residential in scale, forms, materials, construction methods, and details, which echo the existing context. The two-story brick structure has gabled roofs, a vertical expression in the windows and doors, and Craftsman detailing. There is also a small parking area in the back, and the plant material is colorful and drought tolerant.

3 **Carriage Houses** on Ferro Alley between 4th Street and University Boulevard, before 1901

Several brick carriage houses line both sides of the alley. Though converted to rental units, they are a reminder of a way of life in earlier years of the neighborhood.

4 **Gas Station,** 648 N. Stone Avenue, 1936; Cecil Moore

One of a small number of Art Deco buildings in Tucson, this one in white stucco features a conical roof reminiscent of the swirl of an ice cream and a canopy with a curved fascia at the end.

Between Stone and Park Avenues is the **University Boulevard Streetscape,** which, like the 6th Avenue Streetscape, is characteristic of the variety of residential styles popular between 1900 and 1920.

5 Residence **(Law Offices),** 35 E. University Boulevard, c. 1905

Graceful proportions are evident in the south-facing porch, made of five semicircular arches with decorative medallions marking the spandrels. The exterior finish material is stucco. Transformation from residence to offices was easily made owing to the simplicity of the floor plan.

6 **Bayless House,** 145 E. University Boulevard, 1905; Trost & Rust

This is an unusual design in that the entry to the symmetrical house is perpendicular to the dominant gabled roof, causing the two curvilinear Mission-style pediments to form a bracket or bookends on the sides of the house. A full basement constructed of malpais stone and brick contains five rooms, which were used as summer living quarters for the family before air conditioning. The tile roof has two unique dormers that curve slightly upward.

Residence at 521 E.
University Boulevard.

7 Residence, 521 E. University
Boulevard, c. 1900; addition 1936
by Henry Jaastad

The zigzag Art Deco facade barely
turns the corner to reveal the
original bungalow lurking behind.

8 Goodrich House, 645 E.
University Boulevard, 1908; Henry
Trost

In its vertical proportions, light
stucco and dark wood trim,
corner piers, and deep overhangs
on a steeply pitched roof, this
house has a strong resemblance
to the 1904 Dana House by Frank
Lloyd Wright and seems somewhat out of place here. It does,
however, reflect the long-
standing trend, especially at this
time, for Tucsonans to import
styles from eastern and
midwestern sources.

9 Residence, 721 E. University
Boulevard, c. 1905; Henry Trost

A gem of a house. This simple
rectangular house is topped by a
very low pitched pyramidal roof
with deeply projecting eaves. The
south-facing porch is defined by
a low wall with six square but
tapered supports with
Sullivanesque ornament. On a
winter afternoon, the brilliantly
decorated columns in white stand
out sharply against the deep
shade of the porch.

10 Tucson High School
(Roskruge Bilingual Middle School), 501 E. 6th Street, 1908; David Holmes; addition 1919 by Henry Jaastad; addition 1931 by Roy Place

Built as the first high school for Tucson, this two-story structure was originally Neoclassical in style with exterior walls of exposed brick. In two subsequent additions, the building grew to its current size. The present stylistic expression dates to 1931 when the building was covered with stucco and the modest buff-colored portal was added.

Also of note is the **Prairie-style house** at 629 7th Avenue.

Between 9th and 2nd Streets is the **4th Avenue Streetscape,** one of the most lively pedestrian stretches in Tucson. It is a combination of a comfortable scale and a variety of shops and restaurants, with the more recent amenities such as the restoration of the electric trolley, crosswalks, benches, shade trees, and artwork. The architectural character ranges from variations on a Mission theme (including the Salvation Army's sidewalk arcade) to the patios at Caruso's and the curvilinear Art Deco facade at 721 4th Avenue.

Grace Lutheran Church.

11 4th Avenue Shops, 616–620 N. 4th Avenue, 1928; Josias Joesler

In a romantic composition of Spanish Colonial Revival elements, this building varies in height and is topped by tiled gables and a parapet. The storefront features three large arches. It is also a good example of a type of commercial building that included a caretaker's residence over the shop.

12 Round Tower, 553–561 N. 4th Avenue, c. 1931

This is a great corner building in the Mission Revival style, as the windows provide a panoramic view.

13 Grace Lutheran Church, 830 N. 1st Avenue, 1949; Henry Jaastad

Because this church appears relatively modest on the exterior, it is an unexpected surprise to experience the spacious quality of the interior. The wooden beams supporting the high pointed vault echo the rhythm and soaring expression of a Gothic church.

14 **Postal History Foundation,**
920 N. 1st Avenue, 1997; Line &
Space/Les Wallach, FAIA

The reuse for this existing church
building was made possible
through renovation and the
addition of the library block on
the north part of the lot. By
creating a basement level in the
library, a shaded courtyard was
gained at ground level.

15 Santa Catalina Apartments
(Udall Center), 803–811 E. 1st
Street, c. 1910

Originally built as boardinghouses, these two freestanding
stuccoed brick structures have
gabled roofs supported by slender
wooden posts at the perimeter,
creating a continuous porch on
all four sides of each structure.
Segmental arches form the tops
of numerous exterior doors and
windows, typical of this early
residential type.

College Shop, demolished 2001.

16 Arizona Historical Society, 949 E. 2nd Street, 1954–1955; Josias Joesler

The Romanesque stone portal carved by Jules le Flein once graced the first San Agustín Cathedral (p. 77). The portal's semicircular entry arch is flanked by columns. Above this is a pediment supported by stone piers, but the bottom of the pediment is broken and occupied by the rose window. The portal was rescued from oblivion by George W. Chambers when the church was demolished in 1936. He carefully numbered each stone and stored them in rows next to his house at his own expense, until they were reset during the construction of this building. A photograph of the cathedral hangs directly inside the entrance.

17 College Shop, 845 N. Park Avenue, 1956; William Wilde, FAIA; demolished 2001

Perhaps one of the best examples of the type of European modernism practiced by the German architect Ludwig Mies van der Rohe, this building was a composition in stone, marble, terrazzo, glass, and steel. The sleek planar forms appeared to slide by one another, and the I-beam columns were revealed at the entry.

18 First United Methodist Church, 915 E. 4th Street, 1929; T. M. Sundt; sanctuary addition 1977 by Sakellar & Associates

The use of colorfully glazed tiles, wrought iron, and exposed wooden rafter ends is characteristic of the Spanish Colonial Revival, as is the traditional courtyard and bell tower. The height and complex design of the bell tower have made it a landmark. The 1977 addition is a good example of blending contemporary design with a historic building.

19 Campus Christian Center, 715 N. Park Avenue, 1969; Cain Nelson Wares & Cook/Swaim

The exterior of this two-story, concrete frame building is composed of a restrained palette of wood, glass, and stucco, with each expressing a distinct texture. Entry is to the south, along a walkway that runs between this building and First United Methodist Church and through a lush courtyard.

Catalina Park District

The Catalina Park District is centered around the public park created by land set aside in 1902, and the district includes the houses at its perimeter, some of which are listed below.

20 **Residence,** 341 E. 1st Street, c. 1915

House in Western Stick style with characteristic exposed rafters supporting deep overhangs on multiple gabled roofs. This house is a simpler version of the type made popular by the California architects Greene and Greene in their Gamble House. The massing and proportions of this house are good, but it currently suffers from inharmonious paint colors.

21 **Catalina Bed & Breakfast,** 309 E. 1st Street, 1927

This symmetrical Neoclassical Mediterranean Mansion is stuccoed, with porches on east and west shaded by cloth awnings. It is roofed in an unusual green clay tile found in only a handful of Tucson homes.

22 **Residence,** 1003 N. 5th Avenue, c. 1902

The buff-colored ashlar stone and the unique cast concrete columns at the porch are two of the elements of note in this Queen Anne–style house.

23 **Quaker Meeting House,**
931 N. 5th Avenue, c. 1910

This two-story brick Federalist-style house has porches on the east and south with white columns and Ionic capitals. The east porch also forms a balcony over the entrance. The privacy of the front yard is defined by a low wrought-iron fence and gate.

Also of note is the **First Christian Church,** 740 E. Speedway Boulevard, designed by Arthur Brown in 1948 using his characteristic vocabulary of inexpensive materials within the Modern aesthetic (mortar-washed brick, exposed concrete beams, and steel sash windows) and, as in all of his work, responding to the climatic conditions of the desert, in this case with the entry courtyard.

University of Arizona

The 1919 campus plan by John Beattie (Jack) Lyman has many similarities with the plan of the University of Virginia by Thomas Jefferson. Old Main (originally Mines and then University Hall), the first permanent structure, forms the head of an axial composition in which the center is a lawn area defined by the buildings on either side. Unlike Jefferson's plan, the Arizona design is two-sided. The buildings were built between 1885 and 1936, and the area is now known as the West Campus Historic District, with the newer mall to the east. Two other features in this district are Jeffersonian: the secondary rows of dormitories behind the main buildings, and the use of curving paths and streets in contrast with the axial, symmetrical, and classical nature of the buildings.

The entrance to the West Campus Historic District is framed by an opening in the lava stone wall, built in 1916, which encloses a rectangle bounded by Park Avenue and Old Main and by North and South Campus Drives. Within this area, the placement of several notable buildings and the historic landscaping create a sense of an earlier era not dominated by the automobile. In the landscape design, imported species—olives, pines, jacaranda, cypress, and bitter orange—irrigated by flood basins, are clear evidence of an immigrant desire to "transform the desert into an oasis." Plants are used architecturally to define vertical edges or horizontal canopies. For examples, see the 1895 Olive Street trees planted by Dr. Robert Forbes, the arcade of blossoming orange trees between Gila and Maricopa Halls, and the east courtyard wall in the Agriculture Building.

Public Works Administration (PWA) funding provided for much-

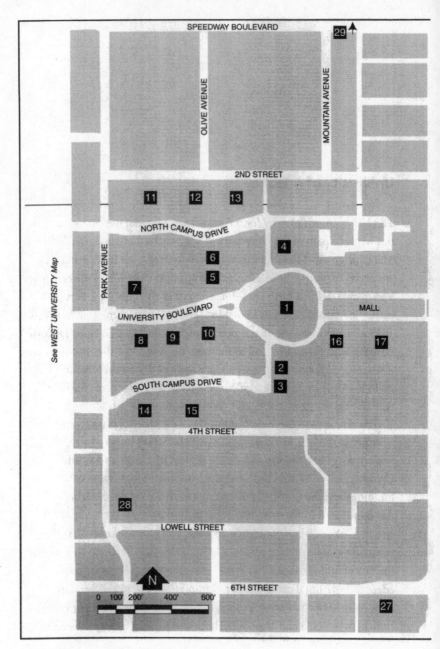

University of Arizona

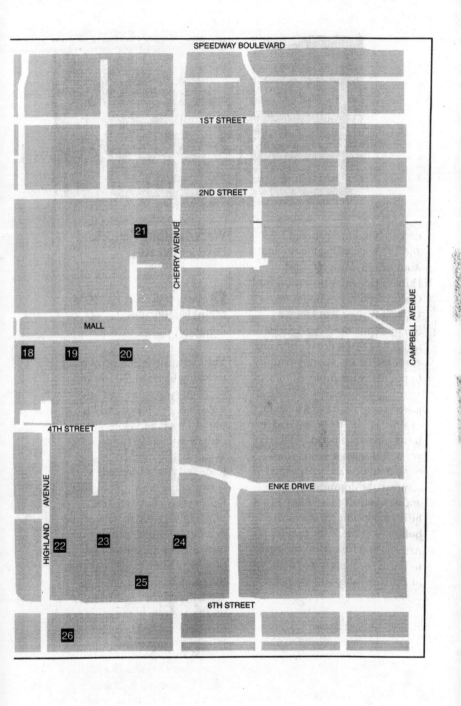

Old Main.

needed buildings between 1935 and 1938, including the original Auditorium, Museum, and Humanities, Administration, and Chemistry/Physics Buildings. University president Homer Schantz convinced the Arizona legislature that a decade of rising enrollments and the opportunity to put many unemployed to work were reason to accept the federal government's offer of $800,000, of which only 70 percent had to be repaid over a period of thirty years. Although several prominent architects are represented on campus, the dominating figure and aesthetic is that of Roy Place; he is responsible for over forty buildings at the University of Arizona and for establishing a uniform vocabulary and quality of craftsmanship still aspired to today.

West Campus Historic District [NRHP]

1 Mines, University Hall **(Old Main)** [NRHP], 1891; James Creighton

The University's first permanent structure blends a Queen Anne vocabulary of stone and brick walls, wooden posts, and high-pitched roofs and chimneys with climate-conscious features such as its partially sunken ground floor and shaded verandah surrounding the entire building. During the late 1960s, this building survived threats of demolition, which prompted a campaign to document and preserve campus buildings and the parklike environment; in 1985, the efforts resulted in the creation of one of the country's first National Register Historic District for university campuses, composed of thirty-five University of Arizona buildings.

Herring Hall.

2 Agriculture **(Forbes) Building,** 1915; Bristow & Lyman

The San Diego architects were selected in a competition based on their floor plan and facade drawings. The most popular style of the period for campus architecture, the Classical Revival, used eight Ionic columns for the portico, a low-hipped tile roof, and Classical ornament at doors and windows. The U-shaped plan, open to the east, provides one of the best courtyards on campus.

3 **Herring Hall,** 1903; David Holmes

In the tradition of turn-of-the-century campus architecture, this hall is a Classical Revival building with a portico that consumes the entire west front. While monumental in form, it is humble in both size (40 feet by 80 feet) and the fact that it and its Roman Doric columns sit on the ground instead of being raised on a podium. The columns are actually made of concrete and set on a plain stone base. Although the interior has been poorly remodeled, it is scheduled for renovation.

4 Mines and **Engineering,** 1917–1918; J. B. Lyman

Lyman won the commission for this building through a design competition and was then contracted to act as agent to hire day labor furnished by the University, as well as to purchase materials. Roy Place was brought to Tucson to do the design revisions and construction administration. The three-story structure is built of reinforced concrete with steel supports inside the eight Doric terra cotta columns. The floor plan is a square doughnut, with the cornice line wrapping around the entire building and the roof dramatically deemphasized.

5 Science Hall **(Communications) Building,** 1909; Holmes & Holmes/David Holmes, designer

Built as the first Science Hall, this structure has several similarities with the Douglass Building (p. 156) facing it across the West Mall, most likely because Holmes was involved in the final design of the Douglass Building. Both buildings are three stories, the lower two of which are exposed Flemish bond brick; the upper floor is cream-colored stucco with a brick diamond pattern. Both are symmetrical horizontal blocks using the regular rhythm of vertical windows with a suggested base and capital in a contrasting material or color. Both buildings have tiled hipped roofs, but the roof on this building has a much deeper overhang, the rafters are not expressed, and its "tile" is actually pressed tin in the shape of Spanish clay tile.

Arizona State Museum.

6 Humanities Building (Center for English as a Second Language: CESL), 1935; Roy Place

A two-story classroom building in the Italian Romanesque Revival style, the CESL Building employs many of the details that make the style appealing. In particular, the dark recessed entry is framed and punctuated by two white columns with ornate capitals, which become on the floor above a tripartite composition with arches and abstracted Corinthian columns. In addition, there is a vertical expression in the two-story-high arches that frame the windows. The arches are semicircular, and some voussoirs are white in contrast to the red brick. Brick corbeling in a continuous arch pattern accentuates the upper wall of the gable. A somewhat surprising feature is the "Pueblo Deco" style of the terra cotta spandrel panels below the second-story windows.

7 University Library (Arizona State Museum, North Building) [NRHP], 1923–1927; Lyman & Place

This symmetrical building, modeled after the Boston Public Library, is one of the buildings that established Roy Place as the campus's architect. The original design included a formal reading room on the second floor, relegating the books to a closed storage area accessible to librarians. While the public areas occupy the three-story brick-and-steel structure, the book stacks are housed in a five-story steel structure in the center of the building. The reading room, which seats 200, is one of the most elegant interior spaces in Tucson, dominated by two-story arched windows along the south wall, decorated ceiling beams, a polished concrete floor, and mahogany bookshelves lining the room. The exterior of the building mixes the Classical

Revival symmetry with an emerging vocabulary that became the signature of Place's University buildings, including the use of arches as a dominant facade feature, masterful brick detailing (including dogtooth), and glazed terra cotta ornament, such as the frieze of opened books on the south facade. There have been several subsequent additions.

8 Anthropology **(Arizona State Museum South),** 1935; Roy Place

The fact that the building is partially sunken is a direct result of the dual public and private functions and creates a grand stair to the main public space. The style of the entry facade is Italian Romanesque Revival, the elements of which include heavy masonry walls with semicircular arched openings, articulated voussoirs, columns, and capitals either of basket weave or Corinthian in design. The three center arches feature a row of turned, or dogtooth, bricks, which catch sunlight. An unusual feature, also seen in the CESL Building, is the decorative spandrel panel below the windows. At the time this building was designed, the understanding of the conservation and display of artifacts was very different than it is today. The basement was used for storage and processing of artifacts, while the main floor was altered and then abandoned for display because the light from the numerous windows was both uncontrollable and potentially harmful to the artifacts. (And it's a pity, because the singular space with its open balconies is delightful.)

9 Auditorium **(Centennial Hall)** [NRHP], 1936–1937; Roy Place, with M. M. Sundt, contractor; renovation 1985 by John L. Mascarella & Associates, with L. G. Lefler, Inc., contractor

This second auditorium, which originally held 2,800 seats, was renamed to celebrate the University's 100th anniversary. Although the decision to renovate the building in 1985 was indisputably correct, the original Italian Romanesque Revival facade was somewhat weakened by the enclosure of the open entry arcade. As the openings were filled in with glass to extend the lobby, the powerful impact of the deep shadows was lost. The original interior acoustical ceiling was designed by Roy Place in collaboration with music professor Rollin Pease, and was considered excellent. Interior renovations in 1985 addressed problems of accessibility and functional needs in exiting, stage, lighting, and restrooms and restored the grand interior to its original beauty.

10 Library and Museum
(Douglass Building), 1904;
Russell, Mauran & Garden

It is the unique design of the central facade that continues to delight its viewers. The tiny entry between two very closely spaced Doric columns appears to be sinking beneath the weight of the composition of the doors, window, and balcony above. Atop the second-story balcony projection is a simplified pediment with acroteria, behind which is a round window surrounded by dark brick on a light stucco background. The rest of the building is generally classical, symmetrical in form, with brick bearing walls in an expressed Flemish bond, repeating vertical windows, and a clay-tile hipped roof. The 1948 addition at the rear uses the same brick pattern (the header bricks are darker than the runners), but it has a parapet roof and asymmetrical massing.

Although mostly intact, the major changes to most of the historic residence halls described in the next five buildings have been in the enclosure and removal of the traditional sleeping porches or in renovations that have changed the quality of some of the interior spaces.

11 **Gila Hall,** 1937; Roy Place; P. S. Wombach, contractor

Built on the original site of the 1893 President's Residence, the U-shaped plan of this three-story brick dormitory creates a private courtyard on the north side. The white terra cotta base and framed door entry, with an ornamented balcony above, contrast with the red brick of the building. The horizontal is emphasized through the contrasting base, a patterned brick course above the second floor, and a strong overhang at the eave of the clay-tile roof. As in all of Roy Place's work, the brick coursing is inspired—patterned and varied, never dull. Gila Hall was the last campus building constructed with PWA funds.

12 **Maricopa Hall,** 1920;
Lescher & Kibbey and Lyman &
Place

In 1918 the Phoenix architects
Lescher & Kibbey hired Lyman &
Place to do the construction
administration on this hall. The
third floor was added by Lyman
& Place in 1921. It features a
prominent Classical Revival
portico with eight paired and
stylized "Egyptian" columns,
behind which the brick rectangle
of the building sits on a concrete
base scored to represent stone.
The generous arched openings at
the first floor once held French
doors.

13 **Yuma Hall,** 1937; Roy Place;
J. J. Garfield, contractor

Completed a few months before
Gila Hall, Yuma is identical in
size and floor plan but of a very
different exterior expression.
There is an interesting mix of
Italian Romanesque Revival
elements—round arches with
voussoirs alternating in white and
red, and a series of corbeled
arches at the cornice line—with
other elements such as the
Renaissance Palladian window
over the entrance. There is also a
hint of Art Deco in the gleaming
white tops of the projected entry
bay. Yuma Hall was built on the
site of a smaller dorm, dating
from 1907, by Henry Jaastad.

14 Cochise Hall, 1920–1921; Lyman & Place

The large scale and elaborate ornament of the two-story Classical Revival raised porch will typically make one pause to look at the eight finely crafted Corinthian columns.

15 Arizona Hall (South Hall), 1913; David Holmes

The best feature of this residence hall is its south-facing, U-shaped courtyard, which warms dorm rooms in the winter but is shaded by the graceful jacaranda trees in the summer. South Hall could also be seen as a simpler alternative to the strict adherence to Classical Revival forms and ornament of other campus buildings from this period.

East Mall

The mall east of Old Main, as designed by Roy Place in 1931, had a formal central urban space defined by the buildings placed along the outer edges of the separated parallel drives. Between the drives was an enormous lawn. Once a grand public social space, this will soon change with the creation of a huge rectangular courtyard cut into the ground to provide light and air for the Integrated Learning Center, which is being built under the mall.

16 Administration Building (Robert L. **Nugent Building),** 1937; Roy Place

The original building was a simple two-story brick rectangle with a pitched roof, the facade facing the mall at the gable end. The Italian Romanesque Revival features include the second-story arch above the entry, composed of an inner and outer arch with alternating colored voussoirs on the inner arch. Above this, a series of corbeled arches accentuate the raked roofline. The ground-floor entry and balcony above, in contrasting white terra cotta, are simpler but very similar to those at Gila Hall, built in the same year. This small recessed entry has two benches in the deepest, coolest shade. The brick pattern below the second-story windows visually extends the horizontal line of the balcony.

17 Chemistry-Physics **(Chemistry) Building,** 1936; Roy Place; M. M. Sundt, contractor; additions 1948 and 1962

Built one year after the Humanities Building, the multiple Romanesque Revival characteristics here are similar: columns with Corinthian capitals, round arches with contrasting white and red brick voussoirs, and the arched brick corbeling along the gable ends. But here, an extremely vertical expression is created by a series of deeply recessed arches on the facade, and the terra cotta tile panels feature a diamond pattern.

18 Chemistry and Biological Sciences, 1992; Anderson DeBartolo Pan/Jack DeBartolo & Jim Richard, designers

"Chem-Bio" and Life Sciences South (p. 167) can be understood as characteristic of the early 1990s in that they are expressions of the juncture between two generations, between modernism and a postmodern regionalism— the conflict between the universal and the specific. Typical of modernism, both building entries are removed and obscure. Chemistry and Biological Sciences even exhibits Le Corbusier's *pilotis* and an insular building mass, but these build- ings also reflect a sense of place in their material palette (brick and concrete), in the rhythmic fenestration pattern of individual windows in a solid wall, and in the massing of Life Sciences South, which acts as a welcoming entrance to the science mall. Both buildings provide shade; the vertical fins in Life Sciences shade the north windows from early and late sun angles, and the somewhat frightening elevated four-story mass of Chemistry and Biological Sciences shades the square of ground below.

Main Library.

19 Men's **(Bear Down) Gymna-sium** [NRHP], 1926; Lyman & Place/Roy Place, architect; Clinton Campbell, builder

19 Men's **(Bear Down) Gymna-sium** [NRHP], 1926; Lyman & Place/Roy Place, architect; Clinton Campbell, builder

Once the first men's gymnasium was outgrown, this structure was built to accommodate a much larger student population; it is used today for informal basket-ball games. Although the classi-cally symmetrical brick exterior with its large barrel vault suggests a brick structure, there is actually an internal steel structural system, including the joists supporting the gym floor, and internally exposed steel bow trusses for the roof. The semicir-cular arched entry is framed with a glazed terra cotta tile in a very delicate bas-relief pattern.

20 **Main Library,** 1976–1977; Friedman & Jobusch/John Whitmire, designer

This building contrasts with the brick vocabulary of its context through the use of a tan and textured, prefabricated concrete wall panel system set in a concrete waffle slab floor structure. Red brick was incorpo-rated as a paving material in the inviting and well-proportioned entry plaza, which directs the visitor through to the ground-floor lobby. The interior is dominated by an open-stacks system of books, in contrast to the inaccessible stacks of this building's predecessor (p. 153), and provides comfortable reading spaces adjacent to the building's windows, whose orientation and shading devices are well designed for the climate.

21 Steward Observatory, 1921–1923; Lyman & Place

Built on the highest point of the University's flat mesa to accommodate the 36-inch reflecting telescope, the white terra cotta tile exterior reflects heat and keeps the instruments inside cool. A Classical Revival expression can be seen in the use of implied pilasters and an entablature on this small octagonal building. The dome itself was designed by Godfrey Sykes.

22 La Paz Dormitory, 1995; Moule and Polyzoides, architects; *inaccessible/published*

This building is the first of the larger "Highland District" master plan of multi-use buildings incorporating the principles of New Urbanism on the campus. It marks a significant and commendable change in the understanding of campus dormitories as urban elements rather than "manor estates." The building provides greater density by building out to the boundary of the site, including a loggia covering the public sidewalk, but its attempts to mitigate climate through shading devices and courtyards are less successful as workable examples of solar design. The building also suffers from a confusing floor plan that leads to newcomer disorientation.

23 Arizona Stadium

This unique complex of diverse functions and facilities is best understood in a chronological description of elements and their subsequent additions: **West Stadium,** 1929; Roy Place; Orndorff Construction, contractor. Prior to completion, the original stadium structure, which accommodated 7,000 seats, was quickly renamed a "building," for which more money was appropriated to enclose 18,000 square feet underneath the bleachers. This space provided offices for the Arizona Pioneers Historical Society, Arizona State Museum, Tree-Ring Laboratory, and the Drama Department's first theater. The Mission Revival west facade of poured-in-place concrete, with an elaborate terra cotta portal around the central entrance, is still visible underneath the 1965 addition of 10,000 seats by Roy Place's son Lew Place, which itself is highlighted by graceful pinpoint connections in the structural piers. **Scholarship Suites,** 1989; Anderson DeBartolo Pan. Located above the West Stadium, this structure contains four levels of climate-controlled seating and is supported by concrete beams cantilevered off of four enormous concrete columns that double as elevator shafts. The glass-faced east facade gracefully arcs with the curve of the stadium form.

24 **East Stadium,** 1938; Clinton Campbell, contractor

25 **South Stadium,** 1949; Place & Place

A smaller, and more utilitarian, structure seating 3,600 was built on the opposite side of the field for the opponent's fans. The seating was expanded by 4,000 in 1947, and a men's dormitory (now called Sierra Hall) was constructed underneath that mimics, but poorly integrates, the stylistic features of the West Stadium facade. **East Stadium Addition,** 1976; Finical and Dombrowski. This two-tiered superstructure of poured-in-place concrete is an extension of the now-dwarfed 1938 stadium. The fluid and sculptural quality of this structure belies its size and is a focal point for the Cherry Avenue entrance to campus from Speedway Boulevard. In 1985, a facility for Optical Science's Mirror Casting Laboratory was skillfully integrated into the east facade of the stadium structure by Seaver/Franks Architects.

The dual function of stadium seating and men's dormitory housing was extended to create Pinal and Navaho Halls on the south side of the stadium. This 6,000-seat addition connects the two previous buildings and blends the stylistic characteristics of the West Stadium with restrained Art Deco motifs formed in the poured-in-place concrete walls. This facade is accented by the word "Arizona" inscribed at the top of the corner towers, making a distinctive presence on 6th Street.

26 **Student Recreation Center,** 1400 E. 6th Street, 1991; Parkin Architects, design architects, and IEF Group, architect of record

From the exterior, the expression of this building is postmodern; it displays a volumetric form in pastel-colored stucco that obscures the internal concrete and steel structure, and the exterior of the barrel vaulted roof is sheathed in a standing-seam metal. It sits firmly on the ground and incorporates a bus stop into the design on 6th Street. Inside, there are plenty of high ceilings and glass walls at the main hallway or concourse, which visually connects spaces vertically as well as horizontally and makes the interior appear much larger than it is. There are enough corners and alcoves to find private areas within a highly public building.

27 **Mansfeld Middle School,** 1300 E. 6th Street, 1929–1930; Roy Place; J. J. Garfield, contractor; addition 1995 by IEF Group

The distinctive pink color and tower have come to symbolize this Spanish Colonial Revival school. Several additions, including a cafeteria and a library, were built to accommodate the growing school's seventeen original classrooms and administrative areas. The east wing addition in 1995 also renovated the original building and created the south-facing courtyard.

Aerospace and Mechanical Engineering.

28 Life Sciences South, 1990; Anderson DeBartolo Pan/Jack DeBartolo & Jim Richard, designers

The buildings for Life Sciences South and Chemisty and Biological Sciences (p. 161) were designed not only by the same architectural firm but with the same design team, and within a year of one another. They make a good comparative study.

29 Aerospace and Mechanical Engineering, 1996; Hoover Berg Desmond, design architects, and John R. Kulseth Associates, Ltd., associate architect

Perhaps the most intriguing aspect of this building is the suggestion of alternative points of view regarding the placement of the building mass along Speedway Boulevard in the denser areas of Tucson. The rooms along Speedway create a wall that clearly defines an urban edge and creates a buffer for the inner courtyard and the other half of the building. There is something wrong with our zoning codes if it prevents the building from actually sitting at the sidewalk and providing a south shade canopy for numerous pedestrians. The two-and-a-half-story structure is a concrete frame with concrete block and brick in a simple running bond at the exterior walls and accented

with perforated metal awnings,
metal downspouts, and guard
railings of horizontal cables.
There are several formal allusions
to airplanes: the huge curved roof
at the back, reminiscent of a
hangar; the tower; and the angled
canopy at the entry, which is
really too heavy to suggest a wing.
The auditorium is spacious and
appropriately tectonic in expression.

West Side

West Side describes the area west of the Santa Cruz River and is made up of the oldest inhabited area in Tucson; many small historic neighborhoods, including Rio Nuevo South and Menlo Park; and some new development to the southwest.

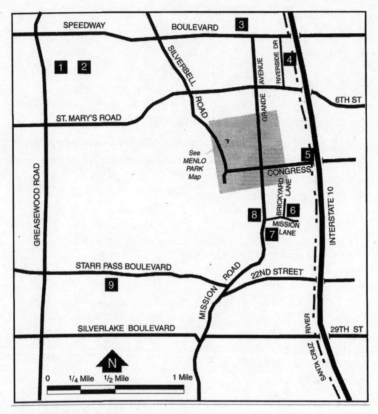

West Side

Pima Community College, West Campus.

1 Pima Community College, West Campus, 2202 W. Anklam Road, 1973; Caudill Rowlett Scott of Houston, including Doug Macneil, with the local firms William Wilde & Associates and Friedman & Jobusch; *published*

According to Bernie Friedman, this project was so large that almost every architect in town worked on it. The large complex of buildings sits respectfully on the contours and features of the land, provides shelter, openness, and shade, yet uses bold reinforced cast-in-place concrete forms in a symmetrical layout to create a strong civic presence. The use of rough concrete and powerful forms is an example of Brutalism. The building's sections are not as logical as the floor plan suggests, making it confusing to many students, but it does provide several excellent multi-level courtyards.

2 Pima Community College, West Campus Center for the Arts, 2202 W. Anklam Road, 1990–1991; John R. Kulseth Associates, Ltd./Mike Harris and Chris Carson, designers

The concrete walls of the three main buildings—Recital Hall, Art Gallery, and Proscenium Theater—open onto the narrow pedestrian street that serves as an intimate and pleasing outdoor lobby with entry at one end and a tiny open theater on the other. Attending a performance at the Proscenium Theater is a must as the old shoebox form works very well here, especially the side "boxes" and balcony seats and the bleacher seating at the back. The curtain of dark velvet uses fiberoptic lights to represent constellations.

Project Potty.

3 El Rio Neighborhood
Center, 1390 W. Speedway
Boulevard, 1973; Robert Swaim;
Antonio Pazos, muralist; addition
and renovation 1996 by Albanese
Brooks Architects, Paty Marquez,
project architect

Individual stuccoed masonry
buildings form a central courtyard, with walkways covered by
very large wooden trusses. The
plan for future expansion was
realized in 1996, which included
classrooms, offices, a branch
library, and outdoor spaces
including a theater.

4 Project Potty, Santa Cruz
River Park, 1993–1996; Line &
Space/Les Wallach, FAIA; *published*

For Wallach, the challenge, and
the fun, of this project was the
development of a prototypical
public restroom that could be
seen as a sculptural object. In
reinvestigating the functional
needs of this building type, the
solution seems self-evident. It is
essentially a durable kit-of-parts
that does not rely on electricity
for ventilation, and shade trees
are grown with the graywater
from the outdoor sink. The
simple structure is concrete block
with brightly colored tile; stucco;
and painted, galvanized, corrugated roofs. Wind-driven
turbines provide ventilation, and
night lighting is via internal
lamps set inside the glass block.
These "potties" are being located
in the linear park system currently under development by the
Pima County Transportation
Department along the Santa Cruz

and Rillito Rivers and along the Tanque Verde, Pantano, and Cañada del Oro Washes.

5 Garden of Gethsemane

This intriguing outdoor garden was built to display Felix Lucero's sculptures of the Last Supper and other religious subjects. There is a strongly surreal juxtaposition of the multi-level courtyard overlooking the Santa Cruz riverbed, as one is surrounded by images of the life and times of Christ, a high-voltage tower, and the daytime abodes of the homeless.

Rio Nuevo South

"Rio Nuevo South" is simply a new name for one of the oldest areas of settlement in the Tucson Basin; it includes the next three entries.

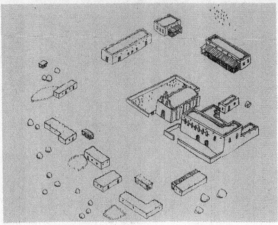

Convento site, reconstructed view.

---

6 Site of San Cosmé del Tucson (San Agustín del Tucson; **"Convento"**), Mission Lane and Brickyard Lane, 1770–1818; demolished 1950s

This is the site of the *pueblito*, or small community, that grew up around the Spanish *visita;* it is known by many names, including San Cosmé, the name given by Father Kino in 1699; San Jose, 1762; and finally San Agustín, 1774. The fact that construction on the *visita*, which was founded by Father Kino in 1699, did not actually begin until 1770 is evidence of the risky nature of building in a location at the farthest edge of the Spanish frontier. Kino established the church at the site of an existing Pima settlement consisting of about 300 people. Their home, located between Sentinel Peak and the Santa Cruz River, had a year-round water supply and well-established agricultural fields. In 1770, under the direc-

tion of the Franciscan Father Francisco Garces, the Pimas began to build a granary, an adobe structure with a stone foundation. Construction of the brick church took place between 1772 and 1773. Like San Xavier, it faced south, was plastered inside and out, and was topped by a dome. The interior featured walls covered with frescoes and painted statues of the saints. Unlike San Xavier, this church was much smaller, at only 35 feet long by 20 feet wide. Built between 1797 and 1810, the enormous two-story adobe administration building, later named the "Convento," was 90 feet long and 40 feet wide (see photograph, p. 11). It housed the priests and some of the functions of the industrial school, and many of its second-story arches were still intact when Americans arrived in the late 1800s. The entire compound, including kitchens, tannery, carpenter shop, smithy, and areas for soap and tallow production, spinning, and weaving, was surrounded by an adobe wall. Rapid deterioration of the site and the Convento building resulted from a variety of factors, including the expulsion of the Franciscans, lack of funding from Mexico, and the growth of the Presidio. Further destruction followed with the earthquake of 1887 and the use of the Convento as a stockyard by Sam Hughes. The final, and perhaps most harmful, blow came with the use of the land south of Mission Lane as a landfill in the 1950s, completely poisoning what remained of the *pueblito.*

7 Site of the Mission Orchard and Gardens, southeast corner of Mission Road and Mission Lane

The orchard and gardens were located southwest of the main buildings of the Convento and at one time were protected by an adobe wall. In the triangular area south of Mission Lane, only this site and a thin strip of land along the southern edge of the lane were not covered by landfill.

8 Site of Solomon Warner House and Mill [NRHP], Mission Road, 1875; mill demolished 1929

Warner, trained as a stonemason, built his house and flour mill with foundations of "A" Mountain stone and the walls and roofs of adobe and timbers. By 1883, the mill's dam held 300 acres of water and was stocked with fish, which attracted birds and visitors. In 1929, Stephen Ochoa took the building apart as it was a hazardous play area for children.

9 Cholla High School, 2001 W. Starr Pass Boulevard, 1966; Nicholas Sakellar, FAIA; addition 1979 by Nicholas Sakellar, FAIA, and Dino Sakellar

This school is a Modern building reminiscent of Le Corbusier in its use of white stucco walls and ribbon windows. These windows do not have intermediate mullions between sheets of glass or at the corners, and they angle outward from bottom to top. The campus buildings enclose a courtyard with an outdoor theater. Green glazed brick is used at the stair towers, and columns at the ground level support overhanging upper levels and provide shaded areas below. Classroom buildings are interlocking hexagons once open for team teaching but now enclosed.

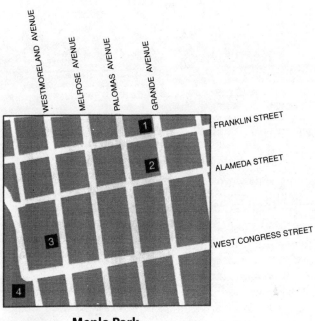

Menlo Park

N

600'

Menlo Park [NRHP]

Developed by Henry E. Schwalen and Manuel King, and named after a community Schwalen had read about in California, Menlo Park was one of the earliest planned communities in Tucson; it lies between "A" Mountain and the Santa Cruz River and between St. Mary's Road and Congress Street. When Schwalen moved his family to Tucson from Wisconsin in 1904 as a remedy for his tuberculosis, he bought a 14-acre ranch with an adobe house. Schwalen and King subdivided the land, laid out the streets and lots, put in water mains, provided graveled streets (some with curbs and sidewalks), and planted native ash trees. Schwalen even donated the land for the elementary school. Gas, light, and telephone service were provided by Tucson Gas and Light and Mountain States. But it was Schwalen's desire for "a residence park for fine people"

that drove the creation of deed restrictions on property value, site setbacks, and race, which alienated many potential buyers. "Negroes" and Mexican Americans were not allowed to buy property in Menlo Park, but Mexican Americans could buy land or homes in South Menlo Park.

The unique character of this residential neighborhood, built between 1905 and 1942, was shaped by a geography of limited area, but one that also provided an unusual building material in the volcanic lava stone quarried from "A" Mountain. Of the six surviving lava-stone houses, three are in this neighborhood. The stone quarry closed in the 1930s under pressure from the city of Tucson, and a citizens committee formed to save the mountain. There are also other examples of many of the popular styles of the period: bungalows, which make up about half of the historic buildings; Spanish Colonial

Bray House.

Revival; Ranch; and the singular Prairie-style Bray House. Homeowners and residents of sanatoria and apartments enjoyed picnicking along the Santa Cruz, attracted by the clean water and cool cottonwoods. At the north edge of the neighborhood, the DeVry Brick Company made bricks by hand, and many of the homes in Menlo Park and the buildings at the University of Arizona used bricks purchased from DeVry.

1 Bray (Bray-Valenzuela) **House** [NRHP], 203 N. Grande Avenue, 1917; William Bray, architect

When it was built, this Prairie-style house was the most elaborate residence on the most prominent street in the neighborhood. Bray was originally from England and worked in the office of Roy Place before moving from Tucson to California. The house that he built for his family is in the style made popular by Frank Lloyd Wright in Chicago and, in particular, is reminiscent of Wright's Unity Temple. The double-width walls of imported buff-colored bricks form cubic volumes, the highest at the living room. Around these volumes runs a strong horizontal projecting band of wood at the roofline below the top of the parapet. Pieces of a plaster frieze, which capped the parapet and may have been painted gold, slowly fell off, and today there is nothing left of the frieze. The ornamental stonework in the exterior brackets, interior fireplace caryatids, and urns was designed by Bray and manufactured in Tucson. The addition in the back was built in 1988.

2 Dodson-Esquivel House

[NRHP], 1004 W. Alameda Street, c. 1921; James Dodson, builder

This Spanish Colonial Revival house features the typical asymmetrical facade, with smooth stuccoed walls and Moorish ornament including intertwined geometric forms and twisted concrete columns on the cast concrete portal framing the main window into the living room. But really stunning are the seven very large elliptical urns, which look like spinning tops, that are used to accentuate the corners and high point of the portal. Larger urns mark the entrance gate and red pressed-metal roofing looks like Spanish tile.

Boudreaux-Robinson House.

3 Boudreaux-Robinson House (Copper Bell Bed & Breakfast), 25 N. Westmoreland Avenue [NRHP], c. 1910; Leon Boudreaux, owner-builder, and Mr. Kurtz, stonemason; addition 1927 by Manuel Miranda, stonemason (mason of the University of Arizona gateway)

Located on what was originally Santa Cruz Avenue, the first floor of this three-story stone house was built sometime before 1910 and was based on a design by Henry O. Jaastad. In 1927, the house was doubled in size by the addition of a second story using a different type and size of stone. While the original deep purple malpais came from the "A" Mountain quarry, some of the newer stone is reddish in color and is used for a horizontal band that marks the transition to the second floor. The masonry features irregular stones and joint lines, and the hipped roof is covered with Spanish tile. A bold arched entryway wraps around to the south; originally it was a porte cochere, but it is now a patio. Try to ignore the addition at the back.

4 House, 1408 W. Congress Street, c. 1910

Another good example of a house made with "A" Mountain stone.

Also of note is the 1903 **Desert Laboratory,** on Tumamoc Hill (1675 W. Anklam Road), designed by David Holmes. The thick walls of volcanic stone, deep overhangs, and an efficient roof ventilation system are design strategies used in a manner that is an appropriate response to the desert.

Midtown

Midtown subdivisions developed as a natural extension of growth north, east, and south of Tucson's early city limits and represent a spectrum of socioeconomic neighborhoods. In some cases, such as Sam Hughes [NRHP], El Encanto Estates [NRHP], and Colonia Solana [NRHP], affluent neighborhoods were ensured through the enforcement of deed restrictions, whereas in other neighborhoods the character is working class, as in Barrio San Antonio, which was home to many of the early railroad workers.

ROGER   ROAD

1

RIVER   ROAD

0   1/4 Mile   1/2 Mile   1 Mile

PRINCE   ROAD

FT. LOWELL   ROAD

2

CHERRY AVE

AVENUE

BOULEVARD

COUNTRY   CLUB   ROAD

3

BLVD

WAY

GLENN   STREET

CAMPBELL

TUCSON

GRANT   ROAD

ALVERNON

4

WAVERLY   ST

8

7

ELM   STREET

VINE   AVENUE

5

WARREN   AVENUE

6

SPEEDWAY   BOULEVARD

10   LINDEN   ST

BLVD

DODGE

PIMA

9

ST

PALO VERDE

11

See
SAM HUGHES
Map

5TH   STREET

12

6TH   STREET

CALLE   PORTAL

CALLE
BELLEZA

16

See
BARRIO SAN ANTONIO
Map

BROADWAY   BOULEVARD

13

15

14

17

RANDOLPH   WAY

18

Midtown

Tucson General Hospital.

1 **Tucson General Hospital,**
3838 N. Campbell Avenue, 1963–
1970; Arthur Brown, FAIA

Although the present generation
has little familiarity with the
work of Tucson's pioneer of solar
design, this building is a great
introduction. In addition to
Brown's trademark mortar-
washed brick facades, the south-
facing wall features a delightful
and inventive golden aluminum
shading device.

2 **Tucson Creative Dance
Center/Mettler Studios,** 3131 N.
Cherry Avenue, 1963; John H.
Howe

The architect of this building was
an apprentice to, and worked
with, Frank Lloyd Wright at
Taliesin West until Wright's
death. His design is true to his
master with organic forms that
appear to rise out of the ground.
The original copper roof over the
brick walls has now oxidized to a
green color and forms a low
profile, which adds to the organic
quality of the building on the
land. The intimate scale of the
interior also mimics Wright and
is applied, in particular, to the
circular performance space with
audience seating on the perimeter.

Tucson Interior Design Center.

CNWC Architectural Office.

3 Tucson Interior Design Center, 3656 E. Fort Lowell Road, 1980; Line & Space/Les Wallach, FAIA

This excellent example of a small retail shopping center began with the redefinition of a run-down 25,000-square-foot building by the addition of 50,000 square feet of new retail and storage space. Located on a corner site, access and parking incorporate shade trees, planters, and fountains. The interior has multiple floor and ceiling levels, which create discrete areas within one large building so that the effect is one of variety and visual connection but also physical separation. In addition, there are several interesting fountains inside, the best one at the atrium area due west from the entrance: A vertical tiled water channel steps forward as it descends so that the water slides quietly down the face and disappears.

4 CNWC Architectural Office (Office Building), 2552 N. Alvernon Way, 1974; Cain Nelson Wares & Cook/John Morrison, designer

Originally built as the office for the architectural firm of Cain Nelson Wares & Cook, the interior was designed without columns, made possible by long-span steel trusses that are expressed in the interior and exterior in a simple and straightforward manner. This building is an early example of energy-conscious design with earth-bermed walls for thermal control, deeply recessed glazing on the south, and east and west walls without windows for passive solar design.

Arizona Health Sciences Library, south elevation.

Arizona Health Sciences Library, brickwork detail on south elevation.

5 **Arizona Health Sciences Library,** University Medical Center, end of Warren Avenue at Mabel Street, north of Speedway Boulevard, 1992; NBBJ/James A. Gresham, FAIA

Like many medical facilities that have grown beyond the boundaries of their initial campus, University Medical Center (UMC) has suffered from a lack of clarity in master planning and implementation. The bold location and striking image of this building, right in the middle of Warren Avenue, are the result of some surprising and perhaps contradictory urban design factors. The singular importance of the library to UMC required a prominent structure and placement, yet the master plan designated the second level, removed from the ground, as the concourse. The site for the library was unspecified, and the location for the future research building was to the west of the existing

building. Deciding that there wasn't a strong reason to keep Warren Avenue open, Gresham set the four-story brick structure squarely in the street, connected to the main building at the ground and second level. The civic scale and expression of an arcade at the ground floor are both powerful and confusing as there is no public access from the arcade. Of the three disparate facades, the north and south provide incredible views and a good amount of natural light. The south facade is formally the most successful in the brick curtain wall's perfect mimicry of the mullion and shadow pattern of the central window. If you arrive by car, park in the **Visitor's Parking Structure,** also designed by Gresham, which is south of the main entry on Campbell Avenue. It is easy to find with its curvilinear wall of patterned brick. A light well the length of the west side brings light and air into the lower levels. The design

Arizona Inn.

of the top level includes planters and trellis structures to provide shade. To visit the library, take the stair at the southwest corner of the structure, cut through the Life Sciences North Building, and head west.

6 **Arizona Inn** [NRHP], 2200 E. Elm Street, 1930; Merritt Starkweather, FAIA, architect, and Isabella Greenway, owner

This complex of buildings, cottages, and open spaces has become a model for garden resort hotels. Established originally on the outskirts of town, this hostelry provided an early oasis of comfortable outdoor living for the increasing numbers of winter tourists. Similar to traditional Mediterranean complexes, the layout of one- and two-story building forms of pitched and flat roofs creates a protective perimeter from the current suburban neighborhood and focuses attention on the interior court-yards, gardens, and hotel guest rooms, similar to a secluded village. Unique to this complex is the sense of scale, which varies from large, formal open spaces and public rooms, such as the library and dining room, to intimate reading niches and passageways found throughout. The interior and exterior details, such as fireplaces, exposed wooden trusses, furniture, balconies, and the distinctive pink wall color, are all done in a simple, consistent manner. Other examples of suburban garden resorts are the **Lodge on the Desert** and **Hacienda del Sol.**

7 Rancho Santa Catalina **(Potter Place),** 2301 E. Elm Street, 1924

The Mission Revival house has an unusual green glazed tile roof. The gabled roof of the port cochere is echoed in an entry gable topping white stucco walls with simple openings having segmental arches. The landscape design of the grounds is gracious with a mix of native and exotic vegetation. The house was built for Leighton Kramer, who was one of Tucson's early boosters; he built a polo field immediately east of Campbell Avenue, which was the site of the Fiesta de los Vaqueros rodeo from 1925 to 1940. The current name came from its subsequent owner, Dickson Potter, who converted the residence into a finishing school for girls.

8 Ball/Paylore House, E. Waverly Street, 1952; Arthur Brown, FAIA; *inaccessible/ published*

Singularly responsive to the needs of the clients and the climate, this small house provides both a nontraditional house plan for two residents and a large shaded patio area for outdoor living. Phyllis Ball and Patricia Paylore were both librarians at the University of Arizona, and they found the typical house for the average American family unsuitable for two independent adults who wanted to share a home. Furthermore, they were intent on "avoiding the trite, conventional and the dull" that they found in most of the homes that were being built in the early 1950s. The core area of the house— living room, kitchen, dining room, and library—is contained within a hexagonal plan, and a brick fireplace at the center supports wooden beams that radiate out to the exterior walls. The bedrooms are placed on the northwest and northeast sides, with the entry at the north. The south three faces open up to glass walls and the patio beyond, which has movable corrugated aluminum shade screens on a track at the outer edge of the slab. After thirty years of living in the house, they threw a party for the architect and the builder to celebrate its success.

Catalina High School.

9 **Catalina High** (Magnet) **School,** 1835 N. Dodge Boulevard at Pima Street, 1955; Scholer, Sakellar & Fuller, architects; J. J. Craviolini and L. C. Anderson, contractors; saved from demolition 1992, Bob Vint, Jim Gresham, FAIA, Kirby Lockard, FAIA, Guy Greene

When this high school campus was designed, the architectural firm was one of the first in Tucson to work in the post–World War II modern architectural vocabulary, which rejected the romanticism of revival styles. Controversial when it was designed (and still controversial today), this campus used materials and forms not seen before in Tucson, including exposed steel and curvilinear roofs and walls. The building's qualities of sensitivity to the desert climate and straightforward design aesthetic won the firm a regional design award and national publicity, which attracted many of today's best practicing architects to Tucson.

10 **Catalina American Baptist Church,** 1900 N. Country Club Road, 1960; Charles Cox

The defining element of building character here is the use of thin-shell concrete in a hyperbolic paraboloid form that is a "super-roof"—that is, a roof that also forms part of the walls. This dynamic roof form opens to the north and south with glass, creating a striking interior space.

Benedictine Sanctuary.

11 Benedictine Sanctuary,
800 N. Country Club Road, 1939–1940; Place & Place/Roy Place

This Spanish Colonial Revival structure includes the private functions typical of a monastery: church, cloister, dormitories, and refectory. However, the church is open to the public and well worth the visit as the interior space is gracious and expanding, cool, and fairly quiet given its location on a major street. The high central nave is flanked by side aisles, and the marble columns support groin vaults. The ceiling vaulting looks convincingly like brick but is actually acoustical tile. It is one of the last buildings designed by Roy Place before his firm began designing in the Modern style. The revivalist vocabulary of arches, clay-tile roofs, and tower is consistent with many of Place's previous buildings and conveys a quality of permanence.

12 Faith Lutheran Church,
3925 E. 5th Street, 1950–1951; Arthur T. Brown, FAIA, architect; Fred Jobusch, structural engineer; James Blackmore, general contractor; *published*

The sheer originality of the use of overlapping, hollow-core, precast, and prestressed concrete units to make both the roof structure and the finished ceiling is remarkable. The precast units are supported on an A-shaped structure of built-up steel trusses with a sawtooth profile. The spacing of the steel trusses is 22 feet on center, and they rest on the foundation.

13 **Tucson Clinic,** 116 N. Tucson Boulevard, 1953; Scholer, Sakellar & Fuller; *published*

This is one of Tucson's first International-style buildings, expressed in its material palette of brick, steel, and glass as well as the fact that it addresses the climatic needs of the desert through its floating roof planes and deeply recessed ribbon windows. The original plan incorporated many architectural innovations for its time, including separate patient and staff corridors, an outdoor play yard in the pediatrics ward, and skylit interior spaces. This two-story building also had to maintain a sensitive scale to the surrounding residential neighborhood and comply to one-story zoning requirements by submerging the rear two-story facade. Parking for this large clinic was hidden from the neighborhood at the rear in the area opened by the sub- merged two-story facade and screened from the street with low brick landscape walls.

Broadway Village.

14 **Broadway Village** Shopping Center, southwest corner of Broadway Boulevard and Country Club Road, 1939; Josias Joesler

This eclectic Spanish Colonial Revival shopping center was intentionally designed as a set of distinct building elements around a plaza space meant to evoke a miniature "village." It was novel for relegating its parking to the back of the property in an age of retail strips and street parking. The resulting pedestrian experience is enhanced through the scale of building forms, openings, and plaza space, which are accentuated by hand-painted decorative tile.

Starkweather Residence.

El Encanto Estates [NRHP] and Colonia Solana [NRHP]

Saddling the north and south sides of Broadway Boulevard between Country Club Road and Randolph Way, El Encanto Estates and Colonia Solana were designed in 1928 as a conscious break from the gridiron subdivisions sprawling across the Tucson Basin after World War I (see pp. 26–27). Although there are individual residences of note, the essence of these neighborhoods is the environment that was created to enhance the homes. In El Encanto Estates, the street pattern is a formal, symmetrical design in the Neoclassical tradition with equally formal landscaped lots, large lawns, and nonnative vegetation. In contrast, Colonia Solana's curvilinear street design follows the contours of the land created by a natural arroyo and uses the natural desert vegetation. Both create a unique sense of place whose integrity has been maintained.

15 Starkweather Residence, 30 E. Calle Belleza, 1932; Merritt H. Starkweather, FAIA

As the overseeing architect and designer of sixteen residences in El Encanto Estates, Starkweather promoted the use of the Spanish Colonial Revival style. Curiously, his house distinguishes itself from this stylistic uniformity by using a combination of Pueblo Revival and Art Deco characteristics, which would later be labeled "Pueblo Deco." This is one of Tucson's rare examples of this stylistic blending where the irregular massing and wall coloring have Pueblo influences, but without the characteristic vigas, and the vertical and stepping decorative features are aligned with the Deco style.

El Conquistador Hotel; demolished 1968.

16 Site of El Conquistador Hotel **(El Con Mall),** 1925–1928; Henry Jaastad/Annie Rockfellow, designer; demolished 1968

The victim of bad timing, this sprawling and romantic interpretation of the Mission and Spanish Colonial Revival styles could not survive the Great Depression, went bankrupt in 1935, and suffered continued financial trouble until the 1960s. The structure of this luxurious tourist hotel was 140 feet long, the tower was 45 feet high, and there were forty guest rooms with separate baths and spectacular views of the Santa Catalina and Santa Rita mountain ranges as there wasn't anything to obstruct either view in 1928. The arcaded structure was built of brick, with stucco and terra cotta ornament and a red tile roof; the construction cost was approximately $500,000. One of the most unique features on the exterior was the incorporation of bas-relief images of

saguaro, ocotillo, and barrel cacti in the entablature, with prickly pear capitals on Baroque twisted columns. The hotel included a lobby, a curio shop, and a gracious dining room that could seat 300 guests. The dining room had a large fireplace, a balcony for an orchestra, columns, "Spanish-style" chandeliers, and ceiling beams that were colorfully decorated. Officially the project of the office of Henry Jaastad, Annie Rockfellow was the design architect, and the drawings are similar to others in her hand. She considered this her finest design, calling it her "prize" or her "ultimate design." Two fragments of the building survive at separate locations: The porte cochere is at the entrance to the Sin Vacas gated community, E. Ina Road just west of Campbell Avenue; the copper dome is located at the Casa Blanca Shopping Center on the northeast corner of Oracle and Rudasill Roads.

RGA Engineering Building.

17 Water Tower [NRHP], S.
Randolph Way near E. Broadway
Boulevard, c. 1929; Roy Place,
architect; John W. Murphey,
builder; restored 1994 by M3
Engineering & Technology/Bob
Vint, preservation consultant

This handsome tower was
designed to cover a large water
tank supplying El Conquistador
Hotel and the new subdivision of
Colonia Solana. Although the
tower was a functional necessity,
the Spanish Colonial Revival
covering was intended to draw
attention to the subdivision, the
architect, and the builder. It is 30
feet square at the base and 65 feet
tall, is stuccoed, and has an
octagonal clay-tiled cupola at the
top ornamented with arched
windows and twisted columns.
The wrought-iron weather vane
depicting a prospector and his
donkey is almost 4 feet in height.
Truly a landmark for Tucsonans.

18 RGA Engineering Building
(Office Building), 877 S. Alvernon
Way, 1974; Cain Nelson Wares &
Cook/John Morrison, designer

Originally built for an engineering firm, this building conveys
the bold forms and clean details
typical of the architecture of Cain
Nelson Wares & Cook. The
simple exterior palette of brick,
stucco, and glass belies the
concrete and steel structural
system, which supports the
cantilevered second floor. Deeply
recessed openings oriented to the
north and south appropriately
address climatic considerations,
and the ground-level entry patio
provides a comfortable transition
between the noise of the street
and the interior offices. A bridge
over the patio connects the north
and south wings.

Also of note is **Child & Family Resources** (formerly Barrows Furniture Store) at 2800 E. Broadway Boulevard, designed by Ralph Haver in 1957. The structural wooden beams forming a flat barrel can be seen through the north window wall. At 3033 E. Broadway Boulevard is **Bank One Branch Bank,** with dynamic sculptural form designed by Bernie Friedman in 1971, and just to the west, on the south side of the street, stand the saintly statues atop **Table Talk.** At 2240 E. Lind Road is the two-story **Lockard Residence,** designed by Kirby Lockard, FAIA, in 1968, which uses exposed concrete block in an elegant design aesthetic repeated a generation later in the work of Arthur Perkins (see **Manlove Studios** and **15th Street Studios** below, in the "Barrio San Antonio" section).

Sam Hughes [NRHP]

The western portion of the Sam Hughes neighborhood was originally called University Manor, but it began to be popularly called Sam Hughes after the Hughes Elementary School was built in 1927. Most building occurred between the 1920s and the 1950s, and by 1929 about half of the lots were built on. It is a huge neighborhood at 218 acres. Blocks are about 450 feet square with lots in which homes face north and south on the streets, one or two parallel alleys, and a few houses facing the ends of blocks on the avenues. The best alleys are the dirt ones with garages that are shaded by mature eucalyptus or Aleppo pine. The gentle slope of the neighborhood is accommodated through a variety of low retaining walls.

The character of the neighbor-

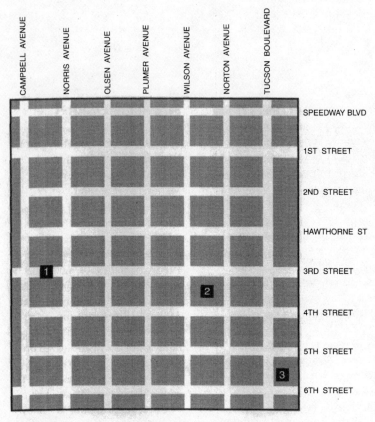

CAMPBELL AVENUE
NORRIS AVENUE
OLSEN AVENUE
PLUMER AVENUE
WILSON AVENUE
NORTON AVENUE
TUCSON BOULEVARD

SPEEDWAY BLVD

1ST STREET

2ND STREET

HAWTHORNE ST

3RD STREET

4TH STREET

5TH STREET

6TH STREET

Sam Hughes

600'

hood was regulated through deed restrictions in effect until 1964, including minimum property value, mandatory heights and setbacks, restrictions on inhabitation of garages, and restrictions on types of animals and ethnic groups allowed.

Architectural style is best described first and foremost as eclectic, with every style—and just about every combination of styles—built between 1920 and 1950 represented. There are very few classic or "pure" examples of any of the styles; rather, what is evident is an incredible individuality, which includes attached elements such as ramadas, porches, and walls and a profusion of landscape material both exotic and native. The worst intrusions are the recent high walls built at property lines.

One of the problems for visitors is that there is no public parking except east of the school. We recommend that you tour by bicycle or take an evening stroll.

For example, starting at the intersection of 4th Street and Norris Avenue: On the southwest corner at 1950 is a Sonoran Revival; at the northwest corner is a Craftsman house with rough textured brick. Continuing east on 4th Street to Olsen Avenue, the southwest corner at 2046 has one of the best examples of a pressed-tin "tile" roof in the Mission Revival style. In the next block east, at 2143, is an example of a Pueblo Revival built in 1928. Continue to Wilson Avenue and turn north to visit the school, then proceed north to Hawthorne Street and east to Plumer Avenue, where you will see Hawthorne Court, a good example of a typical courtyard rental complex with six units in the Moderne style. This arrangement is found in many styles, from Spanish and Mission Revivals to bungalow courts. Also of note, on the northeast corner of 4th Street and Treat Avenue, is a pair of houses in the Moderne style built by Joesler in 1936.

1 **3rd Street Streetscape,**
from Campbell Avenue to
Country Club Road

By far the most appealing street
in the neighborhood, it is best
experienced by bicycle as one
needs to travel from Campbell
Avenue to Country Club Road
for the full effect, and it is closed
to automobile traffic.

Moving from west to east will
evoke a sense of decade-by-
decade time travel: from a street
lined with palms and citrus trees
forming a rhythmic edge and
foreground for a dense fabric of
revival houses to more widely
spaced trees standing guard in
front of bungalows or Deco
houses. By Treat Avenue, most of
the houses are the low, horizontal
Ranch style, with very large and
open front and side yards; the
street trees no longer include
palms; and citrus eventually gives
way to native paloverdes. The
McInnes House, at 2917 E. 3rd
Street, is a very simple Modern-
style residence built in 1959 by
Arthur Brown, FAIA, utilizing an
insulated, lightweight aluminum,
hyperbolic paraboloid roof.

2 Hughes Elementary School, 700 N. Wilson Avenue, 1927; Roy Place; A. Jacobson, contractor

The form and stylistic vocabulary of this Spanish Colonial Revival building evoke more an image of a church than a school. The prominence of the two-story administration building is clearly expressed with the grand scale created by a tower and centered entry doors, both incorporating semicircular arches. The classroom buildings have the feel of California Mission architecture with low-pitch, clay-tile roofs. Although there have been many additions and remodels, the original building still maintains its character and remains the center of the Sam Hughes neighborhood.

3 Rincon Market, 2502–2518 E. 6th Street, 1945; attributed to Merritt Starkweather, FAIA; renovation 1986 by Paul Weiner, Bob Lanning, and John Collins

This brick building, with parking behind and on the east side, has a wonderful interior space with exposed trusses that were opened up with steel beams and columns in the 1986 renovation. The continuous porch along the south wall includes seating and meets the sidewalk at the property line.

Cheng-Olson Studio.

Barrio San Antonio

1 **Manlove Studios,** 1250 E. Manlove Street, 1988; Hoffman Perkins Design/Arthur Perkins

The first collaboration by this team, this simple group of artists' live-work studios faces the street and provides good views to the north. The studios are entered from a central courtyard, which is landscaped with mature desert trees. The studios are built of gray concrete block with steel sash windows. Relatively low and small in scale, this complex fits well in a neighborhood of older American Territorial homes and industrial buildings.

2 **15th Street Studios,** 1335 E. 15th Street, 1991; Hoffman Perkins Design/Arthur Perkins

The second design/build project in this neighborhood by this team is a six-unit infill housing complex with separate work studios for artists. The apartments are aligned on a central walkway. Private porches and yards are entered from common courtyards planted with oaks. The material palette is restrained, in the best sense of the word, with concrete block, steel casement windows and lintels, flat roofs with shallow overhangs, and tin waterspouts. The intimate scale, crisp design, and privacy make this a highly attractive rental. The **Cheng-Olson Residence and Studio,** designed by Renée Cheng and Eric Olson, on the northeast end of the complex, is a larger house but uses the same formal and material palette, with a glazed double-height living area facing north.

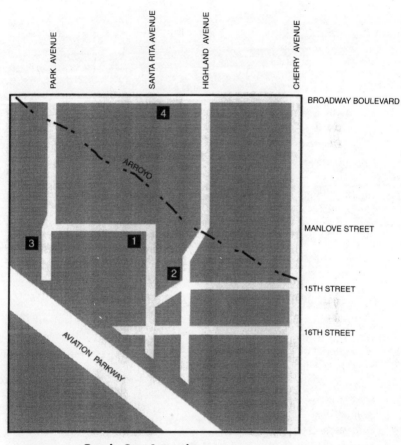

PARK AVENUE
SANTA RITA AVENUE
HIGHLAND AVENUE
CHERRY AVENUE

BROADWAY BOULEVARD

ARROYO

MANLOVE STREET

15TH STREET

16TH STREET

AVIATION PARKWAY

Barrio San Antonio

600'

3 **Project M.O.R.E. Alternative High School,** 440 S. Park Avenue, 1996; Burns & Wald-Hopkins/Dave Burns, designer

This small high school for Tucson Unified School District is built of tilt-up concrete panels on the exterior. The interior courtyard is shaded by perforated steel roof decking on steel trusses. Rain is directed away from the courtyard through the channels in the decking, with the perforations creating a sense of lightness in the material quality of the ramada. Fresh air flows under the ramada and through the breezeway. This is an excellent example of inexpensive materials and construction technology in the service of good design.

4 **Miles** Exploratory **School,** 1400 E. Broadway Boulevard, 1920–1921; Lyman & Place, architects; J. J. Garfield, contractor

The courtyard plan of this Mission Revival building is ideal for the small elementary school because outdoor activities can be held in a defined area. The facade is graced by a Palladian arched entry flanked on either side by the rhythm of deep-set and vertically proportioned windows against smooth white walls. The original school had nine classrooms around the courtyard; later additions in 1928 and 1930 were considerable, and it was again renovated in 1996.

Fort Lowell and East Side

Fort Lowell [NRHP]

The Fort Lowell Historic District is a large area that includes prehistoric Hohokam ruins as well as American-era structures built during and after the occupation of the fort. Most of the remaining structures from the fort itself are in Fort Lowell Park or along Fort Lowell Road west of Craycroft Road.

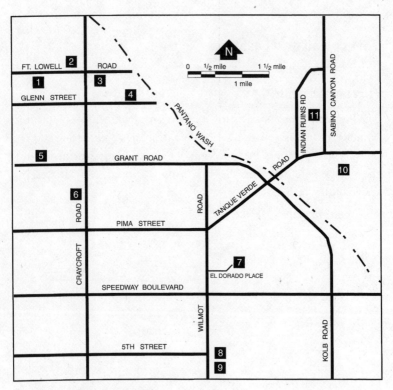

FT. LOWELL **2** ROAD

0 1/2 mile 1 1/2 mile
1 mile
N

1

GLENN STREET

3

4

PANTANO WASH

5 GRANT ROAD

TANQUE VERDE ROAD

ROAD

INDIAN RUINS RD

SABINO CANYON ROAD

11

10

6

CRAYCROFT ROAD

PIMA STREET

7
EL DORADO PLACE

SPEEDWAY BOULEVARD

WILMOT

KOLB ROAD

5TH STREET

8

9

Fort Lowell and East Side

1 **San Pedro Chapel,** 5230 E.
Fort Lowell Road, 1932; attributed
to Alonso Hubbard, architect and
contractor; renovation 1995 by
Bob Vint

In 1931, the village of El Fuerte
commissioned the third chapel
for this location. It was built by
the residents using earth from the
site and is significant as a
contextual remnant of the older
neighborhood. The 1995 renovation included structural stabilization, plaster finish, and a new
corrugated-metal roof.

2 **Quartermaster and Commissary Storehouse,** 5483 E.
Fort Lowell Road, 1875

These lime-plastered adobe
structures display the flat roofs
and wooden lintels typical of a
Sonoran row house. The unusual
stepped parapet is the result of
erosion. Farther west, also on the
north side of the street, is the
1873 Sutler's Store building, now
a residence, and the combined
remains of the 1891 Sutler's
Storehouse and Riallito House.

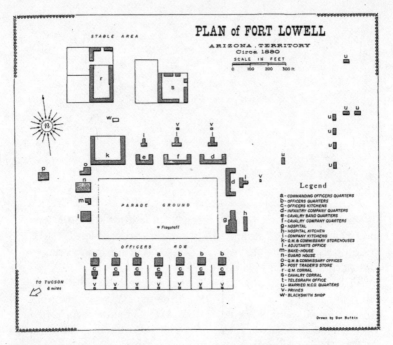

PLAN of FORT LOWELL

ARIZONA TERRITORY
Circa 1880

SCALE IN FEET

0   100   200   300 ft.

STABLE AREA

PARADE GROUND

□ Flagstaff

OFFICERS ROW

TO TUCSON
6 miles

Legend

a - COMMANDING OFFICERS QUARTERS
b - OFFICERS QUARTERS
c - OFFICERS KITCHENS
d - INFANTRY COMPANY QUARTERS
e - CAVALRY BAND QUARTERS
f - CAVALRY COMPANY QUARTERS
g - HOSPITAL
h - HOSPITAL KITCHEN
i - COMPANY KITCHENS
k - Q.M.& COMMISSARY STOREHOUSES
l - ADJUTANTS OFFICE
m - BAKE-HOUSE
n - GUARD HOUSE
o - Q.M & COMMISSARY OFFICES
p - POST TRADER'S STORE
r - Q.M. CORRAL
s - CAVALRY CORRAL
t - TELEGRAPH OFFICE
u - MARRIED N.C.O. QUARTERS
v - PRIVIES
w - BLACKSMITH SHOP

Drawn by Don Botkin

3 Site of Fort Lowell **(Fort Lowell Park),** 1873–1891

Conflicting interests between military activity and settlement by newly arriving American families in the area that is now Armory Park, southeast of downtown, forced the relocation of the former Camp Lowell to this distant location. This large military reservation was established in 1873, as it was deemed "necessary for securing grazing and control of the watercourse" in support of the soldiers who would defend settlers against Apache raiding parties. Located around the 700- by 400-foot tree-lined parade ground were the officers' quarters with kitchens, soon followed by a guardhouse, bakery, offices, storehouses, corrals and stables, cavalry and infantry barracks, hospital, and eight laundresses' quarters. These were all adobe structures, roofed with vigas probably from the Rincon Mountains, savinas, and dirt. The interior walls were coated with lime plaster made from kilns located in the foothills of the Rincon Mountains, now Saguaro National Park East. The defeat of the Apaches led to the closure of the fort in 1891.

Plan of Fort Lowell, c. 1880.

Commanding Officers' Quarters and Kitchen **(Fort Lowell Museum/Arizona Historical Society),** 1873

Reconstruction of these adobe structures took place in 1962–1963. The kitchen building also included a dining room, servants' quarters, and a pantry.

Cottonwood Lane, 1873–1891

Replanted in 1962–1963 near the original site, which marked the southern edge of the parade ground, these trees were originally irrigated by ditches. A protective ramada was built in 1952 for the **Hospital Ruin,** originally built in 1875. There are also several Classic-period **Hohokam Ruins** from c. A.D. 600 here.

East Side

The development of the eastern basin of Tucson began with ranch houses on early homesteads and intentionally isolated facilities including sanatoria and airfields. After World War II, Tucson's population boom accelerated development of residential subdivisions eastward and was quickly followed by the religious, office, and civic buildings that supported them.

4 **Orchard River Townhomes,**
5701 E. Glenn Street, 1971–1972;
Robert Swaim

An excellent example of low-
impact site design that gracefully
incorporates many of the trees
from the original pecan orchard
that stood here near the Rillito
River. Not only did this sensitive
design preserve many of the trees,
but by grouping townhomes and
carport parking areas, the
complex was given a pedestrian
and natural feeling that is
delightful. The townhomes
themselves are oriented north-
south, with polished concrete
floors, concrete block walls,
clerestory windows, and private
patios.

5 **Erickson House,** 5301 E.
Grant Road, 1926–1927; Henry
Jaastad

Now part of Tucson Medical
Center, this building was originally the director's house and is
one of the few remaining
structures from the original
Desert Sanatorium of Southern
Arizona. The complex served the
many health seekers who flocked
to Tucson and aided in the
development of a local sanatorium industry. It was built in the
Pueblo Revival style combining
adobe walls with steel beams
concealed behind cement plaster.

6 **Craycroft Towers Apartments,** 1635 N. Craycroft Road, 1972–1974; F. P. Cole & Associates, Architects & Engineers; renovated 1994 by Collaborative Design Group; Lambert Construction, Inc., contractor

Built by the city of Tucson for public housing, the apartments are efficiently planned to create the feeling of a larger interior space. The only drawback is the very low ceiling height. The exterior structure and details are simple yet bold within a modern aesthetic that responds to the need for shelter and shade in a desert environment through patios, balconies, and overhangs.

7 **Stone Ashley** (Pond Mansion), 6400 E. El Dorado Circle, c. 1930; Grosvenor Atterbury

Originally built as a house for Florence Pond on her 320-acre estate, arrival is made along an alley of mature Italian cypresses, which reinforces the fusion of building and landscape architecture. The stone structure is several stories in height and takes advantage of the steep slope by providing a sunken garden in the Italian Renaissance style. Lushly planted and accented with water features, the garden is enclosed by a stone wall. The guest houses, designed in 1949 by Bernie Friedman, have since been demolished in the conversion of part of the mansion property into El Dorado Lodge.

St. Michael's and All Angels
Episcopal Church.

Wilmot Library.

8 St. Michael's and All Angels Episcopal Church, 602 N.

Wilmot Road, 1953; Josias Joesler; addition 1964 by Gordon Luepke and Ed Morgan; renovations 1991 by Bob Vint; Fine Arts addition 1993 and Classrooms and Parish Center addition 2000 by Bob Vint

The form and materials of this Pueblo Revival church were inspired by the 1760 Mission San Jose in Trampas, New Mexico. It has a single spacious nave enclosed by adobe walls with rounded corners, is protected by smooth earth-colored plaster, and is covered by a flat roof whose huge wooden beams are exposed on the interior. Joesler used weathered materials to make the building look older, but it is the integration of building and arcades with courtyards, shade trees, benches, and fountains that is noteworthy.

9 Wilmot Branch of the Tucson-Pima Public Library, 530 N. Wilmot Road, 1964; Nicholas Sakellar, FAIA

This branch library epitomizes Sakellar's interpretation of modern design for the desert. Deep overhangs and high clerestory windows create the illusion of a floating roof plane, emphasizing the building's low horizontal position on the desert. These ramada-like forms cover the two principal spaces, a landscaped entry courtyard and an open floor plan with an uninhibited interior space that allows visual access throughout the library. The focus of the interior space is a sunken reading area with two walls of floor-to-ceiling windows overlooking a garden, which erases the distinction between exterior and interior spaces.

10 Morris K. **Udall Recreation Center,** 7200 E. Tanque Verde Road, 1990; Albanese Brooks Architects/Doug Macneil, design consultant

A fairly simple exterior of concrete block conceals a spacious interior supported by exposed steel trusses. The clean construction detailing and the integration of public art are also commendable.

11 **Indian Ridge Estates,** begun in 1956 by developer Robert Lusk

This subdivision has several variations of the Perfect Arizona Type (PAT) house and was a rare example of a Tucson-based developer's attempt to create a subdivision appropriate for the climate and culture of Tucson.

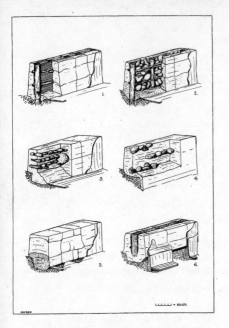

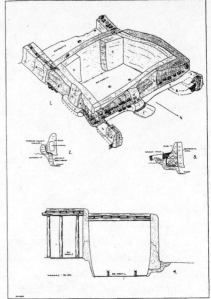

Site of University Indian Ruin,

c. 13th–14th century; *inaccessible except by appointment through the University of Arizona/published*

At the juncture of the Pantano and Tanque Verde Washes lies an enormous rounded mound of earth covered with creosote that protects the remains of this settlement. The excavation of this site in 1940 uncovered the remains of a Classic-period Hohokam village with earlier-period rectangular pit houses, sitting beside a grouping consisting of massive walled rooms and courts and several large earthen mounds. Only one of these mounds was excavated, revealing a large adobe house built on top of another house in which the rooms had been filled with earth to create the base for the upper rooms. The construction technology at Indian Ruin is truly remarkable in its constant experimentation with structural techniques, which related to the composition of the materials (including adobe, wood, stones, and caliche) and how they were used in foundations, walls, roof structures, and finishes.

Roof structures were supported by these composite bearing walls and intermediate wooden post supports. Most impressive of all is the use of caliche as a waterproof finish material for the interior walls and floors. Indicative of the ingenuity encouraged by limited resources, these early construction methods are echoed later in the houses of Spanish settlers in the area beginning in the seventeenth century.

University Indian Ruin, drawing of wall types.
University Indian Ruin, drawing of wall construction.

Note: the following examples are not shown on a map, but they are easy to find:

Bank One Banking Center, Williams Centre, 5210 E. Williams Centre Circle, 1985; Architecture One/Phil Dinsmore, FAIA

This nine-story office building is an elegant, sculptural expression of polished granite and glass in a context defined by low-density stucco buildings. The angular forms, clean details, and soft color palette provide a precedent for subsequent midtown multi-story buildings.

Lutheran Church of the King, 2450 S. Kolb Road, 1958; Edward H. (Ned) Nelson, FAIA

The original church building was ahead of its time in its modern treatment of light, space, and structure. A sawtooth roof allowed both the interior space to be free of structural columns and the creation of triangular clerestories to bring natural light inside. In a masterful use of utilitarian materials, Nelson created an intricately patterned brick screen to shade the east and south facades from direct sun during morning services.

Sherwood Village Office Buildings, 8230 E. Broadway Boulevard, c. 1963; Nicholas Sakellar, FAIA

The primary feature of this building is the way that the cantilevered shade structure not only integrates parking spaces and offices but wraps around two sides of the building. The simple metal structure is supported by cables anchored to massive piers. The office entries are sunlit and landscaped.

Swaim Residence and Office,
1700 N. Harrison Road, 1968;
Robert Swaim; *inaccessible/
published*

Inserted into a mesquite bosque
are two handsome modern
structures built of planar walls of
formed concrete and glass
opening onto covered porches,
with cedar siding and decking.
The use of an 8-foot module of
space and structure provided
orderly flexibility. The second
story in the office structure is
reached through the open stair
tower.

Regina Cleri Center, 8800 E.
22nd Street, 1955; Terry Atkinson

Originally built as a seminary,
this small campus is formed
around a courtyard. Buildings of
pale orange brick include covered
walkways with clay-tile roofs
carried on wooden beams. In an
excellent example of passive solar
design, each of the three original
classroom and dormitory wings
has its own south-facing covered
walkway and courtyard. The
most prominent feature from
22nd Street is the blue Spanish
Colonial Revival dome rising
above a landscape design that
preserves a natural desert buffer
zone along the street. A much
more lush experience is created
in the courtyard with the use of
olive, palm, eucalyptus, and
Italian cypress trees.

Civano, Houghton Road just
south of Irvington Road, construction begun 1981; Moule &
Polyzoides, Architects, the city of
Tucson, and the Civano Development Company

Originally named "Solar Village,"
this 818-acre subdivision is the
city of Tucson's first experiment
in encouraging sustainable design

principles. The idea began with a proposal by John Wesley Miller, a local home builder, to then governor Bruce Babbitt to build a model solar village. To encourage development of this type, subsidies were made available from city, state, and federal sources. The original idea has evolved to include many of the elements of sustainability, with the ideal being that a community could employ minimal use of unrenewable resources and minimal output of waste or pollution. One of the key features of this or any sustainable community is mixed-use zoning that encourages pedestrian and bicycle travel to and from work, shopping, and restaurants. Civano requires very high energy-efficiency standards for construction and maintenance of homes, but, unfortunately, the streets were not aligned to orient the houses for passive solar design, so instead they are all required to be plumbed for active solar water systems.

Agua Caliente Ranch (Roy P. Drachman **Agua Caliente** Regional **Park**), Soldier Trail at Roger Road, 1984; stabilization and adaptive reuse 2001 by Bob Vint

Agua Caliente Creek and the hot springs were used by Archaic-period hunters and gatherers, Hohokam, and the soldiers from Fort Lowell. By 1873, the cattle ranch established there was known as "Agua Caliente Rancho," and by 1878 it was promoted as a respite for city dwellers, which continued until the 1950s. Pima County purchased the 100 acres that included the ranch in 1984 and is in the process of restoration through grant funding and public support. The lush oasis, with spring-fed ponds, cotton-woods, fan palms, and lawns, is supported by this unusual abundance of water. The existing buildings renovated in 2001 included the ranch house, converted to the visitor's center, and the caretaker's cottage, now a meeting room.

texture—wood, split-faced concrete block, and stone—echo the surrounding desert.

Barrett Residence, 12420 Makohoh Trail, 1988; Collaborative Design Group/Frank Mascia; *partially accessible* (can be seen from the road)/*published*

This contemporary version of an early ranch house sits in the foothills of the Santa Catalina Mountains overlooking Agua Caliente Creek, on the clearing that had been the holding pen for cattle. Under a huge roof of corrugated blue-gray metal, the enclosed rooms and porches move in and out of the line of the roof. The material color and

Catalina Foothills

Suburban development of the Catalina Foothills began in earnest in 1928. A combined homestead and auction purchase of 7,000 acres of land by John W. Murphey began one of the earliest master-planned communities in southern Arizona. Murphey knew that his vision of a community of affluent and prominent citizens could be realized only through the provision of municipal services, transportation, and a public school. The centerpiece and gateway for the community was St. Philip's Plaza, which included a church (p. 223), restaurant, offices, and a studio for the painter Hutton Webster, all surrounding a public park. Preservation of the stunning foothills topography, views, and natural vegetation was accomplished through design and deed restrictions. The development by John and Helen Murphey and their architect, Josias Joesler, known as the Catalina Foothills Estates, featured rural Mexican-style homes with arches, breezeways, courtyards, brick and stucco, decorative glazed tiles, and wrought iron.

Murphey's development drove Tucson's expansion northward, and other low-density foothills developments soon established the entire Catalina Foothills as an affluent residential area. This popularity soon led to higher-density developments and increased transportation demands. Today, much of the original rural character of the Catalina Foothills has been lost—an ironic consequence of its success.

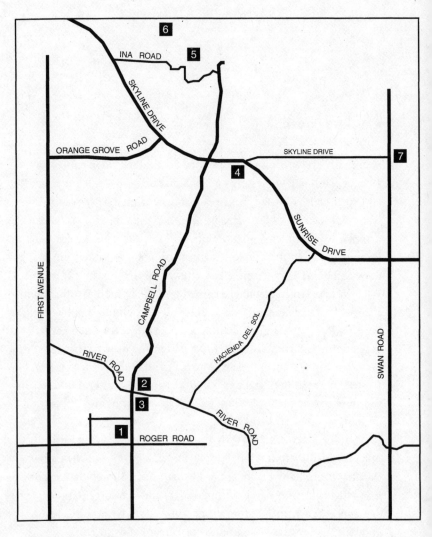

Catalina Foothills

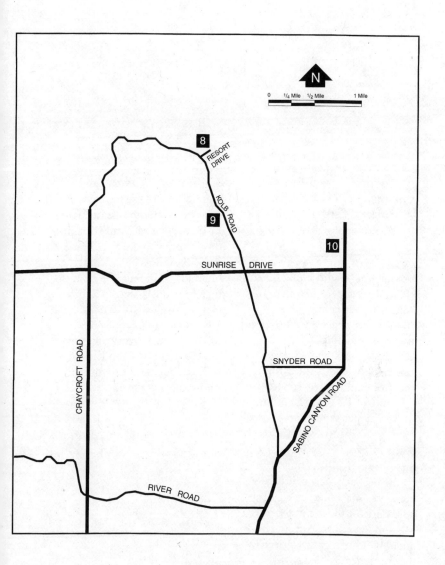

1 Campbell Avenue Farm
(University of Arizona Campus Agricultural Center), 4101 N. Campbell Avenue, 1910–1935

Purchased in 1909 as an 80-acre instructional facility along the Rillito River for the University's College of Agriculture, this property has collected a number of unique buildings. The 1910 Residence/Workman's Cottage on Campbell Avenue is the earliest known extant poured-concrete residence in Tucson. The utilitarian vernacular expression of this residence contrasts with the use of the Mission Revival style for the other agricultural buildings on the property. The unattributed 1914 Machinery Shed set the precedent for the use of the Mission Revival style in subsequent buildings, characterized by the curvilinear gabled parapet, white stucco walls, and corrugated-tin roofs. The 1917 octagonal Water Tower was designed by J. B. Lyman and remains one of the few remaining disguised water towers in Tucson. In 1935, Henry Jaastad's architectural firm, with designer Annie Rockfellow, was contracted to build four buildings for the farm, including the U-shaped Equine Complex (Horse Barn), which includes a cupola roof vent. Rockfellow's designs continued the use of the Mission Revival style, giving the entire complex a unified appearance.

St. Philip's in the Hills
Episcopal Church.

2 St. Philip's in the Hills Episcopal Church, 4440 N. Campbell Avenue, 1936; Josias Joesler; addition 1957 by Gordon Luepke; addition 1998 by Cain Nelson Wares & Cook/Ned Nelson, FAIA

This church was designed as part of a complex of buildings surrounding a park that was meant to mimic a Mexican village center and provide an anchor for the development of the Catalina Foothills Estates. The church depicts Joesler's interpretation of the Spanish Colonial Revival style in the use of arcades and court-yards as well as rusticated building materials to convey a sense of antiquity. The spacious interior of the church features exposed wooden beams, elabo-rate tin lamps, and wall niches, but the principal focus of the space is the arched window behind the altar that looks out to the desert and the Santa Catalina Mountains. Unfortunately, conditions around the building have changed dramatically; what was once a quiet park is now the crossroads of the high-speed, high-volume arteries of River Road and Campbell Avenue.

Muscular Dystrophy
Association National
Headquarters.

3 Bank One Branch Bank,
4398 N. Campbell Avenue, 1978;
James A. Gresham & Associates/
James A. Gresham, FAIA, designer,
and Gordon Heck and Stan
Schuman, design consultants

A single-story, mortar-washed,
burnt adobe structure that tips its
hat to the nearby Joesler buildings, across the street to the west,
including its use of wrought iron
and ceramic tile. A small entry
courtyard serves as a transition
space from outside to inside. The
addition of oversized concrete
lintels brings a modern boldness
to its otherwise modest expression.

4 Muscular Dystrophy Association National Head-
quarters, 3300 E. Sunrise Drive,
1992; Anderson DeBartolo Pan

A model of "barrier-free design,"
there are no curbs, ramps, or
narrow corridors. The decision to
create an edge following the
curve of Sunrise Drive allows the
building to be seen instead of
obscured by a sea of parking. The
parking lot is placed behind the
building, follows the natural
slope of the site, and is entered
through a break in the building at
ground level. A sandstone veneer
covers the exterior, and it is
roofed with artificially weathered
copper. Recipient of design and
accessibility awards.

5 **Hansen Residence,** Ina Road and Campbell Avenue, 1994; Line & Space/Les Wallach, FAIA; *inaccessible* (can be seen from Campbell Avenue and Ina Road)/ *published*

The interplay between the sunlit forms, textures, and deep shadows on the south face of the house reveals the integration of the structure into the rugged hillside, but the hard edges, cold color, and strong horizontality of the concrete beams create a sharp contrast. As in all of Wallach's work, the modernist characteristics are evident: planar walls anchored by the weight of concrete or stone, texture and color integral to the materials, and transitional spaces between inside and outside used to mitigate huge differences in light and temperature. Natural vegetation is preserved and watered by roof runoff. Similar in floor plan to the Arroyo House (p. 226), with its separation of public and private areas connected by a glass-enclosed hallway, this house is a completely different experience because the entrance is perpendicular to the hallway.

Arroyo House.

6 **Arroyo House,** Rancho Sin Vacas (gated community), 1988; Line & Space/Les Wallach, FAIA; Richard Ebeltoft, structural engineer; *inaccessible/published*

In building his own house, Wallach was able to use two elements that many clients would have considered too risky. The first is the separation of the public and private spaces on either side of a deep arroyo connected by a bridge. The second bit of structural bravado is seen in the cantilevered fireplace hearth that penetrates a glass wall. Preservation of wildlife habitat and vegetation of the arroyo and the capturing of cool air that flows down the arroyo through the bridge windows are among many of the advantages of this bold design.

7 **Gallery in the Sun,** 6300 N. Swan Road, c. 1950; Ted De Grazia

This hand-built gallery was designed by De Grazia and constructed under his supervision. It is decorated with the paintings of De Grazia and has thick adobe walls, buttressed corners, and rounded building forms that evoke the architectural expression of New Mexico, but the gallery is done in more of a folk tradition. The Mission in the Sun chapel building is open to the air, creating a peaceful, contemplative space. The isolation this complex once enjoyed has been compromised by the growth of homes in this part of the foothills.

Ventana Canyon Resort.

8 Ventana Canyon Resort,
7000 N. Resort Drive, 1985; Fizzell, Hill, and Moorehouse, Architects

The building by the San Francisco firm for this destination resort hotel complex sits companionably in the rugged mountain surroundings and uses the natural features to provide a vocabulary for the built forms. It also has a strong resemblance to the San Marcos-in-the-Desert resort hotel, an unbuilt project designed in 1928 by Frank Lloyd Wright. Corrugated wall patterns and building forms were constructed using split-faced masonry block matching the color of the rock outcroppings, whose palette of rustic materials is carried into the interior. The development was constructed with an ethic of minimal disturbance to the desert vegetation, and this philosophy is applied throughout the complex, which is itself slowly being covered with vines. A portion of the building spans an existing canyon stream, which has been channeled and incorporated as a principal element in the resort. Windows frame views to both the mountains above and city below.

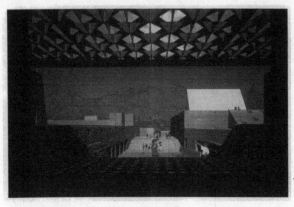

Ventana Vista
Elementary School.

9 Ventana Vista Elementary School, 6085 N. Kolb Road, 1994; Antoine Predock, design/Burns and Wald-Hopkins, architect of record; *published*

The goal of this design was to create an "extraordinary place for learning" with a relatively low budget. The criterion was met: As the campus steps up to match the steep incline of the site, its simple angular forms create the four areas within the school. Class-rooms are organized around three age-group "villages" in addition to a building that houses administrative offices and the multi-purpose room forming an entry "canyon," with the library at the center of the composition. Patterns of sunlight and shadow on these large and stark forms create an ever-changing image. However photogenic, this campus must be walked to experience the canyons, views, and spaces, and be sure to see the solstice wall, which marks the path of the sun and significant calendar events. Although shaded areas are provided, more would have been better.

10 **Canyon View Elementary School,** 5725 N. Sabino Canyon Road, 1989; NBBJ/James A. Gresham, FAIA

This school campus has been recognized for the careful manner in which the small groupings of classrooms were placed on the site. The natural beauty, native plants, and arroyo are preserved and celebrated through this sensitive design. Buildings are connected by a covered walkway and bridge over the arroyo while material choice and color also complement the landscape. Against the earth-colored concrete block, which is rough at the base and smoother above, color accents are provided at the windows, shade structures, and bridge by brick coping, and there are lively trim colors in blue, lavender, and orange.

Also of note are two houses designed by Judith Chafee, FAIA, which are both inaccessible but published. **The Jacobsen House,** built in 1977, is characterized by an expanding and contracting of space starting from its south-facing courtyard entry; then, after passing through a low vestibule, the interior expands into a higher space. Kitchen, study, and bath form a central core from which the Miesian planar walls extend. Rooms are separated from the core by internal patios. The studio and living room sit at an angle from the rest of the floor plan to capture views of the Santa Catalina Mountains. A mountain of glass-faced bookcases in oversized steps creates a reading-area loft above. Earth-toned concrete floors and beams provide a harmonious contrast with the cool white walls and the warm wooden bookcase steps and interior doors.

Chafee's **Rieveschl House,** built in 1988 by the contractor James Hamilton with David Eisenberg supervising construction, is a dramatic house formed of cast-in-place concrete that straddles a ridge with its long connecting hallway. At the entry one can access the guest suite or the studio by moving up the cascading stairs to the north or by taking the opposite direction with the long vista to the main house, which is cantilevered high above the site. Chafee's masterful handling of levels and spaces in this house brings to light the fluidity of space itself. As in all of her work, we see a delicately balanced material palette of warm woods and cool concrete, but the rock fireplace surround seems out of place and uncharacteristic. The house is on the Smithsonian Institution's tour of architecture of the Southwest.

The 1979 **Stamm Residence,**

4341 E. Coronado Drive, uses the
formal vocabulary of modernism
as practiced by Richard Meier to
capture views of the desert and to
create dramatic interior spaces.

Northwest

Development began in the Northwest in the 1920s because the milder, frost-free climate in this particular area and abundant well water were ideal for growing and exporting citrus and dates, as well as sufficient grasses for grazing cattle. Citrus groves, and all but the 49 acres of what would become Tohono Chul Park, became subdivisions with names like "Catalina Citrus Estates."

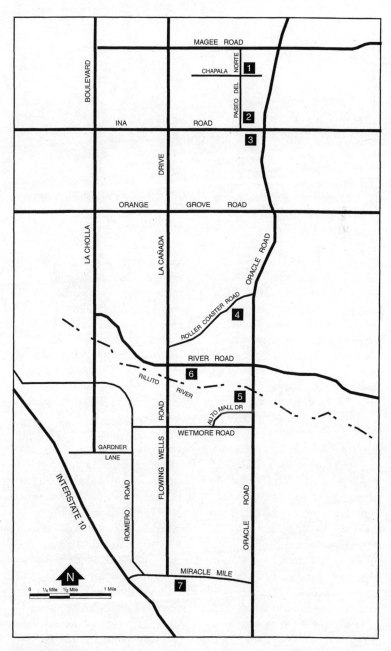

Northwest

1 **St. Andrew's Presbyterian Church,** 750 W. Chapala Drive, 1962; Ned Nelson, FAIA

The dominant A-frame roof structure is supported by laminated wooden beams resting on precast-concrete Y-shaped columns both inside the nave and extending to the entry porch. The structure is buttressed by exterior stone walls of deep reddish black color. Although interesting in its structural expression, the sharp edge of the top of the interior of the A-frame becomes an unwanted focal point, whereas in the 1959 church designed by Carlo Scarpa with E. Gellner, to which this is clearly related, the juncture is more open and seems to be the source of light. The interrelationship between the building and the site is commendable—a seamless composition of multiple-level seating and intimate shaded courtyards with the building raised on a stone base.

2 **Tohono Chul Park,** 7366 N. Paseo del Norte, dedicated in 1985

Truly a desert island in the middle of suburban development, the land of this 49-acre park was inhabited by the Hohokam about A.D. 70–1150, served as a cattle ranch and homestead in the 1920s, enjoyed the view of a citrus grove to the south, and was a winter home to many families. Today, the park includes an Exhibit House, Tea Room, demonstration gardens, classrooms, trails, ramadas, and many excellent examples of minimal water use and living in the desert. The **Exhibit House** was built in 1937 by Paul Holton, based on plans by Santa Barbara architect Chester L. Carjola. The house has thick adobe block walls, made on site, and is Sonoran in form, but the modern interventions carefully inserted during its complete renovation in 1984 are refreshing. The **Tea**

Room (Sullivan Residence), designed as a residence for the property's owner by Lewis Hall in 1963, is centered around a generous yet intimate courtyard into which all the rooms open. The building is constructed of burnt adobe block and exposed wooden rafters and is accented with colorful ceramic tiles.

3 Casas Adobes Shopping Center **(Casas Adobes Plaza),** 7101 N. Oracle Road, 1954–1964; Gordon Luepke

This development funded by Sam Nanini began with the corner service station and is an early example of "strip development," where adjacent shops are built parallel to, but set back from, the street, with parking in the front. This one is a bit more palatable because the variety in form and material is contained within a uniform vocabulary and scale. There are two small patio or courtyard areas and an almost continuous arcade along the front. Materials include adobe, brick, and stucco, and there are columns in either concrete or wood, wooden beams, and colored tile. For an alternative shopping center layout, see Broadway Village (p. 193).

Avalon House, courtyard;
demolished 1983.

4 Dove of Peace Lutheran Church, 665 W. Roller Coaster Road, 1969; Kirby Lockard, FAIA

A quietly elegant and award-winning church that defies the common belief that good design cannot be built on a low budget. The sanctuary is a simple expression of a centralized altar form reflective of the Lutheran liturgy, whose altar is lit by a multi-sided monitor expressed as an abstract crown on the building's exterior.

5 Site of Avalon House, 4519 N. Oracle Road, 1914–1927; *demolished 1983*

Not a trace remains of this fairly large Spanish Colonial Revival home; it was built over a period of time so that additional wings eventually formed a remarkable Moorish-style courtyard measuring 50 by 30 feet. It had a continuous arcade on slender columns, capitals and architrave with bas-relief plasterwork, and brightly colored mosaics on the walls and floor. The traditional Moorish geometric tiles were imported from Spain in 1926 with the laborer to install them. The glass roof seen in archival photographs may have been original or added later when the house was sold to the Adair Funeral Home.

6 **Project Potty,** Rillito River Park, near La Cañada Drive, 1993–1996; Line & Space/Les Wallach, FAIA; *published*

See description and photograph in West Side (p. 172).

7 **Ghost Ranch Lodge,** 801 Miracle Mile, 1941; Josias Joesler/ Gordon Luepke

An example of the motor court with drive-up casitas around formal gardens. This building type is associated with the period of tourism when roads such as the Miracle Mile were the principal routes in and out of Tucson.

Also of note: On the northeast corner of one of the busiest intersections, at La Cholla Boulevard and Ina Road, is the Sullivanesque **Bank of America** by James A. Gresham, FAIA, with a formal facade facing Ina Road but the entry courtyard accessed by parking on the east. Not easily accessible is the winter residence built for Margaret, Countess of Suffolk. The house, now the **Immaculate Heart Elementary School** at 410 E. Magee Road, was designed in 1937 by Richard A. Morse using the clean lines of the Modern style; it was published in *Architectural Record* in January 1941. The brick structure has stuccoed exterior insulation, painted a "warm brown to harmonize with desert," covered porches, roof decks, and steel sash windows. Inside, the public rooms have travertine floors, and the interior detailing is "without trim" in only two tones of color—"pale sea green" and ivory—exactly those of Le Corbusier's 1929 Villa Savoye.

South Side

Ask any number of Tucsonans to define "the south side of Tucson" and you will get as many answers. Generally, it is the area south of 22nd Street between I-19 and Alvernon Way. However, there is also the city of South Tucson, a 1-square-mile area between I-10 and the railroad tracks and between 25th and 40th Streets. The distinctly Mexican character of this area can be seen by driving on 6th Avenue south of 22nd Street and 12th Avenue south of Ajo Way. Vestiges of the American popularity of S. 6th Avenue in the 1930s, when it was originally the main road to Nogales, are visible in the neon-lit motor courts, restaurants, and rodeo grounds along the streetscape. Both streets convey their Mexican character through the eclectic variety of folkcraft businesses (iron-smiths, tinsmiths, mural artists) and their contemporary counterparts (meat shops, bakeries, tortillerias, produce vendors). Driving through the residential neighborhoods reveals a deeply religious population that displays its conviction publicly. This vernacular residential landscape is often defined by the transparent yet enclosing material of chain-link, in which the open space is intentionally not vegetated and where a yard shrine or other religious sculpture is prominently featured—a remnant of the Spanish tradition of space defined by materiality. These landscapes are rich in color, detail, and fluidity. Though this area has suffered from a lack of investment by banks and developers, it is being provided with municipal funds for improvements to enhance these vibrant streetscapes.

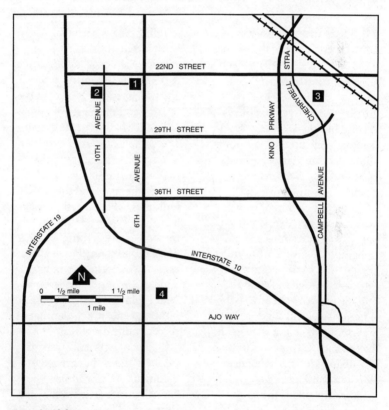

South Side

Santa Cruz
Catholic Church
and School.

1 Santa Cruz Catholic Church and School [NRHP], 1220 S. 6th Avenue, 1919; Manuel G. Florez, contractor

In 1916 Henri Granjon, the second bishop of the diocese of Tucson, drew up the plans for a monastery for Carmelite friars based on a convent in Avila, Spain. The church originally served a population of very poor Mexican and Native American families within a huge triangular geographical area "from 7 miles west of Vail [Arizona] to the Mexican border and from the middle of 17th Street to Sasabe." The adobe blocks for this enormous structure were made by the Papago (now the Tohono O'odham) Indians living near the Mission San Xavier at a cost of $10 per 2,000. It is the largest adobe structure in this area at 50 by 200 feet in floor plan and approximately 33 feet in height. Mudéjar influences are apparent in the minaret-like bell tower,

standing 80 feet high and constructed of brick, and the exterior walls of white stucco with ornament limited to the entry. The repeated finials at the parapet and the pattern in the walls add rhythm to the exterior. The complex includes a cloister (courtyard) on the south side of the church, the adobe Carmelite Hall to the west, and the school buildings, which together create an urban feel. Inside the church, the single nave features windows of Victorian stained milk glass, cherry-wood trim at windows and baseboards, and pilasters with capitals forming a continuous gilt entablature. The altar recedes quite deeply into the west wall, through several layers of pilasters and arches carried on columns with Corinthian capitals, but it is bisected by the dropped ceiling, which was added later. Above the altar is a dome with small stained-glass windows.

Main Post Office.

2 Southside Presbyterian Church Sanctuary Addition,
317 W. 23rd Street, 1993; Jody Gibbs, architect/Gibbs & Vint, construction administration/ Cobre Building Systems, Tim Puntennev, president

In this addition to an original building by Art Brown, the facade became the point of connection, creating a small courtyard with the new sanctuary. The exterior is a deep earth-colored stucco over concrete block with rounded parapet walls, rusted metal, and wood. The new sanctuary has a centralized floor plan, fusing the Native American kiva or round house with the Renaissance ideal. This central space has a continuous *banco* or built-in bench in plaster colored with iron oxide. Tactile accents are supplied by the live ocotillo fence, saguaro-rib ceiling, and ponderosa-pine beams.

3 Main (Cherrybell) Post Office, 1501 S. Cherrybell Stravenue, 1972; Cain Nelson Wares & Cook

A good Brutalist building; facing slightly south of west, both east and west facades are layered to provide shade on the glass. The entry portico creates a deep shade and is proportioned so generously that it feels like a civic building.

Veterans Affairs Medical Center.

4 Veterans Administration Hospital **(Veterans Affairs Medical Center)**, 3601 S. 6th Avenue, 1929; Roy Place

The original gracious campus plan, with its blend of native and exotic landscaping (creosote and palms) and beautiful open spaces, was the perfect setting for the Spanish Colonial Revival buildings in pink stucco and bright accents, forming shady arcades and cool courtyards. Park near the chapel and walk through the original entry into the main courtyard just north of the palm-lined entry drive on 6th Avenue. It may still be possible to see the screened sleeping porches by walking north beyond the chapel, but they are presently being enclosed.

Also of note is the **ERL**

(Environmental Research Laboratory), located on Cortona Road near Tucson Boulevard, near the entrance to Tucson International Airport. You can see several full-scale models of passive solar designs, alternative building materials, cooling towers, ramadas, and fountains, among other exhibits.

Tucson Environs

There are numerous buildings of significance in the vicinity of the
Tucson Basin. The following entries include general locations and
sometimes directions.

Ramada House.

Ramada House, 1975; Judith Chafee, FAIA; George Mehl, contractor; *inaccessible/published*

This is the best example of the work of Chafee that is still standing. A huge shade structure of round timbers and closely spaced two-by-fours on end evokes the pattern of ocotillos while covering the entire house and creating an entry patio at the south. The supporting posts of the ramada are laid out in a formal grid and pierce the house, providing a continual internal reference to the structure outside. The Modern rectangular plan is oriented east-west, and its three levels follow the slope of the site. The private rooms are at the high end of the site, with the public rooms at the lower end. Entrance is in the middle, with a living room that juts out of the house with a full-height bay window that lets the viewer step into the view. At this level, a courtyard is also brought into the house.

San Xavier del Bac Mission Church [NRHP], San Xavier Road, Tohono O'odham Indian Reservation, 1783–1797; Ignacio Gaona, master builder; restorations 1906 by Henri Granjon; restorations 1937–1951 by E. D. Herreras, FAIA; conservation 1989–2000 coordinated by the Patronato San Xavier; 1992–1997 interior conservation team led by Paul Schwartzbaum, with Carlo Giantomassi, Vincenzo Centanni, Donatella Zari, Marco Pulieri, Paola Zari, Ridvan Isler, and Svitlana Hluvko; exterior conservation team, Bob Vint, architect, and Morales Construction Company

Attributed to the combined efforts of master builder Ignacio Gaona, artisans from Querétaro, Mexico, and the local native population, this mission church remains one of the finest examples of Spanish Colonial architecture in the United States. This is the third of three churches built on this site; the first was

San Xavier del Bac Mission Church.

begun by Jesuit missionary Eusebio Francisco Kino in 1700.

The power of San Xavier surely begins with the image of a massive but beautifully proportioned and articulated structure of brilliant white seen against the rich colors of an endless desert. Part of its attraction is, and always has been, its remoteness—its presence as a sacred place in a land so utterly foreign to Spaniards and Americans alike, but one wonders what the experience was for the native Pima and Papago Indians.

San Xavier is characteristic of the Spanish Colonial missions in that it is a provincial adaptation of the late Baroque designs of Mexico, but in this case it is also stylistically fifty years behind. Most were built under the supervision of priests, each of whom was at once architect, contractor, foreman, and building supply agent. These churches were shaped by the severely limited resources and the dedication and ingenuity of the priests. Daily concerns revolved around shortages of building materials, availability of skilled labor, securing funding from Mexico, and protection against attacks by native populations.

San Xavier's twin towers flank a Churrigueresque carved-stone portal with layered broken and curvilinear pediments, framed by the two pair of *estípites* on either side of the facade. The 3- to 4-foot-thick walls in stuccoed brick, and the original floor of polished mortar, kept the interior cool. The combined Baroque characteristics of fluid, dynamic interior space and elaborate surface ornamentation make it an architectural experience of complexity and richness. Wood, plaster, and paint create the illusion of marble and majolica tile. The Latin Cross floor plan is covered by a series of shallow vaults leading to the dome over the crossing. The four windows of the dome illuminate the

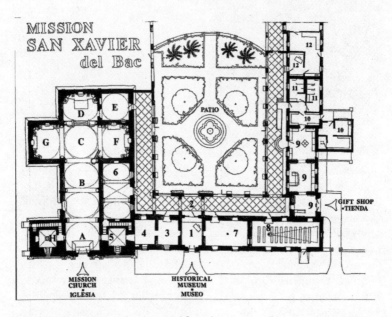

MISSION
SAN XAVIER
del Bac

D   E

G   C   F

B   6

A   5   4   3   1   ·   7   8

PATIO

12

12

11   11

10

10

9

9

9

GIFT SHOP
·TIENDA

MISSION
CHURCH
·
IGLESIA

HISTORICAL
MUSEUM
·
MUSEO

San Xavier del Bac Mission Church, ground-floor plan.

retablos of the sanctuary, the east and west chapels, the painting within the dome, the sculptured moldings, and figures on the walls below. The extensive restoration begun in 1988 has restored this building to its original brilliance. Also see the 1995 **San Xavier Elders' Center,** built of volcanic stone and 1/4 mile west of the mission, also by Bob Vint, architect, and Eric Means, contractor.

McMath Solar Telescope at Kitt Peak Observatory, Ajo Way (Highway 86), 25 miles southwest of Tucson, 1967; Skidmore, Owings & Merrill/Myron Goldsmith, designer; *published*

Among a whole family of blindingly white geometric forms, which are the various observatory buildings, is the powerful modern structure housing the solar telescope. The vertical leg is almost 100 feet high, and the diagonal arm is 200 feet long above ground and another 400 feet below.

Blackwell House,
c. 1980;
demolished 1998.

Tucson Mountain Park, 1933–1942; Clinton F. Rose, landscape architect

The enormous park that follows the ridgeline of the Tucson Mountains was developed by Pima County and the National Park Service with the help of the Works Progress Administration (WPA) in the 1930s. This historic landscape embodies a singular design ethic incorporating historic structures, prehistoric archaeological and rock-art sites, mines, features of the natural environment, topography, views, and new structures such as roads, trails, parking areas, and picnic ramadas. Architecturally, the structures are similar in style and construction and blend into the landscape. For information on the **Rock-Art Sites** of Hohokam petroglyphs, maps are available at the office on Picture Rocks Road, at Saguaro National Park West headquarters.

Site of Blackwell House, Gates Pass Road, 1979; Judith Chafee, FAIA; demolished 1998; *published*

Not only was this house one of Tucson's best examples of Critical Regionalism—the mix of history, climate, culture, and modern architecture—but it was also the portrait of Chafee herself. It was a good house that embodied her love for this place: "The idea is to pick up the deep underlying wisdom that's come from generations of living there [in a particular place]. Plus using your modern know-how in construction techniques." It revealed the strength and rigor of her knowledge of construction in the intersection of the concrete block walls and precast beams. Like most of her desert houses, it was an interior spatial delight and included framed views to the outside. It tempered the climate with passive solar design through site orientation, thick walls, overhanging shade structures,

Johnson House.

natural ventilation captured or created by form, and recycling of rainwater from the roof. The demolition of the house was at the heart of intense and divisive debate that placed preservationists and architects on one side and the general public and the Pima County Parks and Recreation Commission on the other. The primary objection was that its bold modern forms marred an otherwise "pristine" landscape.

Johnson House, Tucson Mountains, 1974; Judith Chafee, FAIA; *inaccessible/published*

Built for Chafee's mother, the house rises in three steps with clerestory windows running the full length of the structure and facing north. The kitchen, dining room, and living room wrap around a mechanical core, whereas the bedrooms are removed and private. The interior is softly lit and has low heat gain. The form is clean and bold with a restrained color and material palette. Walls are mortar-washed white over concrete block inside and out. Neutral-colored concrete slabs above the south windows and entry door provide shade. Gray concrete water channels and floors also complement the white walls.

Rancho de las Lomas, 4500 W. Speedway Boulevard, 1936; Margaret Spencer

This rambling complex of cottages and towers was one of Spencer's few Tucson works. Originally designed as a guest ranch on 140 acres, each of the thirteen buildings blends sensitively into the surrounding desert landscape and is constructed of native stone with windows strategically placed to frame views of the Tucson Mountains and the rolling foothills.

Rammed Earth House, Tucson Mountains, 1992; Paul Weiner, architect/builder, and the design team of Rick Joy, Lauren Clark, and Suzi Weisman; *inaccessible/ published*

The horizontal layering and color of the massive rammed-earth walls match the landscape. These walls both shelter the house and extend into the landscape beyond the enclosure of rooms. In addition, they are used to create two breezeways that cut entirely through the house. Both owner and design team studied the natural beauty of the land for over a year before the design began. In addition to the exposed rammed earth inside and outside, the materials include sandblasted and etched concrete and aluminum, native weathered rhyolite, sandblasted weathered steel, and exposed fir and cedar timbers.

Arizona-Sonora Desert Museum Restaurant and Art Gallery.

Arizona-Sonora Desert Museum Restaurant and Art Gallery, 2021 N. Kinney Road, 1994; Line & Space/Les Wallach, FAIA; *published;* also **Main Entry Plaza,** 1994, Bob Vint, architect, and Eric Means, contractor

The most accessible of the buildings designed by Les Wallach and built by his design/ build team, this project is a study in the complex relationships between the interior and the exterior. Wallach's work must be considered Critical Regionalism as it is both modern and intensely responsive to place. The modern impulse to dematerialize the boundaries between inside and outside is apparent where the floor and ceiling planes extend beyond the plate-glass walls; it is also shown at the corners, where two sheets of glass meet without any structural member. This dynamic spatial quality is continued throughout the structure and into the transitional spaces at the perimeter, particularly the dining terraces, which seem both outdoor and indoor as they are protected, shaded, and air cooled. Wallach's material and color palette is also a blend of modern and regional traditions: The modernist unpainted concrete, wood, and metal are joined by richly colored stone or stucco walls in vivid varieties of purple, magenta, and a rich deep blue. Desert vegetation and trickling water are captured in the dining terraces and in the sloping walls. Small-scale details (such as the singular blue stone in each monolith or the guardrail made of ship hardware) contribute to Wallach's vision—a building in dialogue with its spectacular landscape.

Also noteworthy is the **parking lot:** Its permeable surface has low heat gain, absorbs some water, and the water runoff feeds native plants integrated with the lot that provide evaporative cooling and shade.

Acacia Elementary School.

Vail

Like many small towns in Arizona, Vail (25 miles southeast of Tucson) was a water stop along the railroad, and it remained a small town until recently, when inexpensive and explosive housing development jumped outside of the city limits and created a desperate shortage of schools.

Acacia Elementary School,
12955 E. Colossal Cave Road, 1990; Cain Nelson Wares & Cook, architects of record, and Dominique Bonnamour-Lloyd, design architect

The first new elementary school for the Vail School District is remarkable for the synthesis of a modern aesthetic with responsiveness to regional factors. It is also proof that an extremely low budget can produce a good building that continues to function well. The shade canopies that encircle the courtyard plan create an intimate space that protects small children and provides a cooler micro climate. With the straightforward plan, simple volumes, and basic materials—concrete block and steel—the architect has provided variety in texture, color, and shadow. Attention to detail gives the whole a well-crafted appearance.

Desert Willow Elementary School.

Desert Willow Elementary School, 9400 E. Esmond Loop Road, 1995; Albanese Brooks Architects/Dominique Bonnamour-Lloyd, design architect

Similar in plan to the earlier Acacia Elementary School (p. 251), the entry is flanked by the kindergarten and the administration building with the multi-purpose room at the other end of the composition. But in this case, the composition is manipulated so that the primary circulation is on a covered curved internal street that bisects the courtyard, whereas at Acacia the location of the primary circulation is at the courtyard perimeter. The library is the only building sitting in the courtyard. Classroom buildings are made of concrete block with steel window frames and canopies. All exterior surfaces are painted one of four intense colors: cobalt blue, orange, teal green, or salmon. Overall, this is a rich, powerful, and poetic design.

Shrine of Santa Rita in the Desert, Colossal Cave Road at Old Vail Road (I-10, exit 279), 1930; H. E. A. Figgé

A small Catholic church built in memory of the renowned Japanese scientist Dr. Jokichi Takamine by his widow, Caroline Beach. Still an active church, the Mission Revival exterior leads to a single-room interior with a high ceiling and stained-glass windows on both sides. The stations of the cross are represented in glazed California tile. In addition, Beach's landscape design complements the natural desert.

Profiles of Tucson Architects

Although there have been many Tucson architects who were prolific, prominent, and successful in serving their clients' needs, this section profiles the architects whose accomplishments stand out for their profound impact on the architecture of Tucson. In an effort to have a measure of historical perspective, architects who are currently practicing are not included.

Henry Trost.

Henry Trost (1860–1933)

Henry Charles Trost was born in Toledo, Ohio, where he graduated from art school and later worked as a draftsman for local architects. He left Toledo in 1880, and after working in Colorado, Texas, and Kansas, moved to Chicago in 1887, then the center of international architectural ferment. There, Trost was greatly influenced by Louis Sullivan and Frank Lloyd Wright and may have worked for a short time with Wright in Sullivan's office. Elements identified with both architects appear in Trost's later work—though it is incorrect to categorize him squarely with either. It is not until his 1899 arrival in Tucson, via Colorado, that evidence of his prodigious professional output begins to appear.

Trost promptly received a number of commissions in Tucson, including residential, institutional, and civic buildings. In 1903, Trost moved to El Paso and formed a partnership with Robert Rust to maintain the Tucson office, which, in 1905, was forced to close after Rust's sudden death. In El Paso, Trost formed, with his brother, the firm of Trost and Trost, for which Henry Trost served as the chief designer and produced over 200 commissions spanning a wide range of building function and style. With distinguished designs not only in Arizona and Texas but in New Mexico as well, Henry Trost became prominent as a regional architect of great merit. Although he lived in Tucson for only four years, Henry Trost left an indelible mark. Stimulated by the economic growth of the Southwest, by its vigorous mingling of cultures from Spain, Mexico, and elsewhere, and by its spectacular landscape and demanding climate, Trost designed buildings drawn from both revival and modern architectural movements, but, in the end, he contributed that which would come to be seen as distinctly his own.

Henry Jaastad.

Annie Rockfellow.

Henry Jaastad (1872–1965) and Annie Rockfellow (1866–1954)

Heinrik (Henry) Olsen Jaastad was born in Norway, emigrated to the United States in 1886, and moved to Tucson in 1902. He was trained as a cabinetmaker, worked as journeyman carpenter, and completed a correspondence course in architecture in 1908. When he opened his office in 1908, Jaastad advertised himself as an architect and contractor, with mostly residential commissions, eventually expanding to include religious (thirty-five churches in the Southwest), commercial, and institutional buildings. He is credited with introducing fired-clay brick into the standard building practice of turn-of-the-century neighborhoods like the Barrio Historico. Jaastad is better known for his active political and public life as city councilman, beginning in 1924, and mayor, from 1933 to 1947.

Until his retirement in 1957, Jaastad's office was responsible for over 500 projects and relied on the skills of many unrecognized associates, including Annie Graham Rockfellow, Prentice Duell, D. Burr DuBois, and Eleazar D. (Ed) Herreras.

Among these, the arrival of Annie Graham Rockfellow in 1916 was the most profound, marked by a dramatic shift in design competence from plain, utilitarian expressions to those representing current academic styles, including the many period revival styles popular in the country. Rockfellow, known as both "Annie" and "Rocky," first arrived in Tucson in 1895 from Rochester, New York. She originally came to fill a two-year teaching position at the University of Arizona and returned again in 1909. In 1915, she permanently closed her architectural office in Rochester and attended the Panama-California Exposition in San Diego where the new Mission Revival and Spanish Colonial Revival styles were promoted as a regional architectural expression. When she joined the office of Henry Jaastad at the age of fifty, she brought with her an architectural education from the prestigious Massachusetts Institute of Technology (1887) and twenty-nine years of experience in design and construction. Rockfellow was the second woman to graduate from MIT and was also the first woman architect registered in Arizona. She was an avid traveler and documented the architecture of Mesa Verde and other ancient sites in the Southwest.

The good working relationship between Jaastad and Rockfellow lasted for twenty-two years, during which Rockfellow took part in all aspects of the office's projects, though her primary role was that of chief designer. She preferred to design commercial and governmental work and didn't much care for residential design because it was often subject to delays as clients considered options. Stylistically, her definition of what she considered "appropriate" for the Southwest included solar orientation, thick adobe walls, and a preference for vigas, perhaps for the dramatic shadows they cast, or perhaps because they reveal the structure.

In a long and active life of building design and construction, she also wrote articles about architecture and in 1932 presented radio monologues about architecture on KVOA Tucson. In 1938, at the age of seventy-one, Annie Rockfellow retired from Jaastad's office and moved to Santa Barbara, California, a place surrounded by Spanish Colonial architecture.

Roy Place.

Roy Place (1887–1950)

Roy O. Place was born in San Diego and, after graduation from high school, moved to San Francisco to work as an architectural draftsman for the California State Engineering Department. He later joined the firm of Sheply, Rutan and Coolidge—who were responsible for the architectural imprint of Romanesque Revival at Stanford University—where he worked for three years in Chicago and Boston before moving to Los Angeles in 1913.

In 1917, Place moved to Tucson to supervise construction on the University of Arizona's Mines and Engineering Building designed by John Beattie (Jack) Lyman, a San Diego architect whose first Tucson commission was the 1914 Agriculture Building working in partnership as Bristow and Lyman. Lyman and Place formed a partnership in 1919 and constructed over twenty buildings in Tucson before Lyman left the firm in 1924. Place then worked as sole practitioner until 1940 when his son, Lew, joined him in partnership to form Place and Place Architects.

Place was responsible for some of southern Arizona's landmark public buildings. His use of the Renaissance and Spanish Colonial Revival styles was typical of the period, but also exhibited a high level of craft and graceful formal compositions equal to their status as civic and public architecture. In his role as the University of Arizona's chief architect during its initial period of expansive growth, he established a consistent architectural vocabulary, which included red brick as a unifying element. After World War II, the firm embraced modern architecture, influenced by Place's son, Lew, but these buildings are not as compelling as the earlier work of Roy Place.

Josias Joesler.

Josias Joesler (1895–1956)

Josias Thomas Joesler was born in Zurich, Switzerland, in 1895 to an architect father and was raised in Arosa, Switzerland. His education included the study of architecture in Bern, engineering in Heidelberg, and history and drawing at the Sorbornne in Paris. He worked and traveled extensively throughout Switzerland, Germany, Italy, and Spain as well as in North Africa and Latin America. After moving to Los Angeles in 1926, Joesler was introduced to John and Helen Murphey, partners in a growing Tucson building and development company. The Murpheys had a vision to build residential developments in Tucson that emulated the prestigious resort communities of Los Angeles and Santa Barbara, which attracted wealthy residents from the East. To compete with those communities, the Murpheys needed an architect who could interpret this vision in the form of buildings that portrayed the various historical revival styles popular in other parts of the West. In 1927, they found their architect when they hired Joesler, beginning a thirty-year relationship of patron-architect that lasted until Joesler's death in 1956.

Joesler designed over 400 projects encompassing residences, commercial buildings, and churches that express an eclectic approach toward design with elements borrowed from historic as well as contemporary architecture. Joesler used revival styles to provide an illusionary link to other cultures and places and often blended these with local building traditions, resulting in a distinctive regional image. But he also experimented with many other styles including Contemporary Ranch, Art Deco, and regional variations of the International style.

Today, much of Joesler's recognition as an architect stems

Arthur Brown.

from the promotion of his homes by the real estate market, particularly in the Catalina Foothills, as representing a "Tucson style." These homes, built for some of Tucson's early elite, are exemplary: in their preservation of the landscape, whereby homes were integrated with the natural topography and plants were preserved; in the use of courtyards, which created a cooler microclimate; and in the orientation of the houses, so that spectacular views were captured.

Arthur Brown, FAIA (1900–1993)

Arthur Thomas Brown was born in Tarkio, Missouri, to a professor father and artist mother. After graduating from a local college with a degree in chemistry, he received his architectural degree from Ohio State University in 1927. He was hired as a draftsman in the renowned Chicago firm of David Adler, where he gained firsthand experience with the work of Louis Sullivan and Frank Lloyd Wright, which had a lasting influence on his thinking. During the depression, Brown was hired to work on the 1933 Century of Progress Exposition, for which he designed auxiliary buildings and signage. In 1936, Brown came to Tucson, a town of barely 15,000 people. He quickly found work with Richard Morse, with whom he established a partnership three years later. By 1941, Brown had opened his own architectural practice, which he maintained until he retired in 1991. In 1961, he became the first Arizona architect to be invested in the American Institute of Architects (AIA) College of Fellows, one of the highest honors bestowed on an American architect. His son, Gordon Brown, who joined as partner in 1970, continues to practice and maintains his father's passion for quality architecture.

Brown is credited with the first passive solar-designed school in the country, Rose School in 1948, incorporating techniques that have only recently become popular. His genius was also exhibited in his inventions, through which he demonstrated the innovative use of inexpensive materials and modular housing forms. These were presented in numerous design competitions for such companies as General Electric and Corning Glass and drew considerable attention as the United States struggled to meet the explosive demand for new, cost-effective housing in the late 1940s and early 1950s. Ideas such as subterranean houses, subfloor radiant heating, aluminum and foam insulated roof components, revolving patio covers, and hyperbolic paraboloid shade structures established his reputation as a modernist with a sensitivity to the desert environment of Tucson. He rejected revival styles popular in Tucson during his career as dishonest and challenged himself to design "without style." Art Brown described himself as an architect, an artist, and an inventor—an amalgam whose design legacy remains vibrant and influential to this day.

Nicholas Sakellar.

Nicholas Sakellar, FAIA (1918–1993)

Nicholas Gust Sakellar was born to a Greek immigrant family in Indiana, was raised in Ohio, and graduated with an architectural degree from the University of Michigan in 1941.

After serving in the U.S. Army Air Corps during World War II, Sakellar worked briefly in Cleveland and married his architect wife before moving to Tucson in 1948.

In 1950, Sakellar contributed his design talents to the newly established firm of Scholer, Sakellar and Fuller. During its six-year partnership, this well-balanced team won numerous design awards and contributed greatly to the modern expression in Tucson, long defined by historic revivalism, during one of its busiest periods of growth. Seeking more creative freedom, Sakellar left the firm in 1956 to open his own office, eventually called Nicholas Sakellar & Associates. He continued his bold design reputation and acquired residential, commercial, institutional, and master-planning commissions throughout the rest of his career.

Beginning in the mid-1960s, Sakellar broke away from a more purist modern expression of intersecting planes and began to develop a more sculptural vocabulary, where curvilinear forms and massive cantilevered planes became more prominent. Experimenting with new materials, he used technology to fuse his design aesthetic with the climatic extremes of the desert. Sakellar was joined by his son, Dino, in 1981 to create the current firm of Sakellar & Associates and was invested in the AIA College of Fellows in 1986.

Perhaps just as significant as his forty-year career and 250 commissions is the generation of

Judith Chafee.

architects who came to Tucson because of his design reputation. These include Kirby Lockard, FAIA, James Gresham, FAIA, James Merry, and John Mascarella, all of whom developed their own reputations for design excellence and continue Sakellar's tradition of modern design in the desert.

Judith Chafee, FAIA (1932–1998)

Judith Davidson Chafee was born in Chicago and moved to Tucson at the age of five. Her delight in, and respect for, the desert can be attributed to a Tucson childhood living in an adobe house and learning firsthand about sun angles, cool washes, and prevailing breezes. From her mother, a Harvard-trained anthropologist, Chafee learned to respect the indigenous cultures of Arizona and the wisdom they demonstrated in building for the desert. An additional advantage for Chafee was being the only child in a world of intellectually stimulating encounters, including Margaret Sanger, who later founded Planned Parenthood, Eleanor Roosevelt, and Frank Lloyd Wright.

Chafee's high school years were spent at the Parker School in Chicago, then on to Bennington College in Vermont, earning a bachelor's degree in visual arts, and in 1960 a master's degree from Yale's Graduate School of Art and Architecture. Upon graduation from Yale, Chafee stayed in New England working for a veritable who's who in mid-twentieth-century American architecture: Paul Rudolph, The Architects Collaborative (TAC), Eero Saarinen, and Edward Larabee Barnes. For three years she had her own practice with projects in New York, Massachusetts, Connecticut, and Pennsylvania, before the frustration of cutthroat competitiveness and perhaps a longing for the stark beauty of the desert helped to form her decision to return to Tucson in 1970. She opened a small "atelier" doing primarily residential work and quickly built a national reputation for synthesizing modern design ideology with a critical understanding of the desert's indigenous qualities.

She traveled extensively throughout her career and in 1977 was awarded the prestigious midcareer National Endowment for the Arts Fellowship to the American Academy in Rome. From 1973 until her death, Chafee also taught architectural design at the University of Arizona, instilling in her students the value of place, climate, and culture. In 1983, she was invested in the AIA College of Fellows—Arizona's first woman so honored.

The Tucson buildings of Judith Chafee are unequaled in their power and originality. She created dynamic spaces through the continuity of inside and outside, expressed the power of the structure, did not use formal references to previous styles, and achieved balance through a limited color and material palette, echoing the modern age and the resilience of the desert.

Glossary of Styles and Terms

Styles

In *A Guide to Architecture in Los Angeles* (Peregrine Smith, 1977), David Gebhard and Robert Winter came to the conclusion that "style is the vocabulary and ultimately the language of architecture, and you can only eliminate it by eliminating architecture itself."

The use of the word "style" will make most practicing architects extremely uncomfortable, a discomfort surely based in modernist ideology, which rejects any sort of historicism, particularly the use of historical vocabularies as a "dress" slipped over a structural frame. In the context of modernism, "style" is defined as something that can be applied or removed and is therefore dishonest. A clear example of this "dishonesty" is the Gothic Revival stone cladding that covers the steel frame of the 1925 Chicago Tribune Tower or, closer to home, the current use of Puebloesque stucco and protruding vigas over wood-framed houses.

It is necessary to consider a redefinition of the word "style" itself, because if we limit its use to only those architectural expressions that are "dressed," then we lack a word to describe *all* architectural character-istics shared by a particular culture, place, and time. Those characteristics must include more than the exterior appearance of buildings to be useful in understanding cultural values. At the core of this kind of definition is the idea that cultural and architectural ideologies are also seen in other features, such as the relationship between form and space; construction technology; climate; geography; economics; and politics as well. It is the plural "ideologies" that results in varied expressions within a particular time and place, reflecting a complex rather than monolithic culture. An interesting feature of our time is the ideological difference between the profession and popular culture.

In most places, communal values determine which structures to retain, whether and how they should be transformed, and which to discard. In considering the value of historic structures, the urban historian Kevin Lynch questioned the wisdom of letting chance determine building preservation. Moreover, he called for an evaluation of the underlying intentions and goals of historic preservation itself, a discourse that is still the focus of heated debate today. In this book, structures were included based on present value—that is, as living parts of the city, on the evidence they yield concerning the values and technologies of the past, and on their usefulness as critical tools for judgment in current practice. A building is a living work, yet sometimes the collective need to freeze time in a physical and tangible example may be paramount to the city's need to change.

The inevitable and invigorating transformation that occurs as imported architectural ideologies come to terms with the conditions of the Sonoran Desert is the gift of immigration. Some of our best architecture comes from the infusion of foreign ideologies into the realities of a harsh and breathtaking landscape. Our best work is also born from innovation within an indigenous tradition, from a reinvention of place based on present conditions. Although several current approaches are in the process of evolving, there are two very interesting areas of practice: one that embraces the best of modernism within the parameters of local climate, material resources, and labor, and another that is concerned with global ecology. At our best, we are a balance of tradition and innovation, preservation and a living environment.

We do not recommend an experience of architecture based on exterior appearance; rather, we outline the characteristics necessary to connect a structure to a particular time, place, and culture. Even though very few buildings fit neatly into one stylistic definition, the examples that follow have been selected for their relative purity. Dates in each section refer to periods in Tucson. Styles and related terms found in Tucson are included here for the reader's convenience, and sources for further information are indicated in the bibliography.

Indigenes, Immigrants, and First Structures (c. 800 B.C.–A.D. 1300s)

In several locations in the Santa Cruz floodplain and the Tucson Basin, archaeologists have found the remains of simple "pit structures" built by the first farmers of the Sonoran Desert between 1200 and 800 B.C. More complex and intensified architectural activity in the Tucson area is presently dated from as early as 800 B.C. in the large villages of the people of the Cienega phase (c. 800 B.C.–A.D. 150). Evidence of round freestanding pit structures, storehouses, communal structures, plazas, and cemeteries was found in their villages along the Santa Cruz River. All of these early architectural forms depended on readily available materials, with the primary impetus to temper the climatic conditions by creating semipermanent shelter. To this end, the "pit structure" made use of the more consistent temperature of the earth, rather than that of the air, by digging into the ground 14 to 18 inches, thus keeping the room warmer in the winter and cooler in the summer. Walls were made by anchoring

Santa Cruz Bend site; aerial view of the early farming village where archaeologists found more than 175 houses dating from 800 B.C. to A.D. 150.

willow saplings into a circle in the earth and gathering them together at the top. The saplings were then covered with smaller plant material or grasses with a cap and base of puddled adobe. At the Santa Cruz Bend site, there is an early example of a structure of identical construction but larger than all of the others and possibly used for communal and ritual purposes.

After A.D. 450, with the introduction of the Hohokam to the Tucson Basin, several new features were added to the existing architectural forms, including ramadas and ball courts. The pit structure and the ramada were the primary built forms; the latter was the center of Hohokam family life, which was mostly spent outdoors. Ramadas were built of sturdy wooden posts and beams, with a shade cover of saguaro ribs and brush. Woven side panels of plant material were occasionally used for additional shade. Initially,

Hohokam pit structures were similar to those of the early agricultural people but later grew in size and complexity, adding heavy center posts and beams across the top. Walls were still made of plant material, but more of the openings in the walls were filled in with handfuls of mud adobe in a true wattle-and-daub method. The inclusion of caliche-rich mud made these structures a little more water resistant.

The most clearly public or communal structures of the Hohokam are the central village plaza, appearing between A.D. 500 and 600, and the ball court, found in most of the major sites beginning about A.D. 800. In contrast to the rectangular shape of the Mesoamerican ball court, the Hohokam courts were large, elliptical depressions surrounded by earthen embankments. The entire playing surface was sometimes worked with mud and caliche plaster to a smooth finish.

Several remarkable architectural changes occurred in the late or Classic period of Hohokam culture. Structures became more rectangular with flat roofs, individual houses were oriented toward a common space or courtyard, and not all structures were dug into the earth. Walls were built of solid materials: coursed or puddled adobe, stones, and pieces of wood for reinforcement. Intermediate posts were still used for extra support for the heavy timber-and-earthen roofs. The size of rooms was based on the length of wooden members available. Walls and interior spaces became higher, and caliche was often used as a water-resistant finish inside and out. Massive rectangular walled forms were grouped into apartment-like complexes often surrounded by an enclosing wall, suggesting a defensive posture.

Another change came with the building of platform mounds and "great houses." Large platform mounds resembling unfinished pyramids began appearing about A.D. 1100. In the Phoenix Basin, these were initially small, round, earthen constructions, which eventually evolved into large rectangular mounds approximately 200 feet long and 25 feet high. Initially, the top of the mound was plastered; at a later date, structures were added to the top. Located along rivers and irrigation systems, these mounds, and their repeated occurrence, suggest that the form had defensive, ritual, and socio-political implications. One of Tucson's platform mounds (see University Indian Ruin, p. 214) was built by filling in an earlier pit structure with earth to create the platform for the upper level. The best example of a great house is located at Casa Grande, about halfway between Tucson and Phoenix.

Mission San Xavier del Bac, c. 1900, Spanish Colonial.

Spanish Colonial (1757–1821)

Spanish occupation and colonization of the Pimería Alta began in the 1700s and ended with Mexican independence in 1821. Settlements along watercourses were of three types: religious missions, military presidios, and civilian pueblos. Missions included a church, a priest's residence, other structures for food or seed storage and preparation, gardens, and quite often a protective wall around the whole compound. The *visita* did not have a resident priest and was usually smaller, sometimes consisting of a single chapel or church.

Unique to the American Southwest are the two formal types of Spanish Colonial churches, which are distinct from each other both in plan and in section. The first type is a single-cell or "shoebox" form, as seen at San José de Tumacacori, 48 miles south of Tucson. The second type is more closely related to the High Baroque Latin cross plan with a transept between the nave and sanctuary, like that at San Xavier del Bac. Although the light source in the single-cell church is typically a transverse clerestory window that illuminates the altar in the morning, Tumacacori does not demonstrate this feature. The light source of the Latin cross form is provided by windows in the transept dome.

Characteristics of Spanish Colonial:

· smooth surfaces of earth-colored or white lime stucco over brick or adobe block

· bell towers, single or paired and usually tiered

· semicircular arches at the main entry and courtyard

· low vaulting or exposed timbers forming the nave ceiling

· dome with windows over the transept

· elaborately painted wood or plaster *retablos*

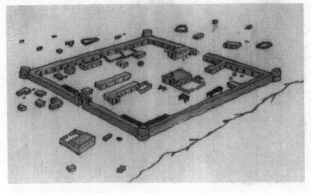

Presidio San Agustín del Tucson, reconstructed view, Spanish Colonial.

Characteristics of Baroque architecture seen at San Xavier:

· contrasting Churrigueresque ornament, especially at the portal and *retablo*

· dynamic interior featuring curved and painted surfaces

Although almost nothing remains, one can imagine the richness of the community at the *visita* of San Agustín del Tucson, now referred to as the "Convento." Because there was no resident priest, this community was something between a mission and a pueblo. The buildings included a granary, houses, kitchens, a tannery, a carpenter shop, a smithy, and areas for other types of industry, as well as a brick church and an enormous structure that was both the priests' residence and an industrial school for the native population. The entire compound and the adjacent orchard were both surrounded by low adobe walls, and the *visita* itself was surrounded by cultivated land.

The Presidio San Agustín del Tucson measured about 900 feet per side with contiguous rooms for storage and quarters built along the interior face of the 2-foot-thick walls, whose parapet created a protected rooftop position for defense against raiding Apaches. The interior was split into two plazas by rectangular blocks of buildings running east to west. Contained within the Presidio were barracks, corrals, a chapel, and a graveyard.

Outside of the Presidio, civilian settlement grew casually. It is clear in the Fergusson Map of Tucson of 1862 (see p. 14) that the pueblo did not follow the more orderly precepts of the Laws of the Indies, especially concerning planning around a plaza. These urban-planning precepts are most apparent in the formation of an urban geography

La Casa Cordova, Sonoran.

of small, compact blocks divided by narrow streets powerfully defined by their contiguous adobe walls. This compact urban form provided the necessary commercial and social amenities, safety from Apache raids, protection from the environment, and privacy within the house or interior yard.

Sonoran: Spanish and Mexican (1850–1890)

The precursor to these massive and contiguous adobe houses was the *jacal* built by Pima, Spanish, and Mexican people as a temporary structure. It was made of small wooden posts and horizontal members with a brush roof. The sides were often filled in with wattle-and-daub or adobe blocks. The roof may have been covered with mud adobe as well.

The early single-room adobe block house in the Sonoran tradition was the basic building unit of the larger urban fabric of barrios. In this tradition, the building is a simple square or rectangle in plan, located at the front property line or street edge and contiguous with adjacent units. Shared walls saved both time and materials. These rows filled the perimeters of blocks, although most corner units housed commercial enterprises: saloon, bakery, or butcher shop. A communal area in the center of the block was used for gardening, livestock, cooking, and outdoor living and was a safe place for its occupants. In the summer, sleeping took place outside or on rooftops. Summer monsoon rains necessitated the use of canales to drain water from the roof, well away from the adobe walls.

The Spanish brought with them a conception of private space that originated in Moorish Spain: Houses expressed the high value Islamic culture placed on the privacy of the home. The planar wall at the street is the absolute dividing line between

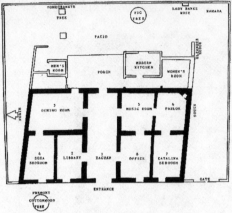

Sosa-Carrillo-Frémont House, typical Sonoran floor plan.

the highly public street and the private home. For the street as a place, this wall was the defining spatial element.

The *zaguán* was originally the entry into the interior of the block, with a gate at the street, through which horses, carriages, and wagons entered and were kept safe from Apache raids. After the defeat of the Apaches in 1886, the *zaguán* was typically enclosed to form a wide central hall that was quite high, some of them 14 to 15 feet, from which the other rooms were entered. These rooms had high ceilings as well, with vents at the top of the walls allowing hot air to rise and escape. Mantas kept insects and dirt from falling onto the occupants.

Examples: Convent Street-scape (p. 99); La Casa Cordova (p. 53). There are no unchanged Sonoran houses; these are the closest examples of a Sonoran house but must be imagined without their later additions, as described under "Transformed Sonoran" below.

Characteristics of the Sonoran house:

· one- or two-room, one-story adobe block either exposed or mud-stuccoed with pounded-dirt floors

· foundation either absent or of stone; may have stone veneer at the exterior wall base

· relatively flat parapeted earthen roof with mud coping supported on vigas with savinas laid crosswise

· canales from the roof penetrating the parapet wall

· hand-hewn lintels, few and small openings, little or no trim, wooden plank doors set back from the face of the building with *reja* at the windows set at the exterior face, no glass

· kitchen often under the back porch or lean-to in the courtyard, which may also include a well, shade trees, outhouse, and a ramada for the eating area

Verdugo House,
Transformed Sonoran.

· fireplaces (corner, adobe) often found in every room except the *zaguán*

Transformed Sonoran (1863–1912)

"Transformed Sonoran" refers to buildings that were modified from the Sonoran as American cultural attitudes and materials began to shape existing structures. The most common change is the addition of a gabled or pyramidal roof, sometimes leaving the canales in place. Arriving in small quantities by wagons, and after 1880 in larger amounts by railroad, came premanufactured building material: bricks for coping, milled lumber for roofs or window and door trim, and tin for roofing membrane.

Examples: Sosa-Carrillo-Frémont House (p. 75); Verdugo House (p. 58); Montijo House (p. 98).

Transitional (c. 1880–1900)

The Transitional style, formerly called "Territorial," is the result of the architectural transformation that occurred as the Sonoran Hispanic traditions began to incorporate non-Hispanic American traditions from the East. The largest impact was felt in changing land-use patterns at the urban scale: from the Hispanic tradition of buildings creating space to the antithetical American emphasis on the building as an object in space. (An excellent analysis of this subject is found in Veregge, "Transformations of Spanish Urban Landscape in the American Southwest, 1821–1900.")

At the scale of the building, Transitional structures incorporate both traditions, identifiable in two periods: The earlier period is noted for its simplicity and use of the Greek Revival pediment, and the later is noted for the use of wooden gabled roofs on adobe walls erected at the time of construction, not as a later addition as in the Transformed Sonoran. The Late Transitional addition of the pitched roof is indicative of at least four changing attitudes: scruples about the civility of the use of the roof as a sleeping area, the perception of a diminished need for a defensive position, a preference for lower maintenance, and, perhaps most important, the desire for a familiar and "non-Hispanic" form.

The Greek Revival style in other parts of the United States began in 1798 with Benjamin Henry Latrobe's Bank of Pennsylvania and was popular until about 1850. In residential examples it was noted for simple volumes with smooth surfaces, low pitched roofs, and trabeated windows; the only external ornament was the pediment over doors and windows. In Tucson, the Greek Revival fused with Sonoran forms and was restricted by minimal means and materials. Although the Greek Revival waned in the East after 1850 because of overuse, imported elements such as the pediment continued to be popular in Tucson until the 1890s, when the Queen Anne style at Armory Park began to supplant them. The use of decorative, applied pediments was a clear example of fashion or perceived cultural identity in architecture. The Late Transitional phase is marked by an even stronger identification with American culture in its preference for freestanding buildings, Victorian architectural elements, and imported landscape material.

Examples: McCleary House (p. 59); Kitt House (p. 118); El Presidio Bed & Breakfast (p. 57).

Characteristics of Early Transitional and Greek Revival:
· building placement at front property line with adjacent units
· walls usually lime-stuccoed rather than exposed adobe block
· expansion of the simple one- or two-room plan into either a *zaguán* or shotgun type

· brick coping at the parapet for buildings with flat roofs

· pyramidal wooden gabled roof with metal sheathing built at the time of construction

· stone veneer, usually "A" Mountain volcanic basalt added to base to stop erosion

· doors set deep but windows and shutters at the exterior face of the wall

· simple wooden trim of milled lumber at windows and doors, use of pediments

· glass added to window openings

Characteristics of Late Transitional:

· whole structure set back from the property line to accommodate the front porch and create zones of separation between public and private

· adobe walls covered with lime stucco

· highly articulated or complex roof forms with deep overhangs for shade

· fired-brick features: coping and chimneys with corbeled tops

· dimensioned lumber used for panel doors, wooden floors, and porches

· sash windows either double hung or divided light, often with leaded glass

· Victorian wooden trim on both the exterior and the interior (lathe-turned balusters and milled-wood brackets supporting roof overhang at top of porch posts)

· landscape material of imported species

American Territorial (c. 1880–1910)

American Territorial was previously called "Anglo-Territorial" and "Anglo-Brick" or "American-Brick." The term "Anglo" was applied to anything non-Hispanic—that is, concepts or materials that were associated with Americans migrating to the Southwest from the East or Midwest. With the arrival of the railroad came not only the

Olcott House,
American Territorial.

American notion of the free-standing pitched-roof house centered in the lot, but an increasing number of prefabricated building materials from bricks and wood to tin roof tiles, ornamental elements, and paint. These houses usually sat on stone foundations with a gabled, pyramidal, or hipped roof. Openings in the walls were topped with either a flat lintel or a segmental arch. Porches consist of wooden floors, rafters, and lathe-turned columns and trim. Dormers and patterned siding on the gables may also be present.

The floor plan in its simplest form is a square in which one corner is devoted to an exterior porch. In more complex examples, the plan may be irregular, with bay projections, and porches may be used to tie an irregular plan together. The major difference between this house form and a Queen Anne is that the Territorial house is simpler in form and is contained under a singular, simple roof. This transplanted structure was not well insulated, thus offering inadequate protection from extreme heat, unlike its adobe predecessor. However, occasionally the porch was located on the south side, providing a passive solar design. "Territorial" refers, too broadly to be clear, to the early years of the period in which Arizona was a territory of the United States, 1853–1912.

Examples: Olcott House (p. 56); McGinty-Laos House (p. 121); Old Main (p. 150).

Characteristics of American Territorial:

· building located at center of lot with front, side, and rear yards
· brick construction, usually on stone foundation
· simple pyramidal roof in residences
· corner porches with turned wooden columns and eave trim
· flat or segmental arched headers at doors and windows

Residence at 228 S. 4th Avenue, Queen Anne Revival.

Queen Anne Revival (1890–1910)

As in the earlier Greek Revival, Tucson versions of Queen Anne seem incredibly mild in comparison with those in almost any other part of the United States. This eclectic style, originating in England, was popularized in America at the Philadelphia Centennial Exposition of 1876 with two houses built by the British government. The style was intended by its creator, Richard Norman Shaw, the most successful English architect of the late nineteenth century, as a picturesque alternative to High Victorian architecture. His desire to suggest country living dovetailed perfectly with the American romantic ideal of the manor house, a beautiful object at the center of an estate. Multiple porches and bay windows reinforce the notion of the house as a freestanding object, not a piece of the urban fabric, and it is here that the greatest impact may be felt in Tucson as these houses step back even farther from the street and from the Hispanic urban form. Gradient layers of privacy begin at the front: from a low fence at the public sidewalk to a planted front yard and then to the porch, acting as the final transitional space before entry into the privacy of the home.

The seemingly endless list of features of the Queen Anne, noted below, reflects the taste for variety and multiplicity that is common in the picturesque. In Tucson, the examples are very modest in their variety but even more so in scale due to the economic burden of importing the majority of building materials from great distances by rail.

One important feature developed by Shaw and faintly echoed in the Tucson examples is the spaciousness of the interior, accomplished by means of large openings connecting rooms to the central hall. In addition, diagonal walls in parlors and

Roskruge House, Queen Anne Revival floor plan.

dining rooms give these houses a feeling of dynamic interior space.

Despite the name, the style did not originate in, or revive architecture from, the reign of Queen Anne.

Examples: Roskruge House (p. 118); Lee-Cutler House (p. 121); Residence at 228 S. 4th Avenue (p. 117).

Characteristics of Queen Anne:

· irregularity of plan
· multiple roof forms of steep pitch
· structure usually brick, sometimes stuccoed
· upper stories projecting beyond ground floor
· vertical elements, such as turrets and paneled or molded chimneys
· wooden verandahs and balconies that wrap around corners
· bay windows, often with leaded glass
· variety of materials, colors, and textures
· diagonal walls used on interior
· small-scale Classical details and elaborate woodwork, especially on the interior

Early-Twentieth-Century Revivals (c. 1900–1930)

The primary period for these revival styles ends about 1930, but there are some notable exceptions in the late work of Roy Place and Josias Joesler. In addition, the use of Pueblo Revival and Spanish Colonial Revival is still seen in residential architecture today.

Neoclassical (1900–1927)

The "Academic Reaction" to provincialism in American architecture began in the mid-1880s, culminating in the spectacular Classical Revival of the 1893 World Columbian Exposition in Chicago. This return to classicism was marked by axial site planning in which buildings of monumental scale

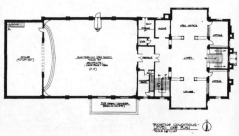

Scottish Rite Cathedral, Neoclassical, facade and main floor plan.

demonstrated an academic understanding of Greek and Roman architecture. This later period of classicism was particularly American, as the corresponding body of work occurred much earlier in Europe. Although cast iron on the interior, the structures in the Court of Honor, the formal core of the master plan, adhered to the following restrictions: They employed a classical vocabulary, they had uniform height, and their plaster was painted white, whereas other buildings that would also prove to be influential—Sullivan's Transportation Building or Brown's Mission-style California Building—were located elsewhere and were quite different in expression.

Defined by symmetry in plan and in the principal facade, the building exhibited a preference for the Greek orders and Roman monumental scale. The building was often on a raised base dominated by a porch or entry

feature supported by columns. The roof was often hidden behind a parapet, and domes were often used. Rich and durable materials such as marble appeared in a variety of building types from religious and civic structures to commercial buildings and residences.

Examples: Scottish Rite Cathedral (p. 108); Carnegie Free Library (p. 109); El Paso & Southwestern Railroad Depot (p. 72); Arizona State Museum (p. 153). The 1899 Kitt House (p. 118) straddles the definitions of the earlier Transitional Greek Revival and the later Neoclassical style.

Characteristics of Neoclassical:
· use of classical proportions and forms with symmetrical facade
· use of pediments, columns with capitals, domes, and Roman or semicircular arches
· frequent use of a raised base

Corbett House,
California
Mission Revival.

California Mission Revival (c. 1895–1930)

Commonly called Mission Revival, this work is based on the architecture of the California missions. It is an interesting example of a formal style based on a vernacular tradition that is itself the result of an earlier adaptation to place that occurred during Spanish colonization. The notion of using the mission as a source of inspiration can be traced in large part to A. Page Brown's California Building for the 1893 World Columbian Exposition in Chicago. The enormous pavilion had most of the features associated with the missions *and* a classical portico on the west elevation, which at first seems peculiar but was in fact featured on the Santa Barbara Mission (1812–1820), based on an illustration from a Spanish edition of Vitruvius in the possession of one of the priests. The other features that seem odd in Brown's version are the "Moorish" dome with its flared base, the Islamic windows, and the rooftop garden with exotic plants instead of a courtyard. The dominant characteristic is the curvilinear pediment forming the gable end of a low-pitched, clay-tiled roof. Also familiar are the semicircular arcades set in smooth white walls. The Mission Revival was quickly replaced by the more elaborate Spanish Colonial Revival.

Examples: Steinfeld Mansion (p. 56); Corbett House (p. 55).

Characteristics of California Mission Revival:

· building set back on site; first floor often above grade and symmetrical in plan

· smooth stucco walls usually painted white

· dominant curved parapet-gable of curvilinear outline

· extensive use of arches, usually semicircular and free of moldings

· in larger buildings, towers or

Pima County Courthouse,
Spanish Colonial Revival.

turrets topped with domes or pyramidal tiled roofs
· clay-tiled roofs of low pitch, either hipped or stopped at ends of shaped gables
· projecting eaves with exposed rafter ends
· balconies
· open porches or porticos with square or rectangular piers
· impost (wall between the arches) marked by a string course at the spring line of the arch
· interiors with wooden floors, white walls, and wooden trim; cabinetry, wainscoting, and stair rails characterized by flat, narrow pieces of unarticulated wood, contrasting with white or off-white walls

Spanish Colonial Revival (1918–1940)

Spanish Colonial Revival is quite similar to, but usually more elaborate than, Mission Revival, especially in the addition of the decorated entry portal, colorful ceramic tile, and the use of ornamental wrought iron. This slightly later revival was the product of the influence of Bertram Goodhue's California State Building of 1913–1915 at the Panama-California Exposition in San Diego, which in all probability was visited by many Tucsonans. Goodhue's model was the Spanish Colonial church of Mexico, not the California mission church. Closer to the center of Spanish government in the New World, Mexican churches benefited from financial resources only dreamed of by the priests of the California missions. As in the Mission Revival, courtyard plans, loggias or pergolas, and gardens create outdoor rooms within the walls of the building, and the bell tower is often used as a vertical landmark.

Examples: Veterans Affairs Medical Center (p. 242); Benedictine Sanctuary (p. 191); Safford Junior High School (p. 119).

St. Michael's and All Angels Episcopal Church, Pueblo Revival.

Characteristics of Spanish Colonial Revival:

· plan featuring courtyards usually open on one side, sometimes pergolas to the garden

· walls usually broad expanses of smooth stucco

· elaborate entry with carved or cast ornament and columns

· bell towers and domes in civic or religious structures

· clay-tiled roofs

· openings usually trabeated but occasionally employing arches

· balconies with iron railings

· window grilles (reja) of wrought iron or wood

Pueblo Revival (c. 1928–1953)
This twentieth-century style is often called "Santa Fe" because it was invented to attract tourists to Santa Fe, New Mexico, after the railroad bypassed the town in 1912 and the population began a rapid and frightening decline. The most influential architects of this style, Isaac Hamilton Rapp

and John Gaw Meem, admired the forms and tactile qualities of the multi-storied pueblos at Laguna and Taos. The vernacular form, with its casual additive nature, was translated into an applied "style" of formal designs, which combined aesthetic qualities of the Pueblo with Spanish elements such as the portal and American building technology such as brick or wood frame.

One of the earliest structures in this style is the now-familiar 1909–1913 remodeling of the Santa Fe Palace of Governors, originally built in 1610. What is less well known is that the archaeologist Jesse Nusbaum chose to ignore the Victorian and territorial Greek Revivals of the original building and "restored" it to an invented image of an earlier period. The new "restoration" was built of brick and stuccoed, with a portal of round wooden columns supporting curvilinear brackets and a stuccoed parapet with exposed vigas. Soon to follow was Rapp's 1915 version of the Spanish Colonial church San Esteban at Acoma (1629–1639) in the form of the New Mexico building at the Panama-California Exposition in San Diego, California. It was a wood frame building covered with stucco. Rapp then used this same design, in brick and stucco, for the 1916 Fine Arts Museum in Santa Fe.

Pueblo Revival has remained a popular residential style in Tucson and elsewhere for its picturesque and romantic qualities: stepped forms in earth-colored stucco, battered walls, flat roofs with rounded and stepped parapets, simple window openings, exposed viga ends creating dramatic shadows, and portales with wooden brackets as capitals. It was created as and remains an applied style quite removed from the people, the place, and the technology of the pueblos. Only two characteristics make it appropriate for Tucson:

the thick walls and the limited window area, which both reduce solar heat gain.

Example: St. Michael's and All Angels Episcopal Church (p. 212).

Characteristics of Pueblo Revival:
· earth-colored stucco on adobe, brick, or wood structure
· battered walls
· flat roofs with rounded and stepped parapets
· vigas, exposed and more often decorative than structural
· portales with wooden bracket capitals
· small and simple vertical rectangles or squares for window openings

Bungalow and Craftsman (1900–1940)

The English bungalow house appealed to Americans for several reasons. The form could be easily adapted to various climatic conditions and was especially good at sheltering its inhabitants

Bungalow.

from sun and rain while providing spacious porch areas that captured cooling breezes and created deep shade. It must have seemed a refreshingly simple design in comparison with that of the Victorian or Queen Anne. Because the house was easy to construct, it quickly became a standard in lightweight wood-frame construction and was affordable for many Americans.

The appeal of this house form to warmer climates such as California and Arizona is no surprise given its origins as a house built to provide temporary shelter during the monsoons in India. (The words "bungalow" and "verandah" are both derived from Hindustani.) The house form, carried to England by returning British colonial administrators and translated into an English country house, was further developed in America. Second only to the cooling porch, the generous attic vents, allowing built-up heat to

escape, were particularly useful in Tucson, providing a distinct advantage before the era of mechanical cooling systems.

The bungalow was so accessible to Americans through numerous publications such as *The Craftsman* (1901–1916) and other architectural or home magazines, the sale of inexpensive sets of working drawings, and mail-order catalog kits that its vocabulary soon became part of the vernacular. One could even order a house from Sears & Roebuck or the Tuxbury Lumber Company that advertised the "Quickbilt" bungalow.

For most middle-class Americans, the bungalow represented the three main points of the Arts and Crafts philosophy embodied in *The Craftsman:* simplicity, harmony with nature, and craftsmanship. The simple, unembellished design with its generous porch and landscaping provided a connection with nature. The interior featured practical built-in cabinets, drawers, and bench seating. Although the interior may seem small and dark today, the evolution of the "parlor" into a spacious and informal "living room" was a new trend that continued to evolve.

The breadth of variations runs from the simplest roofed box to bungalow courts and from the single-story house with a single gable facing the street to two-story houses with perpendicular and multiple gables. The most recognizable form employs two street-facing gables: one covering the roof and another for the porch, which is slightly offset from the house. The most elaborate designs are those of Charles and Henry Greene in California.

Examples: Many variations in West University and Midtown (Sam Hughes); Hinchcliffe Court (p. 62).

Characteristics of Bungalow:
· gabled roof[s] over house and front porch

· partial or full-width porch
· porch roof supported by heavy masonry or concrete piers
· house raised above grade
· exposed wooden rafters
· frequent use of volcanic stone at base and/or for porch piers
· built-in cabinetry

The Western Stick style is a fusion of the Craftsman interest in Japanese wood construction methods, in which the structural system is expressed ("sticks" held together with joinery), and the bungalow form.

Examples: Residence 341 E. 1st Street (p. 145); Hinchcliffe House (p. 61).

Prairie Style and "Wrightian" (1902–1920)

There are a handful of buildings in Tucson that are influenced directly by the early work of Frank Lloyd Wright, illustrating both the earlier phase, usually called Prairie, and the next phase, which looks quite different from

Bray House, Wrightian.

the first and is sometimes called "Wrightian." Unlike every other imported architectural style that took a long time to make its way to Tucson, these arrived very quickly in the person of Henry Trost. The impact of Wright's Prairie philosophy and designs, which emphasized open interior space, is even greater with the later importation of the modern California ranch house by Tucson developers.

The two most distinctive features of the Prairie-style house, in contrast to most houses of the period, are its horizontality and its open interior floor plan. The relatively low exterior profile is created by rectilinear massing and planar forms covered by a hipped or gabled roof with deep overhangs. Exterior elevations feature contrasting material or color on walls that are usually brick or stucco and windows that are divided into patterned panes rather than single sheets of glass. The interior spaces are open to

one another and often surround a central utility core and massive fireplace.

The later "Wrightian" forms were modeled on his 1906 Unity Temple, which was similar to the Prairie house in its massing but was distinguished by flat projecting roofs that extend over the walls while the parapet continues above the roof. In addition, a repeated bas-relief ornament was cast into the face of the concrete piers that stood in between the leaded-glass windows. Trost employed similar massing, flat roofs, parapets, and Sullivan-esque ornament in plaster bas-relief.

Examples: Goodrich House (p. 139); Hereford House (p. 58); Bray House (p. 179); Lincoln House (p. 119).

Characteristics of Prairie:
· frequently, a symmetrical plan
· thick brick walls, often stuccoed
· strong horizontal lines

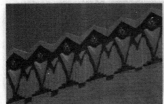
Fox-Tucson Theatre, Art Deco detail.

New Art Deco facade on an older house.

· understated front door (hidden behind porch), often with leaded and colored glass
· interiors with contrasting white (dusty green, burnt orange, gold) walls and natural-finish wood trim in Mission style, built-in closets, cupboards, and bookshelves

Characteristics of "Wrightian":
· asymmetrically balanced plan
· gabled or flat slab roof with deep overhang and projecting cornice
· Sullivanesque ornament sometimes present

Art Deco: Includes Zigzag and Streamline Moderne (1925–1950)

Art Deco takes its name from the pavilions and exhibits of the 1925 Exposition Inernationale des Arts Décoratifs et Industriels Modernes in Paris; its influences were as diverse as the European decorative arts (the tendency of which was to consider all parts and surfaces of a building as decorative elements, usually employing biomorphic forms) and those modern prototypes that were less curvilinear and more geometric, employing bas-relief ornament on planar forms with an eye toward machine production.

Art Deco buildings typically emphasize verticality through multifaceted forms made up of smooth surfaces with low-relief ornament at the entrance and base, the top of building walls, and the spandrels of skyscrapers. Consisting of neo-Egyptian design motifs or patterns or stylized zigzags and chevrons, these ornamental pieces were repeated elements and often employed an overall symmetrical composition. Color is used more often on the inside, where murals, lamps, carpets, curtains, walls, and ceilings are richly decorated. The style was popularized by many architects, including Bertram Goodhue, Eliel

Tucson High Magnet School Vocational Education Building, Streamline Moderne.

Saarinen, and Frank Lloyd Wright, but is perhaps best recognized today in the 1928–1930 Chrysler Building in New York City.

Streamline Moderne, a later variation of Art Deco, belongs largely to the 1930s and is often seen in Public Works Administration (PWA) projects. The Moderne style is characterized by an emphasis on horizontal lines, which suggested movement by the use of rounded, continuous forms associated with new designs for trains, luxury ocean liners, and airplanes.

Even though there are relatively few examples of this style in Tucson, they are surprisingly varied: a simple Zigzag facade, a lavishly elaborate theater, and a good example of the Streamline Moderne.

Examples: Fox-Tucson Theatre (p. 83); Residence 521 E. University (p. 139); Tucson High Magnet School Vocational Education Building (p. 126).

Characteristics of Art Deco:
· vertical emphasis in form and detail
· stepped or faceted forms (not simple volumes)
· bas-relief ornament at entry and top of building
· all interior elements lavishly decorated and richly colored

Characteristics of Zigzag:
· simple stucco forms
· ornamentation of zigzags, chevrons, sunbursts, spirals

Characteristics of Streamline Moderne:
· horizontal emphasis in form and detail
· simple forms with rounded corners and parapets
· round portal windows and horizontal rails (steamship elements)
· use of glass block

College Shop, demolished 2001, International.

Modern (1945–)

It may be useful to think about modernism as a continuum in three phases: European Inception (c. 1900–1930), International (c. 1945–), and Critical Regionalism (c. 1980–). In reality, the origins for the last phase lie with Le Corbusier at about the same time as the second phase began, but his work from that period was not recognized or emulated until the next generation. In addition, the International style was primarily an American invention, which then spread internationally.

Modernism began before the turn of the twentieth century with the use of industrial materials and systems in architecture, but the major period of innovation and development by European architects occurred between the two world wars. At the heart of early modernist ideology was the absolute rejection of the lingering nineteenth-century aesthetic of

historicism—the recycling ad nauseam of historical styles, in particular Greek, Roman, and Gothic—when it was becoming increasingly obvious that an iron or steel structure and prefabrication were much more efficient in both material and labor costs and could be beautiful in their own right.

Although each of the primary architects associated with this monumental shift in design theory—Walter Gropius, Ludwig Mies van der Rohe, and Le Corbusier—had a personal agenda in regard to the purposes, meaning, and uses of architecture, the opinions that they shared resulted in similar formal expressions, which then led to the misunderstanding, in the International phase, of their work as a new "style" in the applied sense. Any shared sense of social responsibility or of being visionaries in a new epoch was largely ignored by the promoters of the formal International style

Tucson General Hospital, Modern.

in America. But it was primarily world politics that helped spread modernism to this country as many of the leading practitioners and educators fled Germany during and after World War II. With Gropius directing the Graduate School of Design at Harvard University and Mies van der Rohe in a similar position at the Illinois Institute of Technology, the next generation of American architects was schooled in the founding ideals of the Modern movement.

In 1932, at the Museum of Modern Art in New York City, Philip Johnson, director of the department of architecture, and the architectural historian H. R. Hitchcock presented the work of European modernist architects to the American public in an exhibition entitled "International Style." In this formalist presentation, one saw work stripped of historical association: There were no pitched roofs, no applied ornament, and no symmetrical facades. Material texture and color sat in for ornament. Spatially, the work was dynamic, eliminating the distinction between outside and inside, and planes were used to demarcate areas, not confine static rooms. In Le Corbusier's definition of the "Machine Aesthetic," structure is expressed and celebrated, as in the example of Gropius's clear glass curtain wall at the Bauhaus, which reveals the concrete structure inside. Le Corbusier's seemingly dismissive attitude toward varying climatic conditions—"one building for all climates"—was promoted, yet he himself recognized and addressed the problem in his design for the Salvation Army Hostel (1929–1933) in Paris. Johnson, Hitchcock, and Mies van der Rohe, who built many glass-walled buildings in America, were not concerned about the use of unrenewable resources to fuel building heat gain or loss because it wasn't yet identified as a

Ramada House, Modern.

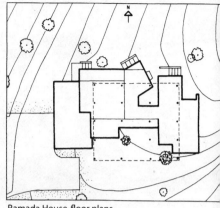

Ramada House, floor plans.

problem in the booming postwar American economy.

The core issue of the third phase of modernism, Critical Regionalism, is the synthesis of European modernist intentions with the cultural, geographical, and climatic concerns of a particular place; thus, this style will produce different formal expressions depending on locale. In some ways, it represents a dissatisfaction with the loss of time and place created by the International style, not only in this country but as it spread worldwide. In Tucson, the response to the harsh sunlight and generally constrained economics has led to some intelligent and innovative solutions.

In a survey of any current text on modernism, Tucson (and Phoenix) is conspicuously absent, with the singular exception of Judith Chafee's Ramada House (p. 244). Indeed, there are no "pure" examples of the earliest phase of modernism in Tucson; instead, a style that originated as the result of enormous social, technological, and political change in Europe is here transformed. Examples: Tucson General Hospital (p. 184); Ramada House (p. 244).

Example of the International style: Transamerica Office Building (p. 81).

Examples of Critical Regionalism: Arizona-Sonora Desert Museum Restaurant and Art Gallery (p. 250); Studio at 400 S. Rubio Alley (p. 101).

Characteristics of International:
· no adaptation to site, "one building for all climates"
· abstract and asymmetrical classicism in form and proportioning systems
· machine aesthetic: expressed structure, use of cantilever
· curtain wall of steel frame and glass on vertical skyscraper or horizontal pavilion

Arizona-Sonora Desert Museum Restaurant and Art Gallery, Critical Regionalism.

· ground floor often open, or lobby only, with building appearing to be raised on stilts

· no formal facade or public "face"

· smooth stucco or curtain wall

· flat roofs

· dynamic spatial arrangement

· extensive use of glass to blur distinction between inside and outside, often with flush-glazed corner detail

· no applied ornament: material color and texture used for variety or articulation

Characteristics of Critical Regionalism in Tucson:

· orientation of building along east/west axis, glass on south/southeast face with adequate roof overhang for passive solar design

· vertical shading structures on east and west faces

· thick and/or heavily insulated walls and roofs

· flat roofs used with bearing wall structures

· texture and color of local materials expressed

· form may adapt to site (or cultural precedent)

· use of courtyard form

· use of natural ventilation

Ranch House (1935–1970s)

It is primarily the California architect Cliff May who should be credited with the creation of the modern ranch house, as he was both designer and promoter of a house form that would accommodate and encourage the kind of familial closeness and hospitality that was part of early Californian Hispanic culture. May based his designs on nineteenth-century California adobe haciendas or ranchos, which were L- or U-shaped in plan, thus creating a courtyard that was in many ways the primary living space of the house. The buildings hugged the ground, with low-pitched roofs and rather understated front

Brown Residence, Ranch House.

facades of simple vertical openings. The relatively open interiors were most probably the influence of the Prairie-style house by Frank Lloyd Wright. May designed many houses in San Diego and Los Angeles in the 1930s that were subsequently published in *Sunset* magazine, but it was in the late 1940s postwar housing boom that the style was exported to other western states and evolved into the more common linear form associated with the popularity of the automobile and the larger lot sizes of suburban residential neighborhoods.

Typically, these single-story houses are low in profile and horizontal in expression, so that the mass of the house is visible from the street. They include highly visible garages, usually part of the house and often under the same roof. In addition, they feature a "drive-through" driveway, which displays the car as a status symbol. The ranch house probably arrived in Tucson via a Phoenix developer of tract housing.

Examples: Colonia Solana and El Encanto Estates in Midtown.

Characteristics of Ranch House:

· expansive front yard (often with a lawn) accentuating the size and horizontality of the single-story house

· exterior walls of fired adobe block, brick, stucco, or wood siding

· very low roof pitch with overhangs

· porches under the main roof of shingle or clay tile

· horizontal or large "picture" windows with decorative shutters

· sliding glass doors connecting to covered outdoor living areas

· minimal or no windows in east/west walls, limiting solar heat gain

· informal interior arrangement of open spaces with low ceilings

Main Post Office,
Brutalism.

· often combined with materials or details from other styles (for example, Spanish Colonial Revival)

Perfect Arizona Type (PAT) House (1950s–1960s)

This Tucson derivative of the ranch house was used by developer/builder Robert Lusk and is characterized by open and flexible floor plans, low pitched roofs with deep overhangs, and, sometimes, passive solar orientation on the lot. In the living and dining areas, ceilings are open to the underside of the roof with the gable end glazed above the line of the wall, which is usually built of burnt adobe or concrete block.

Example: Indian Ridge Estates (p. 213).

Brutalism (1970s)

As is the case with many stylistic periods in architecture, there is often an early formative period soon followed by codification. The young generation of British architects who coined the term "New Brutalism" were deeply disillusioned by the bland and provincial public housing that was promoted and built after the devastation of World War II. Their hope was to regain the critical edge and power of modern architecture that they perceived had evaporated with the war.

Peter Smithson and his wife, Alison, leaders of the younger generation of British architects, began their work in 1949 with the design of the Hunstanton School, developing a kind of architecture that they described as an "ethic not an aesthetic"—that is, an attitude, not a formal dictum.

Ironically, and based on the work of the Smithsons, the term was then applied to architecture in Britain that was monumental in scale and used very rough concrete as its structural and finish material. The work of Le Corbusier was the precursor, as in his 1946–1952 Unité d'Habitation in Marseilles, which was the first use of the *béton brut,* or poured-in-place concrete, in which the impression of the formwork is expressed, illustrating both process and material qualities. This style became popular as a revolt against the sterile monotony of the corporate International style spawned by Mies van der Rohe's glass skyscrapers.

In later examples of Brutalism, the building is seen as a bold and masculine monumental piece of sculpture. Paul Rudolph, architect and chairman of the Department of Art and Architecture at Yale University from 1958 to 1964, was the leading practitioner of this style in America and a source of inspiration and instruction to the next generation of architects.

Examples: Pima Community College, West Campus (p. 171); Tucson Museum of Art (p. 52); University of Arizona Main Library (p. 162); Main Post Office (p. 241).

Characteristics of Brutalism:
· variety in form as a result of the plasticity of cast-in-place concrete
· exposed structural concrete with very rough texture
· expression of infill panels, often in another material such as brick
· support systems of pipes, vents, and ducts often exposed in the interior

Terms

Note: Terms derived from Spanish are indicated by "Sp"; those from Arabic are indicated by "Ar"; "fr." = "from."

acanthus A plant with thick scalloped leaves used as the model for Corinthian and Composite capitals.

acequia [Sp, fr. Ar] Water channel or ditch; used to divert water from the existing rivers and arroyos for daily use and irrigation.

acroterium/acroteria Pedestal situated at the apex and ends of a pediment, often fan-shaped and used to support ornaments or statues.

adobe [Sp, fr. Ar] The word "adobe" has several meanings. It is most commonly used to refer to large molded and sun-dried blocks of clayey mud and water and may include a binder such as manure or straw. The term is also used for the mud mixture itself when used as mortar or for building walls, as in **puddled adobe,** which is set in "puddles" and left to dry, eventually building up to form a wall. In contrast, **adobe masonry** uses blocks set in mortar and is often covered with a mud plaster made water resistant through the addition of caliche or lime.

"A" Mountain stone Volcanic basalt rock from Sentinal Peak, now called "A" Mountain.

arcade Series of arches.

arroyo [Sp] A desert wash, dry except after rainfall, when it can become a torrential river.

baluster/balustrade The supporting vertical member in a stair or balcony rail, and the row of balusters joined by a top rail.

barrio [Sp, fr. Ar] Neighborhood or district; in Tucson, refers to neighborhoods occupied today, or historically, by people of Hispanic descent.

base course The coursing or horizontal rows of stones or bricks at the base of a building, which may reach as high as the sill of the windows.

bas-relief A shallow sculptural carving projecting from the background of which it is a part.

battered wall A wall that slopes

inward as it rises, becoming narrower toward the top.

bearing wall Supports its own weight and the weight of the roof.

bosque Small forested area.

brick bonding The pattern in which bricks are put together with "headers," describing the small end of the brick, and "stretchers," indicating the length. English bond features alternating rows of stretchers and headers; Flemish bond uses rows with alternating headers and stretchers in each row. A running bond features staggered rows of stretchers.

caliche [Sp for "flake of lime"] Naturally occurring calcium carbonate found in local Tucson soil; used by Hohokam and Salado cultures as a waterproof finish coat on exterior walls and floors and as an admixture in puddled adobe.

canal/canales [Sp] Rolled-tin pipe or channel used to drain water from adobe roofs in Sonoran structures, projecting through the parapet and often decorated by a flared opening with ornamental pieces perpendicular to the opening.

cantera [Sp for "quarry"] The word is used in Mexico to denote any type of quarried stone, but in Tucson the term is most often associated with the soft, light-colored volcanic stone with dark speckles that is also called "tufa." Still quarried in Mexico and imported to Tucson.

capital The top or crown of a column. See also **Greek orders**.

caryatid A female figure used as a column to support part of a building.

Churrigueresque A term derived from the elaborately decorated Spanish style of the seventeenth-century Churriguera family, many of whom were architects. This term is also used to describe Late Baroque architecture in Spain, Mexico, and the Americas.

clear aluminum Neither colored nor coated.

clerestory/clearstory From "clear story," windows above the ground-floor level; often seen in the upper part of the nave walls of a church.

coping Cap or cover on a parapet wall used to protect it from water damage; usually made of brick, tile, metal, or concrete.

corbel A brick or stone that projects beyond the one below it.

corbeled table A range or row of arched corbels running just below the eaves of a roof, usually at the gable ends.

Corinthian See **Greek orders**.

cornice From Classical architecture, the top projecting section of the roof. Usually ornamented, this projecting molding of any material occurs along the top of the building, wall, or arch.

courtyard An area open to the sky and enclosed by walls or building; commonly found in Mediterranean, Latin American, and other cultures in arid lands.

cruciform Cross-shaped; characteristic plan for Christian churches formed by the intersection of the nave with the transept.

cupola Small domed structure on top of a dome or roof used to provide light or air to the space below.

curtain wall An exterior non–load-bearing wall that is attached or hung from an internal steel or concrete structural frame and made from any of a variety of materials, including glass or metal alloys (e.g., aluminum, steel, titanium).

dentils Small square blocks of material that alternate with a space of the same size in a linear pattern; seen in Classical architecture, usually at the roofline.

dogtooth Brick turned at a 45-degree angle, which can produce a deep shadow.

Doric See **Greek orders.**

dormer A small structure built on top of a pitched roof with a perpendicular roof of its own; usually used for light, ventilation, and sleeping area in the attic, hence its name.

egg-and-dart molding A decorative band based on alternating eggs and arrowheads found in Classical architecture.

elevation A drawing of the walls of one side of a building, either interior or exterior, with all lines drawn to a scale to show true vertical and horizontal dimension; also used in reference to the vertical plane of a building, as in the "west elevation."

English or Flemish bond See **brick bonding.**

estípites [Sp] A stack of square balusters with a capital on top.

facade The "face" or public front of a building.

flush-glazed A window detail, usually at the corner, in which there are no structural members (**mullions**) supporting the glass.

form/formal The shape and structure of something as distinguished from its substance or material.

gable The triangle-shaped upper part of the end walls in a structure with a pitched roof.

Greek orders A structural system used by the Greeks that employed

columns in three main forms: The Doric is the shortest in width-to-height proportion, the column is fluted, and the capital is a simple curved-disk shape. The Ionic is more slender, also uses a fluted column on a base, but has a more elaborate capital with volutes or curved shapes on either side. The Corinthian is often large in scale and has the most elaborate capital, covered with acanthus leaves terminating in small volutes at the four upper corners.

impost The block that the foot of an arch rests upon; the line of those blocks.

infill The act of building on a vacant lot within an otherwise developed area or neighborhood.

Ionic See **Greek orders.**

jacal [Sp, fr. Nahuatl] A structure similar to a ramada, but with walls of lightweight brush or mud.

latillas [Sp] The more common term for slender wooden poles or twigs, such as saguaro ribs or ocotillo branches, placed across vigas upon which an earthen roof is applied in traditional Sonoran construction. Also called **savinas.**

Laws of the Indies Compilation of decrees by the Spanish monarchy beginning in 1501 to control the campaign of Spanish colonization in the New World, including guidelines for the establishment of new towns whose planning principles reflected the Roman model of an urban grid with a center defined by the open space or plaza around which the major civic and religious structures would stand.

loggia A roofed open gallery or walkway within the form of the building, usually with a wall on one side and columns or posts on the other.

lunette Opening in a wall in a half moon shape, with the flat surface downward.

majolica A ceramic glaze used on pottery and tile in which bright colors are applied to a white base coat.

malpais [Sp] Basaltic lava stone.

manta [Sp] A cloth ceiling used to hide an exposed Sonoran roof system and to prevent insects or dirt from falling.

Miesian Referring to elements characteristic of the work of the Modern architect Ludwig Mies van der Rohe.

mission A complex comprising a church, residence, and school for the purpose of converting the local population and administered by a resident priest.

"Moorish" style/character See **Mudéjar**.

Mudéjar [Sp, fr. Ar] Refers to subjugated Moors living in Christian Spain during the Reconquest, as well as the Islamic architectural characteristics in Christian buildings in Spain and its colonies.

mullion A slender vertical member supporting a piece of glass or wood in a window or door.

nave The main rectangular volume running lengthwise in a church, frequently oriented east-west.

nine-square plan A floor plan based on nine squares, three rooms wide in each direction.

Palladian motif The pattern of windows made popular by the Renaissance architect Andrea Palladio. There are three windows:

The central window has a semicircular arch, and the two side windows, usually narrower than the central window, have a flat head at the spring line of the arch. Also used for attic vents, entry doors, and other features.

parapet Extension of the exterior wall (horizontal, stepped, or curved) above the roof; conceals the roof and often is capped with brick or tile.

passive solar design One of the simplest and oldest forms of adaptation to intense heat, originally used by Native Americans of the Southwest in their cliff dwellings. Relies on an overhanging horizontal element on the south side; the high sun angle in the summer is blocked by the overhang, whereas the lower winter sun angle brings heat into the living area. Insulation and the absence of glass in the east and west faces of a structure deflect interior heat gain caused by the lower angle of the sun in the morning and evening.

patio Outdoor area of contemporary houses, often covered and usually in the back.

pediment Low pitched gable above a portico, also above windows or doors, forming a triangle or the curved segment of a circle.

pergola Covered walkway in a garden. Beams are supported by columns or posts, and plants often are grown on the sides and top. See also **loggia**.

piloti/pilotis Term coined by architect Le Corbusier to denote slender supports seen in a building where the principal floor is above an open ground level.

pit structure Associated with the

prehistoric southwestern cultures, usually a single-room structure dug into the earth to about 12 to 18 inches, supported with wood poles and enclosed with **wattle-and-daub** rising above ground level.

planar Describing a two-dimensional surface, as in a plane.

plaster Exterior or interior finish coat on walls; on adobe masonry, mud plaster has little resistance to water, but when combined with caliche or lime the plaster is water resistant while allowing the wall of organic materials to "breathe."

portal/portales [Sp] A doorway, gate, entrance hall, or colonnaded passageway.

porte cochere From the French, porch (for) coaches, large enough to drive up and drop off passengers under a roof.

portico Porch; term usually used in reference to Greek temples.

post and beam A structure that uses posts (vertical members) and beams (horizontal members), usually of wood, to support a roof structure; also called **trabeated**.

presidio [Sp] A walled garrison containing living quarters and various types of buildings.

puddled adobe See **adobe**.

pueblo [Sp] Settlement, town, or people; Spanish reference to both traditional Native American communities and Spanish new towns.

quoins Originally large stones expressed at the corners of buildings; later imitated in stucco.

ramada [Sp] A post-and-beam shade structure open on all four sides and covered with lightweight brush and sometimes mud.

reja [Sp] Grillwork of iron or wood

at an unglazed window opening, providing security and ventilation; sometimes decorative.

retablo [Sp] A decorative structure of wood or plaster behind or above an altar in Spanish Colonial churches whose purpose was to form a frame for holy statues and paintings of religious figures; often elaborately painted in rich colors and gold leaf.

Romanesque Medieval style of architecture characterized by solid and massive stone forms with round arches.

sala [Sp] Living room or parlor; in Sonoran row houses, it is the basic multipurpose unit of interior space.

sanctuary The most sacred, and usually most remote or protected, part of a church, temple, or mosque.

savinas [Sp] See **latillas**.

segmental arch An arch that is a segment of a circle.

spandrel/spandrel panels Originally applied to the triangular wall space between arches in an arcade or facade, the term is now used in modern buildings to describe the space between floors that is spanned or covered with an opaque material such as brick, terra cotta, concrete, or even glass—thus "spandrel glass."

spring line The horizontal line between the base of an arch and its support.

strawbale house Use of bales of straw, usually to form the exterior (load-bearing) walls of a house. Straw's high insulative value is ideal in hot climates and especially those with diurnal temperature ranges of 30 degrees or more. In addition, the material is an agricultural waste product, easy to work with, and relatively inexpensive.

string course A protruding and continuous molding (often in brick) used to accentuate a horizontal line in an exterior wall; a base, a floor line, the spring line of a row of arches, etc.

stucco Cement plaster used as a weatherproofing coat and sometimes to decorate walls.

Sullivanesque Referring to the decorative ornamentation style of Louis Sullivan (1890–1930), seen in bas-relief terra cotta or plaster. The characteristics include naturalistic foliage combined with geometric shapes and other repetitive motifs; in Tucson, this is found in the architecture of Henry Trost.

terra cotta Cast clay, which is then fired and sometimes glazed; often used for decorative ornamentation on building facades.

toldo [Sp] Lightweight wooden shade structure attached to a Sonoran house above doors and windows and braced with two supports into the wall.

trabeated Referring to a structural system that uses straight horizontal beams and vertical posts, columns, or piers.

transept The section of a cruciform church whose axis crosses that of the nave; sometimes thought of as the "arms" in the figure of the cross.

transom window A window above a door.

vernacular Using architectural forms and materials native to a period or place; usually transmitted through example or practice, rather than obtained through association with academic or foreign sources.

viga/vigas [Sp] Round or rectangular

Sullivanesque detailing on the Second Owl's Club.

wooden beams used to support a flat roof; sometimes exposed on the exterior.

visita A missionary complex similar to a mission that did not have a resident priest—rather, one who "visited."

volute A loosely spiraling scroll.

voussoir The wedge-shaped cut stones or bricks that make an arch.

wattle-and-daub An infill wall in a post-and-beam structure made up of a weave of plant material (wattle) with mud filling in the small holes and forming an exterior plaster (daub).

zaguán [Sp, fr. Ar] Covered entrance hall leading from the street into a courtyard; eventually these were enclosed, creating a spacious semipublic room from which other rooms are entered.

Bibliography

This bibliography is a selected list to direct the reader to the sources used for this publication as well as further reading on Tucson architecture. In addition to the following sources, we relied on the extensive information available from the unpublished materials of the National Register of Historic Places nominations, available from the Arizona State Historic Preservation Office; the collections of the Arizona Historical Society; and the collections of the Arizona Architectural Archives, College of Architecture, Planning and Landscape Architecture, University of Arizona.

Sources on Architects

Brown, Arthur
Arthur T. Brown: Architect, Artist, Inventor. Compiled by Kathryn M. Wayne. Tucson: College of Architecture Library, University of Arizona, 1985. Contains comprehensive bibliography.

Burns and Wald-Hopkins/Antoine Predock
Kroloff, Reed. "Desert Education: Ventana Vista Elementary School, Tucson, Arizona." *Architecture,* Vol. 84, No. 3 (March 1995), pp. 58–67.

Chafee, Judith
Chafee, Judith. "The Region of the Mindful Heart." *Artspace,* Spring 1982, pp. 27–33.
Cheek, Lawrence. *Judith Chafee.* Tucson: Civitas Sonoran, 1999.
"A Desert House Revives Its Region's Traditional Forms." *Architectural Record,* February 1979, pp. 107–110. (Ramada House.)
Freeman, Allen. "Reinterpreting Regionalism: Arizona: Three Architects Who Respect the Desert Terrain and Traditions." *Architecture,* Vol. 73, No. 3 (March 1984), pp. 114–119.
"Streamlined Majesty." *Phoenix Home and Garden,* November 1993, pp. 39–43. (Rieveschl House.)

Gresham, James
"James A. Gresham: Works." *Architecture and Urbanism,* Vol. 134, No. 11 (November 1981), pp. 98–101.

Laudecker, Heidi. "Islands of Learning: Five New U.S. Schools." *Architecture,* Vol. 80, No. 1 (January 1991), pp. 58–71. (Canyon View Elementary School.)

"Patterning Brick." *Architecture,* February 1995, pp. 109–113. (State Office Building and UMC Library.)

Holmes and Holmes
Matthews, Gary David. "Holmes and Holmes Architects, Tucson, Arizona, 1905–1912." Unpublished student paper from the College of Architecture, University of Arizona, 1969.

Jaastad, Henry
McCroskey, Mona Lange. "Henry O. Jaastad: Architect of Tucson's Future." *Smoke Signal,* No. 53 (Spring 1990), pp. 42–53. Tucson: Tucson Corral of the Westerners.

Joesler, Josias
Jeffery, R. Brooks, et al. *Joesler and Murphey: An Architectural Legacy for Tucson.* Tucson: City of Tucson, 1994.

Joy, Rick
Giovannini, Joseph. "Earth Work." *Architecture,* Vol. 87, No. 12 (December 1998), pp. 90–97. (Palmer-Rose House.)

Pearson, Clifford. "In Tucson's Historic Barrio." *Architectural Record,* Vol. 185, No. 4 (April 1997), pp. 70–75. (Convent Avenue Studios.)

"Rick Joy: Convent Avenue Studios, Tucson, Arizona, U.S.A." *GA Houses,* No. 51 (March 1997), pp. 150–157.

"Rick Joy: Palmer-Rose residence, Tucson, Arizona, U.S.A." *GA Houses,* No. 60 (June 1999), pp. 70–79.

"Rick Joy: Osborn Claassen Residence, Tucson, Arizona, U.S.A." *GA Houses,* No. 63 (2000), pp. 140–141.

Underwood, Max. "Rick Joy, Architect: 400 South Rubio, Tucson." *Architecture,* Vol. 89, No. 1 (January 2000), pp. 78–83.

Line and Space/Les Wallach
Crosbie, Mike. *Green Architecture: A Guide to Sustainable Design.* Rockport, Mass.: Rockport Publishers, 1994. (Project Potty.)

"Line and Space in Arizona." *Spazio e Societa/Space and Society,* January–March 1998, pp. 24–28.

"Putting Design Back into Design/ Build." *Progressive Architecture,* December 1995, pp. 60–61.

Moule, Elizabeth, and Polyzoides, Stefanos
Katz, Peter. *The New Urbanism: Toward an Architecture of Community.* New York: McGraw-Hill, 1994, pp. 199–205.

Place, Roy
Cooper, James F., and Lew Place. *Places in the Sun.* Tucson: Westernlore Press, 1989.

Rockfellow, Annie
Kunasek, Kimberly Ann Oei. "Annie Graham Rockfellow." Master's thesis, University of Arizona, 1994.

Scholer, Sakellar and Fuller
"Large Clinic for Group Medical Practice, Tucson, Ariz." *Architectural Record,* Vol. 119 (March 1956), pp. 201–204. (Tucson Clinic.)

Swaim, Robert
"Desert House within a Wild
Mesquite Grove," *Sunset,* January
1971, pp. 56–57.
"Secured in a Desert Oasis," *House
Beautiful,* Summer 1982, pp. 76–77.

Trost, Henry
Engelbrecht, Lloyd C. "Trost in
Tucson." *Tyiglyph,* No. 2 (Spring
1985), pp. 25–31.
Engelbrecht, Lloyd C., and June-
Marie Engelbrecht. *Henry C. Trost,
Architect of the Southwest.* El Paso:
El Paso Library Association, 1981.

Vint, Robert
Arcidi, Philip. "Earthen Vessel."
Progressive Architecture, Vol. 73, No.
5 (May 1992), pp. 128–133. (San
Xavier del Bac restoration.)

Map Sources

Bufkin, Don. Tucson, Arizona
Territory, circa 1880. Tucson:
Arizona Pioneers' Historical
Society, 1962.
Foreman, S. W. Official Map of the
City of Tucson, Situated in Pima
County, Arizona Territory.
Occupying Secs. 12 & 13 Township
14 S. Range 13 E. Gila and Salt
River Meridian. Tucson: S. W.
Foreman, 1872.
Mills, J. B. Map of Tucson, A. T.
(Fergusson Map), 1862.
Roskruge, George J. Official Map of
Pima County, Arizona. N.p., 1893.
Sanborn Map Company. Insurance
Maps of Tucson, Arizona
("Sanborn Fire Maps"). New York:
Sanborn Map Co., 1883, 1886,
1889, 1896, 1901, 1909, 1919, 1948.

Schneider, Gus. George Hand's
Tucson 1870–1880. Tucson:
Privately published, 1949.

General Sources

Ball, Phyllis. *A Photographic History
of the University of Arizona, 1885–
1985.* Tucson: University of Arizona
Foundation, 1987.
Banham, Reyner. *Scenes in America
Deserta.* Salt Lake City: Gibbs M.
Smith, Inc., 1982. (See Chapter 9,
"Marks on the Landscape," about
Tucson.)
Barrio Historico, Tucson. Tucson:
College of Architecture, University
of Arizona, 1972.
Bieg, Jim, John Jones, and Ann
Leviton. *Fort Lowell.* Tucson: Pima
County Planning and Zoning
Department, 1976.
Bonnamour-Lloyd, Dominique. "The
Thick and the Thin: Enclosure for
the Sonoran Desert." *Journal of the
Southwest,* Vol. 40, No. 1 (Spring
1998), pp. 1–24.
Brand, Stewart. *How Buildings Learn:
What Happens after They're Built.*
New York: Viking, 1994. (See
Chapter 9, pp. 132–155, on the
invention of the Santa Fe style.)
Brophy, Blake. "Tucson's Arizona Inn:
The Continuum of Style." *Journal of
Arizona History,* Vol. 24, No. 3
(Autumn 1983), pp. 1–28.
Browne, J. Ross. *Adventures in the
Apache Country: A Tour through
Arizona and Sonora, 1864.* Tucson:
University of Arizona Press, 1974.
(First documentation of Tucson by
a popular American publication,
Harper's Weekly.)

Bufkin, Don. "From Mud Hut to Modern Metropolis: The Urbanization of Tucson." *Journal of Arizona History,* Vol. 22, No. 1 (Spring 1981), pp. 63–98.

Celebrating Tucson's Heritage. Tucson: City of Tucson, 1996.

Chambers, George W., and C. L. Sonnichsen. *San Agustín: First Cathedral Church in Arizona.* Tucson: Arizona Historical Society, 1974.

Cheek, Lawrence W. "The Good, the Bad, and the Ugly: How Did We Manage to Build Such an Ugly City in Such a Beautiful Place?" *City Magazine,* April 1988, pp. 42–51.

Cooper, James F. *The First Hundred Years: The History of the Tucson Unified School District 1, Tucson, Arizona, 1867–1967.* Privately published, 1968.

Deitch, Lewis Ian. "Changing House Types in Tucson, Arizona." Master's thesis, University of Arizona, 1966.

Duell, Prentice. *Mission Architecture as Exemplified in San Xavier del Bac.* Tucson: Arizona Archaeological and Historical Society, 1919.

————. "A Review of the Modern Architecture in Arizona." *Western Architect,* June 1922, pp. 63–77.

Fontana, Bernard L. "Biography of a Desert Church: The Story of Mission San Xavier del Bac." *Smoke Signal,* No. 3 (Spring 1961), pp. 2–23. Tucson: Tucson Corral of the Westerners.

Giebner, Robert C., editor. *Armory Park: 74ff.* Tucson: College of Architecture, University of Arizona, 1974.

————, editor. *Tucson Preservation Primer: A Guide for the Property Owner.* Tucson: College of Architecture, University of Arizona, 1979.

Giebner, Robert C., Allan C. Lamper, and Douglas Hawkins. *Look around Arizona: Architectural Guide to the University of Arizona Campus Historic District.* Tucson: College of Architecture, University of Arizona, 1987.

Gregonis, Linda M., and Karl J. Reinhard. *Hohokam Indians of the Tucson Basin.* Tucson: University of Arizona Press, 1988.

Griffith, James S. *A Shared Space: Folklife in the Arizona-Sonora Borderlands.* Logan: Utah State University Press, 1995.

————. *Southern Arizona Folk Arts.* Tucson: University of Arizona Press, 1988.

Hayden, Julian. *Excavations, 1940, at University Indian Ruin, Tucson, Arizona.* Globe, Ariz.: Southwestern Monuments Association, 1957.

Henry, Bonnie. *Another Tucson.* Tucson: *Arizona Daily Star* publication, 1992.

Historic Areas Committee. *Tucson Historical Sites.* Tucson: Arizona Historical Society, 1969.

Historic Preservation Consultants. *Historic Architecture in Tucson: A Report on the Historic Architecture to Be Preserved as Part of the Pueblo Center Redevelopment Project.* Tucson: City of Tucson, 1969. 2 volumes.

Johnson, Rev. David A., editor. *In the Beginnings: A Bicentennial History of Tucson's Religious Buildings.* Privately published, 1970.

King, Anthony D. *The Bungalow: The Production of a Global Culture.* London/Boston: Routledge & Kegan Paul, 1984.

Lockard, William Kirby. "Buildings of Architectural Significance in Tucson." *Arizona Architect,* October 1960, pp. 24–25.

Mabry, Jonathan B. "Rewriting Prehistory: Recent Discoveries at Cienega Phase Sites in the Santa Cruz Floodplain." *Archaeology in Tucson,* Newsletter of the Center for Desert Archaeology, Vol. 11, No. 3 (Summer 1997).

McAlester, Virginia, and Lee McAlester. *A Field Guide to North American Houses.* New York: Alfred A. Knopf, 1984.

Officer, James E. *Hispanic Arizona, 1536–1856.* Tucson: University of Arizona Press, 1987.

Olvera, Jorge. "San Xavier del Bac: Spanish Mission or Moslem Mosque?" *Dove of the Desert,* No. 4 (Winter 1989), pp. 1–6.

Property Development Services. *Historical Survey of Downtown Tucson Az.* Privately published, 1983.

Sheridan, Thomas E. *Arizona: A History.* Tucson: University of Arizona Press, 1995.

———. *Los Tucsonenses: The Mexican Community in Tucson, 1854–1941.* Tucson: University of Arizona Press, 1992.

Sonnichsen, C. L. *Tucson: The Life and Times of an American City.* Norman: University of Oklahoma Press, 1982.

Stewart, Janet Ann. *Arizona Ranch Houses: Southern Territorial Styles, 1867–1900.* Tucson: University of Arizona Press/Arizona Historical Society, 1974, 1987.

———. "Mansions of Main Street." *Journal of Arizona History,* Summer 1979, pp. 193–222.

Strittmatter, Janet. "Arizona's Vernacular Dwellings." Master's thesis, University of Arizona, 1999.

Tucson, Arizona: The ULI/AIA plan for Action: Preserving Tucson by Planning Its Future: A Panel Advisory Report for Tucson Tomorrow, Inc., the City of Tucson, Pima County, Citizens of the Tucson Area. Washington, D.C.: ULI-Urban Land Institute, 1984.

Tucson: A Short History. Tucson: Southwestern Mission Research Center, 1986.

"Tucson's New Railway Depot." *Sunset,* Vol. 19 (October 1907), pp. 584–586. (Shows rare photos of the original wooden depot.)

Van Slyck, Abigail A. "What the Bishop Learned: The Importance of Claiming Space at Tucson's Church Plaza." *Journal of Arizona History,* Summer 1998, pp. 121–140.

Veregge, Nina. "Transformations of Spanish Urban Landscape in the American Southwest, 1821–1900." *Journal of the Southwest,* Vol. 35, No. 4 (Winter 1993), pp. 371–459.

Wagoner, Jay J. *Early Arizona: Prehistory to Civil War.* Tucson: University of Arizona Press, 1989.

Whiffen, Marcus. *American Architecture since 1780: A Guide to the Styles.* Cambridge, Mass.: MIT Press, 1969.

Williams, Jack S. "Fortress Tucson: Architecture and the Art of War at a Desert Outpost (1775–1856)." *Smoke Signal,* No. 49/50 (Spring/Fall 1988), pp. 168–188. Tucson: Tucson Corral of the Westerners.

———. "San Augustin del Tucson: A Vanished Mission Community of the Pimería Alta." *Smoke Signal,* No. 47/48 (Spring/Fall 1986), pp. 113–128. Tucson: Tucson Corral of the Westerners.

Illustration Credits

History

Reconstructed view of Santa Cruz Bend site, c. 300 B.C. Drawing by Ziba Ghassemi, Center for Desert Archaeology. .

San Xavier del Bac, c. 1900. Photograph courtesy of the Aultman Collection, El Paso Public Library.

"Convento," Mission San Agustín del Tucson, c. 1890. Photograph courtesy of Arizona Historical Society/Tucson, Accession #2535.

Reconstructed view of the Presidio of San Agustín del Tucson, c. 1853. Drawing courtesy of Jack Williams.

Fergusson Map of Tucson, 1862. Map courtesy of the Arizona Historical Society/Tucson.

Roskruge Map, 1893. Map courtesy of the Arizona Historical Society/Tucson.

Silverlake, c. 1890. Photograph courtesy of Arizona Historical Society/Tucson, Accession #18790.

Church plaza, no date. Photograph courtesy of Arizona Historical Society/Tucson, Accession #2887.

Sanborn Insurance Map, 1883. Map courtesy of the Arizona Historical Society/Tucson.

Typical Sonoran and American blocks. Illustration by Mark Barmann.

Tucson subdivision patterns, 1928. Drawing courtesy of City of Tucson.

Pima County Courthouse, c. 1934. Photograph courtesy of Arizona Historical Society/Tucson, Accession #10473.

Aerial view of Tucson subdivisions c. 1950. Photograph courtesy of Arizona Historical Society/Tucson, AHS# PC 177 #1170.

Blackwell House, c. 1980. Photograph courtesy of the Chafee Collection, Arizona Architectural Archives, The University of Arizona.

Architectural Examples

Reconstructed view of the Presidio of San Agustín del Tucson, c. 1853. Drawing courtesy of Jack Williams.

Jacobs House; demolished 1968. Photograph courtesy of Arizona Historical Society/Tucson, Accession #45602b.

Corbett House. Photograph by Bill Timmerman.

First Owl's Club. Photograph by Bill Timmerman.

First Owl's Club, detail of owl design. Photograph courtesy of the Aultman Collection, El Paso Public Library.

El Presidio Bed & Breakfast. Photograph by Bill Timmerman.

Verdugo House, Transformed Sonoran. Photograph by Bill Timmerman.

Second Owl's Club. Photograph by Bill Timmerman.

El Paso & Southwestern Railroad Depot. Photograph courtesy of Arizona Historical Society/Tucson, Accession #14458.

Douglas Park; demolished c. 1974.
Photograph courtesy of Arizona
Historical Society/Tucson, Accession
#15503.

Arizona State Office Building, atrium.
Photograph courtesy of Christopher
Barone.

Arizona State Office Building, north
elevation. Photograph courtesy of James
A. Gresham.

Sosa-Carrillo-Frémont House. Photograph by Bill Timmerman.

San Agustín Cathedral; demolished 1936.
Photograph courtesy of Arizona
Historical Society/Tucson, Accession
#200330.

Pima County Courthouse. Photograph by
Bill Timmerman.

Second Pima County Courthouse;
demolished 1928. Photograph courtesy
of Arizona Historical Society/Tucson,
Accession #59756.

Second Tucson City Hall; demolished
1972. Photograph courtesy of Arizona
Historical Society/Tucson, Accession
#15418.

Transamerica Office Building. Photograph by Bill Timmerman.

First National Bank of Arizona.
Photograph by Anne M. Nequette.

Pioneer Hotel. Photograph courtesy of
Arizona Historical Society/Tucson,
Accession #BS20851.

Fox-Tucson Theatre. Photograph courtesy
of Arizona Historical Society/Tucson,
Accession #B27703.

Consolidated Bank of Tucson. Photograph by Bill Timmerman.

St. Augustine Cathedral, c. 1896.
Photograph courtesy of Arizona
Historical Society/Tucson, Accession
#B32373.

St. Augustine Cathedral today. Photograph by Bill Timmerman.

Southern Pacific Railroad Depot.
Photograph courtesy of Arizona
Historical Society/Tucson, Accession
#92701.

Ronstadt Transit Center. Photograph by
Bill Timmerman.

Convent Streetscape. Photograph by Bill
Timmerman.

Convent Avenue Studios. Photograph by
Bill Timmerman.

Carrillo Gardens; demolished c. 1925.
Photograph courtesy of Arizona
Historical Society/Tucson, Accession
#18790.

Scottish Rite Cathedral. Photograph by
Bill Timmerman.

Carnegie Free Library. Photograph
courtesy of the Aultman Collection, El
Paso Public Library.

Temple of Music and Art. Photograph by
Bill Timmerman.

Healy House. Photograph by Bill
Timmerman.

Residence at 228 S. 4th Avenue.
Photograph courtesy of Arizona
Architectural Archives, The University
of Arizona.

Safford Junior High School. Photograph
by Bill Timmerman.

Tucson High Magnet School. Photograph
by Bill Timmerman.

Tucson High Magnet School Addition.
Photograph by Bill Timmerman.

Ronstadt House. Photograph by Bill
Timmerman.

Deco Facade. Photograph by Bill
Timmerman.

Grace Lutheran Church. Photograph by
Bill Timmerman.

College Shop. Photograph courtesy of the
Wilde Collection, Arizona Architectural
Archives, The University of Arizona.

Old Main. Photograph by Bill
Timmerman.

Herring Hall. Photograph by Bill
Timmerman.

Arizona State Museum. Photograph by
Bill Timmerman.

Main Library. Photograph by Bill
Timmerman.

Aerospace and Mechanical Engineering.
Photograph by Bill Timmerman.

Pima Community College, West Campus.
Photograph by Bill Timmerman.

Project Potty. Photograph courtesy of
Henry Tom.

Reconstructed view of the Convento. Drawing courtesy of Jack Williams.

Bray House. Photograph by Anne M. Nequette.

Boudreaux-Robinson House. Photograph by Bill Timmerman.

Tucson General Hospital. Photograph by Bill Timmerman.

Tucson Interior Design Center. Photograph by Bill Timmerman.

CNWC Architectural Office. Photograph by Bill Timmerman.

Arizona Health Sciences Library, south elevation. Photograph courtesy of Douglas Kahn.

Arizona Health Sciences Library, brickwork detail on south elevation. Photograph courtesy of James A. Gresham.

Arizona Inn. Photograph by Bill Timmerman.

Catalina High School. Photograph by Bill Timmerman.

Benedictine Sanctuary. Photograph by Bill Timmerman.

Broadway Village. Photograph by Bill Timmerman.

Starkweather Residence. Photograph by Bill Timmerman.

El Conquistador Hotel; demolished 1968. Photograph courtesy of Arizona Historical Society/Tucson, Accession #26659.

RGA Engineering Building. Photograph by Bill Timmerman.

Cheng-Olson Studio. Photograph by Bill Timmerman.

Plan of Fort Lowell c. 1880, drawn by Don Bufkin.

St. Michael's and All Angels Episcopal Church. Photograph by Bill Timmerman.

Wilmot Library. Photograph by Bill Timmerman.

Drawing of wall types at University Indian Ruin. Drawing from Hayden, *Excavations, 1940,* courtesy of Southwest Parks and Monuments Association.

Drawing of construction at University Indian Ruin. Drawing from Hayden,

Excavations, 1940, courtesy of Southwest Parks and Monuments Association.

St. Philip's in the Hills Episcopal Church. Photograph by Bill Timmerman.

Muscular Dystrophy Association National Headquarters. Photograph courtesy of Timothy Hursley.

Arroyo House. Photograph courtesy of Glenn Christensen.

Ventana Canyon Resort. Photograph by Bill Timmerman.

Ventana Vista Elementary School. Photograph courtesy of Timothy Hursley.

Avalon House, courtyard; demolished 1983. Photograph courtesy of David Freshwater.

Santa Cruz Catholic Church and School. Photograph by Bill Timmerman.

Main Post Office. Photograph by Bill Timmerman.

Veterans Affairs Medical Center. Photograph by Bill Timmerman.

Ramada House. Photograph courtesy of Glen Allison.

San Xavier Mission Church. Photograph by Bill Timmerman.

San Xavier Mission Church, ground floor plan. Drawing courtesy of Robert Vint.

Blackwell House, c. 1980. Photograph courtesy of the Chafee Collection, Arizona Architectural Archives, The University of Arizona.

Johnson House. Photograph courtesy of Glen Allison.

Arizona-Sonora Desert Museum Restaurant and Art Gallery. Photograph courtesy of Michael Stoklos.

Acacia Elementary School. Photograph courtesy of Cain Nelson Wares Cook.

Desert Willow Elementary School. Photograph courtesy of Steven Meckler.

Profiles

Henry Trost. Photograph courtesy of the Aultman Collection, El Paso Public Library.

Henry Jaastad. Photograph courtesy of Arizona Historical Society/Tucson, Accession #7717.

Annie Rockfellow. Photograph courtesy of Arizona Historical Society/Tucson, Accession #96037.

Roy Place. Photograph courtesy of Stephen Farley.

Josias Joesler. Photograph courtesy of Arizona Architectural Archives, The University of Arizona.

Arthur Brown. Photograph courtesy of Gordon Brown.

Nicholas Sakeller. Photograph courtesy of Dino Sakellar.

Judith Chafee. Photograph courtesy of Mari Schaffer/*Arizona Daily Star.*

Glossary

Aerial view of Santa Cruz Bend site 800 B.C.–A.D. 150. Photograph courtesy of Jonathan Mabry, Center for Desert Archaeology.

Mission San Xavier del Bac. Photograph courtesy of Aultman Collection, El Paso Public Library.

Reconstructed view of the Presidio. Drawing courtesy of Jack Williams.

La Casa Cordova, example of a Sonoran house. Photograph by Bill Timmerman.

Typical floor plan of a Sonoran house. Drawing courtesy of Arizona Architectural Archives, The University of Arizona.

Verdugo House, Transformed Sonoran. Photograph by Bill Timmerman.

Olcott House, American Territorial. Photograph by Bill Timmerman.

Residence at 228 S. 4th Avenue. Photograph courtesy of Arizona Architectural Archives, The University of Arizona.

Floor plan of Roskruge House. Drawing courtesy of Arizona Architectural Archives, The University of Arizona.

Scottish Rite Cathedral. Photograph by Bill Timmerman.

Main floor plan of Scottish Rite Cathedral. Drawing courtesy of Robert Vint.

Corbett House. Photograph by Bill Timmerman.

Pima County Courthouse. Photograph by Bill Timmerman.

St. Michael's and All Angels Episcopal Church. Photograph by Bill Timmerman.

Bungalow. Photograph by Bill Timmerman.

Bray House. Photograph by Anne M. Nequette.

Detail of Fox-Tucson Theatre. Photograph by Bill Timmerman.

A new Art Deco facade on an older house. Photograph by Bill Timmerman.

Vocational Education Building, Tucson High Magnet School. Photograph by Bill Timmerman.

College Shop. Photograph courtesy of the Wilde Collection, Arizona Architectural Archives, The University of Arizona.

Tucson General Hospital. Photograph by Bill Timmerman.

Ramada House. Photograph courtesy of Glen Allison.

Plan of Ramada house. Drawing courtesy of Arizona Architectural Archives, The University of Arizona.

Arizona-Sonora Desert Museum Restaurant and Art Gallery. Photograph courtesy of Michael Stoklos.

Brown Residence. Photograph courtesy of Steve Haines/Photographic Associates.

Main Post Office. Photograph by Bill Timmerman.

Sullivanesque detailing, Second Owl's Club. Photograph by Anne M. Nequette.

Index

Hotel Heidel, 87
hotels and resorts, 18, 22, 28–29, 33; in Armory Park, 114; in Catalina Foothills, *227*, 227; in downtown, *82*, 82–83, 86, 87, 88, 91, 92; in Ironhorse, 128; in Midtown, *187*, 187–88, *195*, 195, 196. *See also* motor courts
Housing Act of 1954, 33
Howe, John H., 184
Hubbard, Alonso, 207
Hughes Elementary School, 197, 201
Hughes House, 55
Hughes, Oden, 120
Hughes, Sam, 175
Humanities Building, University of Arizona, 153, 160
Hummel, Don, 31

Ibarra, Luis, 103
IEF Group, 166
Immaculate Heart Elementary School, 237
immigrants and immigration, 95, 132, 265
Indian Ridge Estates, 213, 294
Indian ruins. *See under* Hohokam culture
infill, 31, 33, 103, 127, 137, 202, 295, 298, 301
International style, 192, 258, 289–91, 292, 295
irrigation systems, 11, 14, 19, 268. *See also* canals
Islamic style and characteristics, 8, 89, 271, 280. *See also* Moorish style and ornamentation; mudéjar influences
Isler, Ridvan, 244
Italian Renaissance Revival style, 82, 211
Italian Romanesque Revival style, 153, 154, 155, 158, 160

Jaastad, Henry O., 23, *255*, 255, 256; in downtown, 85, 90; in other areas,
65, 100, 119, 131, 158, 181, 195, 210, 222; at Tucson High School, 125; in West University, 133, 139, 140, 141
Jaastad & Knipe, 131
Jackson Street, 84
Jacobs, Baron, 52
Jacobs House, 28, *29*, 35, *52*, 52, 69
Jacobsen House, 230
Jacobson, Arthur, 56, 201
Janus & Associates, 111
Jerry's Lee Ho, 96
Jesuits, 10, 11, 245. *See also* Kino, Father Eusebio Francisco
Jobusch, Fred, 191
Joesler, Josias, 27, 219, 223, *258*, 258, 278; in Midtown, 193, 199; in other areas, 212, 224, 237; in West University, 141, 143
John Spring Historic District, 130
John Spring Junior High School, 131
Johnson House, *248*, 248
Johnson House (Manning-Johnson House), 65
Johnson, Philip, 290
Joy, Rick, 101, 249
Julian Drew Block, 92

Keith, Michael, 67
King, Manuel, 178
Kingan House, 60
Kino, Father Eusebio Francisco, 10, 174, 245
Kitt, Katharine, 118
Kitt Peak Observatory, 244, 246
Kitt-Peterson House, 118, 274, 279
Kramer, Leighton, 188
Kruttschnitt House, *57*, 57, 274
Kulseth, John R., Associates, Ltd., 167, 171
Kurtz, Mr. (stonemason), 181

La Casa Cordova, 53, *271*, 272
La Paz Dormitory, 163
La Placita shopping and office complex, 34
Lambert Construction, Inc., 211

parking, designs for, 186, 192, 193, 201, 210, 215, 224, 237, 247, 250–51

parks and gardens: in Barrio Anita, 131; in Barrio Historico, 18, 21, 95, 96, *104*, 104; in downtown, 72–73, *73*; in East Side, 217–18; in El Presidio, 18, 67; in Fort Lowell, 205, 208–9; in Northwest, 232, 234–35; in Tucson Mountains, 247; in West Side, 172, 173; in West University, 145

Paseo Redondo, 65, 66

Pasquale Court, 102

Pasquale, Juan, 102

passive solar design, 38, 256, 260, 276, 283, 292, 294; in East Side, 215, 216, 217; in Midtown, 184, 185; in other areas, 163, 247; in South Side, 241, 242

Pastime Park, 24

PAT House (Perfect Arizona Type House), 36, 213, 294

Patronato San Xavier, 244

Patterson, B. J., 86

Paylore House (Ball/Paylore House), 189

Pazos, Antonio, 172

pedestrian areas, 37, 140; design for, 81, 167, 193, 210, 217

Perfect Arizona Type (PAT) House, 36, 213, 294

Perkins, Arthur, 197, 202

Peterson House (Kitt-Peterson House), 118

Phelps Dodge Company, 72

Pima Community College, West Campus, *171*, 171, 295

Pima County, 31–32, 247

Pima County Courthouse, 28, *29*, 51, *79*, 79, *80*, 80, 82, *281*

Pima County Parks and Recreation Commission, 248

Pima County Transportation Department, 172

Pima Indians, 7, 9, 10, 11, 12, 68, 174, 245, 271

Pimería Alta, 10, 14, 269

Pinal County Courthouse, 118

Pinal Hall, University of Arizona, 165

Pioneer Hotel, 29, *82*, 82–83

pit structures, 4, *5*, 5, 6, 65, 214, 266, *267*, 267, 268

Place, Lew, 164, 257

Place and Place, 82, 165, 191, 257

Place, Roy O., 179, 257, 278, *257*; in downtown, 79, 82, 88; in Midtown, 191, 196, 201; in other areas, 128, 242; at Tucson High School, 123, 126; at University of Arizona, 29, 150, 152, 153–54, 155, 157, 158, 159, 160, 162, 164, 166; in West University, 133, 140. *See also* Lyman & Place; Place and Place

planners and planning, 40, 42, 43, 69, 137. *See also* master plans and planning

Plaza de la Mesilla (Church Plaza), 18, 20, *21*, 34, 68, 69, *77*, 77–78

Plaza de las Armas, 18, 34, 49, 69

Plaza Militar, 49

Plaza School, 108, 119

plazas, 12, 13, 15, *16*, 16, *17*, 17, 23, 270; in Armory Park, 106, 116; in Catalina Foothills, 219; in downtown, *88*, 88; in John Spring, 131; in Midtown, 193; prehistoric, 5, 6, 266, 267. *See also* Plaza de la Mesilla (Church Plaza); Plaza de las Armas

Pond Mansion (Stone Ashley), 211

Postal History Foundation, 142

Poster Frost Associates, Inc., 86, 114, 131

Potter Place, 188

Prairie style, 50, 58, 87, 119, 132, 140, 179, 285–87, *286*, 293

Predock, Antoine, 228

prefabrication and prefabricated materials, 35–36, 42, 276

preservation and preservationists, 34, 35, 41, 78, 248, 265, 266

Presidio San Agustín del Tucson, 12–13, *13*, 14, 15, 23, 49, 50, 51, 68, 175,

About the Authors

Anne Marie Nequette is a Lecturer at the College of Architecture, Planning and Landscape Architecture (CAPLA), at the University of Arizona. She received her Master of Architecture degree from Princeton University in 1986. Nequette practiced in Tucson firms in the design, documentation, and construction administration of schools and civic buildings until the spring of 1996 when she established her own office and began teaching at the University of Arizona. She teaches "Architecture and Society," the University-wide general education course, and architectural design at all levels. Nequette has written interactive tutorials and other reference material on architecture for Internet use. She has also taught "Tucson's Architectural Heritage" through the University of Arizona Extended University and has lectured on numerous occasions on that subject. Her commitment to the architectural education of the community is demonstrated in many other fields as well: mentoring middle and high school students, providing career information for children of all ages, coordinating interactive workshops on architecture with the Tucson-Pima Public Library, volunteering in construction for Habitat for Humanity, and leading numerous tours of historic neighborhoods.

R. Brooks Jeffery is Coordinator of Preservation Studies and Curator of the Arizona Architectural Archives at the College of Architecture, Planning and Landscape Architecture (CAPLA), at the University of Arizona. Jeffery has used his degrees in Architecture and Information Science to document, interpret, and disseminate the significance of the built environment around the world. Between 1985 and 1988, he worked as an architect in the Middle Eastern country of Yemen, within a UNESCO-sponsored program to preserve the architecture of its capital city, San'a. Since 1988, Jeffery has been at the University of Arizona, where he has been involved in the preservation of cultural heritage in Tucson as an educator and advocate. In addition, his preservation research and advocacy activities have extended to projects in Latin America, Spain, and the Middle East.

He serves on the Arizona Historic Sites Review Committee, the Arizona Preservation Foundation, the University of Arizona Historic Preservation Advisory Committee, and was founder of the Tucson Architectural Landmarks program. His recent publications include *Yemen: A Culture of Builders* and *Joesler & Murphey: An Architectural Legacy for Tucson,* as well as articles and presentations on Islamic, Spanish Colonial, and Southwestern architecture.